THE CHRISTIAN LIFE:

CROSS OR GLORY?

2nd Edition

What would a theology look like that takes seriously Paul's words, "I decided to know nothing among you except Jesus Christ and him crucified" (1 Cor. 2:2 ESV)? Steven Hein provides a compelling answer in a book that might be called a "dogmatics of the cross." Rich with insights from Luther's Heidelberg Theses and engaging of issues raised in the culture of autonomous spirituality so dominate in North America, Hein has provided a book that will serve well in grounding seasoned Christians in the word of the cross while also challenging those who have been bored or burnt out with shallow and anemic Christianity to a fresh hearing of the story and promise of the Crucified and Risen Lord.

—John T. Pless
Assistant Professor of Pastoral Ministry and Missions / Director of Field Education
Concordia Theological Seminary
Fort Wayne, IN

You probably have experienced an announcement that your favorite author is releasing his latest book—and it's a book that is about your favorite author's own favorite subject? *How soon can I get a copy?* That is exactly what I thought when I heard the announcement of Dr. Steve Hein's new book: *The Christian Life: Cross or Glory?* (Irvine, CA: 1517 Legacy, 2015).

How so? Over decades, Dr. Hein mastered Luther and classical, Confessional Lutheran theology (he was a professor of that subject at the Lutheran Church—Missouri Synod college in Chicago for almost twenty-five years). Hein delights in, is supremely competent in, teaching this faith *within the confines* of his church/synod, as an "insider" to other "insiders." He would do it 24/7 were that possible. And in particular, Dr. Hein is a master of Luther's view of the Christian life ("sanctification"—the doctrine that other Christians don't believe that Lutherans have, believe or are even interested in!)

Centering on the paradoxical themes found in Luther's *Heidelberg Disputation*, Dr. Hein's book covers all the predictable subjects: law and Gospel, God hidden and revealed, justification *sola fide* and *propter Christum*, the nature of the Christian life/sanctification, and so on. Parts II and III of his book focus in on the war in the Christian between his or her new life and his or her "Old Adam," on what Luther called *tentatio* (trials, temptations, afflictions), on good works as fruit of faith in Christ, on *vocatio* ("vocation, calling, station") and on the Christian being *both* free Lord of all and simultaneously servant to neighbor (Luther, *The Freedom of the Christian*). As in St. Augustine's *Confessions*, he has a final, C. S. Lewis–conditioned chapter on Heaven and Hell (not as taught in dogmatics classes, but rather more "How-do-we-make-sense-of-these?"—cf. Lewis's conversation with MacDonald in *The Great Divorce*.)

The Christian Life is packed with not just Scripture [full text and well-chosen] but illustrative references to Luther and to contemporary Lutheran writers (e.g., the late Gerhard Förde, Dr. Heiko Obermann, and to the yet-living Dr. Ronald Feuerhahn,). To both my surprise and delight, Dr. Hein also makes use of the writings of the late Father Robert Capon (mainline Episcopal, but who had a soundly Biblical and amazing grasp of "grace"—and the almost complete absence of its scandalous content in priests, pastors, churches and seminaries). To the writings of these "greats," Dr. Hein adds his own helpful illustrations throughout his book.

I recommend Dr. Hein's book particularly for those who appreciated Dr. Eugene Edward Veith's *The Spirituality of the Cross* and who want to read more of the same, but written in a deeper and more analytical style. But if you read through *The Spirituality of the Cross* in a weekend, you should probably allow yourself a couple of weeks for Dr. Hein's *The Christian Life: Cross or Glory?*

—Dr. Rod Rosenbladt

If you're looking for a book that puts a "Lutheran spin" the subject of the Christian Life, this isn't it. When it comes to the Christian Life, Lutherans and pop-American Christianity aren't on the same planet, much less the same page. No, this is a uniquely Lutheran book on the Christian Life. It is a life given in preaching, Baptism and the Lord's Supper, lived in the neighbor, and shaped like the Cross. In other words, this book locates the Christian Life not in the Christian, but in the crucified Christ Himself.

—Todd Wilken

THE CHRISTIAN LIFE:
CROSS OR GLORY?
2nd Edition

STEVEN HEIN
edited by
RICK RITCHIE

The Christian Life: Cross or Glory?

© 2015 Steven A. Hein

Scripture quotations set in italics are the author's translations.

Scripture quotations marked (ESV) are from the ESV® Bible (The Holy Bible, English Standard Version®), copyright © 2001 by Crossway, a publishing ministry of Good News Publishers. Used by permission. All rights reserved.

Scripture quotations marked (NKJV) are from the New King James Version®. Copyright © 1982 by Thomas Nelson. Used by permission. All rights reserved.

Scripture quotations marked (CSB) are from the Christian Standard Bible®, Copyright © 2017 by Holman Bible Publishers. Used by permission. Christian Standard Bible® and CSB® are federally registered trademarks of Holman Bible Publishers.

Scripture quotations marked (NASB 1977) are from the New American Standard Bible®, Copyright © 1960, 1971, 1977, 1995, 2020 by The Lockman Foundation. Used by permission. All rights reserved. www.lockman.org.

Scripture quotations marked (KJV) are from the King James Version.

Scripture quotations marked (NIV) are from the Holy Bible, New International Version®, NIV®. Copyright © 1973, 1978, 1984, 2011 by Biblica, Inc.™ Used by permission of Zondervan. All rights reserved worldwide. www.zondervan.com The "NIV" and "New International Version" are trademarks registered in the United States Patent and Trademark Office by Biblica, Inc.™

Scripture quotations marked (NLT) are from the Holy Bible, New Living Translation, copyright ©1996, 2004, 2015 by Tyndale House Foundation. Used by permission of Tyndale House Publishers, Carol Stream, Illinois 60188. All rights reserved.

Published by:
1517 Publishing
PO Box 54032
Irvine, CA 92619-4032

Library of Congress Control Number: 2015942956

Publisher's Cataloging-In-Publication Data
(Prepared by The Donohue Group, Inc.)

Names: Hein, Steven A. (Steven Arthur), 1944– author. | Ritchie, Rick, 1966– editor.
Title: The Christian life : cross or glory? / by Steven A. Hein ; edited by Rick Ritchie.
Description: Second edition. | Irvine, CA : 1517 Publishing, [an imprint of] New Reformation Publications, [2021] | Includes bibliographical references.
Identifiers: ISBN 9781948969680 (hardcover) | ISBN 9781948969697 (paperback) | ISBN 9781948969703 (ebook)
Subjects: LCSH: Christian life—Lutheran authors. | Sanctification—Lutheran Church. | Lutheran Church—Doctrines. | Holy Cross.
Classification: LCC BV4501.3 .H439 2021 (print) | LCC BV4501.3 (ebook) | DDC 248.4841—dc23

Cover art by Brenton Clarke Little

Contents

Introduction

> Grace cannot prevail . . . until our lifelong certainty
> that someone is keeping score has run out of steam and
> collapsed.
>
> —Robert Farrar Capon (1925–2013)

The title of this work, *Christian Life: Cross or Glory?*, is intended
to entice the reader to consider a rather distasteful question: *What
is the relevance of the crucified Christ for daily Christian living?* Should
the glorified risen Jesus or Christ the crucified be the focus of the
Christian's daily walk of faith? Standard religious wisdom believes
that to rub people's eyes, ears, and nose in the bloody cross of Christ
is foolish if we are serious about advancing Christian ideals and fill-
ing the pews on Sunday mornings. For those of gentile religious sensitivities, the crucifixion of Jesus has never been a very popular focus
when seeking to develop a more satisfying relationship with God. To
dwell or focus on the torturous grizzly death of Jesus as carried out by
the ancient Romans has always grated against refined aesthetic and
religious sensitivities. By contrast, however, crosses of various shapes
and sizes have always been popular as religious fashion statements.
Precious metal crosses with almost anything attached to them have
always been viewed positively by believers and nonbelievers alike.
Crosses with anything on them except Jesus, that is. Let's face it. For
most people, including those who call themselves Christians, crosses
that accurately depict what happened to Jesus are a big emotional
turnoff. For this reason, many churches will not allow them of any

shape or size in their sanctuaries, thinking them negative and in bad taste. Much more popular are depictions of a very healthy Jesus in various reverent poses, often standing around serenely with some small children and stray sheep.

Most Protestants and many Lutherans think that it is Catholics who have such things as crucifixes, and as they say, *we are not Catholics*. Moreover, the following theological argument is often presented for absenting the crucified Jesus: *Look, we present an empty cross of Christ because Jesus has already died and left the cross. He is not there any more; He has risen and ascended and is now with the Father in glory.* I have never thought this rationale was very convincing. Have you ever seen a depiction of the Nativity of our Lord that presented an empty feed trough without the baby Jesus, only to be told that it is a celebration of *the empty manger? Jesus is no longer there—He grew up, died, rose, and ascended to the Father in glory.* No, the truth is this: depictions and presentations of the bloody crucified Christ make us feel uncomfortable. Give us a cross in church made out of calla lilies, and let's just direct our attention to the risen Christ in glory.

The desire to avoid any focus on the cross of Christ is nothing new in the history of the church. Such hostility was alive and well in the Apostle Paul's day. The church at Corinth was in turmoil about how it ought to focus its mission and ministry. Many thought that the characteristics and abilities of its spiritual leadership were the pivotal consideration for the health and expansion of Corinthian ministries. They bickered about which leader and what attributes were critically important for spiritual vitality (1 Cor. 1:11ff). Divided into factions, each championed their own spiritual leader—some Paul, some Peter, some Apollos. But a special visionary group thought none of these: *We're going with just Jesus!* This latter group thought that mere earthly leaders were a detriment to success. They would simply follow Jesus and live in accord with what He would do. Forget the apostles, their teaching, and advice; this group would shape the Corinthian spiritual vision guided only by WWJD. They thought that what should be preached is Jesus Christ and Him exemplified.

We learn in 1 Corinthians 1–2 that the apostle Paul would have none of this. Here he set forth the theme for his whole ministry and mission among them. He maintained that in the preaching of the Gospel, *the cross of Christ should not be emptied of its power*

(1 Cor. 1:17). Drawing his line in the ecclesiastical sand, he declared he had *decided to know nothing among you except Jesus Christ and Him crucified* (2:2). For Paul, *Christ crucified* was not simply *a part* of the message, but the whole message and the only message for the Church of Christ. Was Paul deluded here and showing off his naïveté? Did he not realize that this would turn off a lot of spiritual seekers who might otherwise be willing to give the Corinthian church a try? Yes, he understood completely. He labeled the cross *foolishness* to those who are perishing; *a stumbling block to the Jew*, and just plain all-around *foolishness* to the average gentile (1:23). Yet here alone is the wisdom of God for sinners and the only mission and ministry by which we may live with God's graciousness and reconciliation. Apart from the cross of Christ crucified, all focus on Jesus, all talk about the love of God or doing what Jesus would do, simply add up to remaining under God's wrath and condemnation. God has no merit badges, and certainly, no favors for any mission, ministry, or focus on Jesus that hides or supplants the Gospel of Christ crucified.

Who can deny the distasteful flavor of making Christ the crucified the sum and substance of the church's proclamation and life? Crucifixion is an ugly and repulsive form of execution that the Romans reserved for criminals of whom they desired to make an example. We don't like to dwell on the fact that Jesus received just such a shameful, grizzly treatment. *Yes, it happened to our Savior, and we are glad it did. But now it's over and done with so let's move on.* Not so fast! If we take seriously Paul's presentation about our Baptism in Romans 6:3–11, a back-to-the-future perspective of the cross of Christ is necessary. Union with the crucified Christ in His death is what God requires of us if we are to live with Him. While Jesus moved on from the cross and grave, rising to glory, we have not—yet. Our life with God remains stuck for now in nothing but the bleeding charity of God—a bleeding charity provided nowhere else than in the cross of Christ. Our whole perspective of the cross of Christ promises to offend ordinary religious sensibilities. It will argue that the exercise of God's power and justice against all the world's evils will end up with everyone getting what they do not deserve.

Yes, Jesus has had his Easter, but we remain in this life tied to his cross, still awaiting ours. While some would rather die than have a spiritual life so centered, it is God who demands just that, your death, in order for your spiritual life to be rightly centered. Your death to sin is demanded by the very same cross that crucified your Lord. You must die with Christ in order to live with Him. If you want to be a Christian, you need to get crucified. What he got, you get! He got it for a few hours, and you get it for life.

The amazing thing is that in the cross of Christ, two die—Christ and you. And by that death, there is life; two live, Christ and you (Rom. 6:10–11). It's ugly to see and experience, and it's absolutely nuts to think about. Every ounce of reason will tell you that in death, you get death. But the promise of the holy cross of Christ is that in THIS death, you get life—indeed, life eternal. And for the Church at Corinth and all the churches then and now, you don't get saved by the wretched cross and five minutes later move on down the road to glory and a more fulfilling relationship with God. Here, for now, we all remain captivated in and by the divine foolishness of Jesus Christ and Him crucified—here is the bloody cross that alone saves sinners, to be and to stay until we receive our crown of glory. His death to sin and your death to sin; it's a double cross. Satan loses, and you win.

It was Martin Luther who began his movement of recovering the New Testament Gospel by echoing St. Paul's resolve to the Corinthians when he declared, *The cross is our theology.* Searching the Scriptures, Luther discovered that Christian life in this world is lived in union with Christ the crucified. It is cross life now! The question for the reader is this: Are you willing to consider the implications of Christ the crucified where sinners get bloody with Jesus because they are just dying to live? This would require you to swallow Luther's conclusion that the glory story is reserved only for you and all Christians on the occasion of your own Happy Easter. Luther understood that many aspects of the cross life of the Christian reflect realities that are best understood by way of paradox. The Scriptures often present two seemingly opposite realities where both must be embraced and appreciated without the tension between them relaxed or resolved. The dual yet paradoxical realities of sin and grace, dying and rising, Law and Gospel, repentance and faith, sinner and saint, faith and experience, now and not yet—these pairs of opposites describe how many aspects of our faith and experience of life in Christ should be understood.

Cross life begins from the splashing of grace in baptism, which unites the sinner with the death of the crucified Christ (Rom. 6:5ff).

There in the cross, the Christian lives as a dual citizen of this world and the Kingdom of God until he is translated into the glorified risen life of Christ. Luther labeled as theologies of glory all distortions of the Gospel that would promise the Christian elements of glory in this life if he will perfect or offer spiritual things that deserve God's favor. Any promise that would grant to the believer in this life some reprieve or release from the experience of his own sinfulness or that of others and this world, Luther would characterize as a theology of glory. In the chapters that follow, we will explore what Luther described as the Theology of the Cross and sketch out the contours of the life of the Christian as lived in the cross of Christ. The reader may be surprised to find that it looks very much like his own where grace alone gives it any redeeming quality.

In the pages that follow, our purpose is not to inspire or uplift, but rather to inform and then persuade you to reevaluate what constitutes a healthy life in Christ. Our discussion will offer a radically different perspective from that of many best-selling authors concerning how the Christian should measure and evaluate travel along God's path of righteousness. It will endeavor to persuade you, the reader, that by feeding regularly on the Gospel in the Word and the Supper, God promises to have His way with you, and He alone will accomplish all you need for your life in Him to be complete. He is not waiting or requiring you to do anything first (during or after your conversion) to provide you with every blessing of the Gospel. Christian leaders who write and speak about a glorious this-worldly life in Christ, similar to the old beer commercial where the guys are sitting around the campfire with their favorite brew saying to one another; *It just doesn't get any better than this!*—are deceived and misguided! When the experience of our life in Christ does not get any better, we will have left cross life behind and entered that glory of life in the Happy Forever.

Our discussion will explore cross life from different vantage points. *Part One: The Cross Life of the Christian* will begin with an overview of *The Theology of the Cross* as Luther came to understand it in his monumental *Heidelberg Theses* of 1518. Here major paradoxical themes that shape life in the cross will be briefly described to orient the reader for a more robust treatment of them in the chapters that follow. Understanding and appreciating these paradoxical realities will comprise the strategy of how our discussion will seek to engage the reader to consider the overall question of the book: *Christian Life: Cross or Glory?*

From a beginning sketch of cross theology, the discussion will engage the key to understanding biblical revelation: the realization that God is not very nice, and He presents Himself with two faces. He never comes to sinners sweetly to inquire if anyone is interested in becoming a Christian. He hammers them to death with full-strength Law but then raises them up to new life in Christ with pure Gospel. Law and Gospel rightly divided and at full strength are both *the substance* of Christ crucified and *the address* of God that kills and makes alive. What is spoken and what you hear is what you get. If you don't *get it* in God's judgment of Law, you won't *get it* in grace from the Gospel. There just is no other way.

God's address of Law and Gospel renders the Christian a complete paradox—*a simultaneous sinner/saint*—still unrighteous in character, yet holy, righteous, and blameless before God. Christians continue to look disappointing to other people, but just wonderful to God decked out in the robe of righteousness. In other words, they will not necessarily know you are a Christian by your love. Our treatment of the chief article, justification, will explain that getting saved by faith alone means not only a faith apart from works but faith apart from experience. Christians continue to experience all their sinful wretchedness, but the *grace by which you are saved* is held onto by sheer faith alone. Moreover, we will advance the position that the Christian has become completely righteous in Christ. She has it all but always is in need of more.

Our chapter on sanctification promises to be a real let down. It will champion the religiously unpopular position that your godly works never contribute anything toward your growth and maturity in Christ. As baptism creates a new self-fashioned after the Second Adam, fresh Christians are babes in Christ. The new creation is immature but not defective. Sanctification involves God's work of maturing our faith and life in Christ, not reforming it. However, the more mature in Christ, you become, the less mature you will feel. Growth in Christ brings an increasing awareness of your sinfulness. The peace of God passes this disturbing awareness, but it does not replace it. In other words, you get to debate with the Apostle Paul about who is chief of sinners (1 Tim. 1:15).

Part Two: The Experience of Cross Life will bring the discussion into perhaps the most disturbing aspect of Christian living according to cross theology. It was for Luther. What should we expect to experience *from* a healthy spiritual life lived in the cross of Christ? How should unpleasant and unwanted episodes of trials and spiritual distress be understood? Should they be seen, as many books today on Christian life interpret them, as symptoms of spiritual want and poverty? Our treatment will take the unpopular position that trials, tribulations, and spiritual anxiety (*tentatio*) are normal Christian experiences for all Christians, but even more so for those of mature faith. It will continually be reminding the reader to distinguish how the gifts and blessings of the Gospel apply to our life in the crucified Jesus over against our life with the glorified Christ. We will amplify what Luther understood as central to the cross life of the Christian: life in Christ will continue to have the gates of Hell rattling around us, producing spiritual warfare from within and without. Christians are saved by faith alone, but that faith will not be left alone as we sojourn through the valley of the shadow of death. It will be assaulted continually by the unholy triad—the world, the flesh, and the Devil.

The concluding *Part Three* of our discussion will be a bit eclectic. We have called it *Faithfulness in Cross Life*. The matter of good works will be surveyed, arguing that they are the consequence of life and growth in Christ from the impact of the Gospel. Our picture of the works of the Christian follows the botanical model (John 15:1–5). As the branch produces grapes because it does as it was designed to do, so our fruit of faith simply come forth from what we are, branches living and growing in Christ the Vine. We do as we are; we do not become as we do.

The labors of the Christian's vocation distribute the blessings of God, where we live, work, and play. If you have felt that your labors don't do much to convince others that you are a *real* Christian—rest easy. We will argue that the works of the Christian are usually rather common and ordinary—not very distinguishable from the beneficial labors of the unbeliever. Therefore, no, they will not know we are Christians by our love. Moreover, we will maintain that godly works are never for God's benefit for two embarrassing reasons: we do not have anything He needs and, anything we do have that is worth anything, He gave us. Good works are God's secret, and by faith, they

serve Christ by distributing God's blessings to our neighbors who
need them. They will know we are sheep by our love only when our
works are extolled by Christ on the Day of Judgment (Matt. 25:31–40).

The discussion of faithfulness in cross living will challenge
the reader to reflect on how this understanding of cross life should
impact the strategies and substance of the spiritual nurture of our
baptized children. Seriously, can exercises in finger painting and glitter with bunnies and butterflies effectively communicate to young
children the realities of dying and rising in the cross of Christ? We
will contend that Luther's insight in his famous essay, *The Freedom
of the Christian*, should inform a pedagogy that prepares our children to engage the world's fight and the soul's salvation. Such nurture
would embrace the freedom of grace that makes us beggars for life,
yet a bondage of works that binds us to our neighbor.

Throughout our discussion, comparisons and contrasts with
popular accents of alluring glory stories will punctuate the discourse. Our goal is that from a fresh evaluation of what constitutes
normal Christian living, the reader may recognize more clearly how
God has been having His way with him all along. His baptism recreated his life in the cross of Christ and placed him rightly on the
path of righteousness, which includes many experiences that flow
from sojourning through the valley of the shadow of death (Ps. 23:4).
There is comfort for the beleaguered Christian knowing that the
Good Shepherd is faithfully leading him on that path to the green
pastures of glory that surely will come.

For this reason, we will conclude our discussion by examining the contours of eternity and some contrasting characteristics of
Heaven and Hell. Our contention is that the justice of God will reign
supreme forever only in Heaven, where everyone receives what they
do not deserve. Conversely, Hell is that provision of God for those
who demand to be treated according to the fairness doctrine—to
have only what they deserve and are willing to die for it. Only the
lost get what they deserve. Christians deserve neither the cross nor
glory, but both are the inheritance of their baptism, and both come
to us—now and then. It is our prayer that in the pages that follow,
the reader may be renewed in a determination to join the Apostle
Paul in knowing *nothing* but the divine foolishness of *Jesus Christ
and Him crucified*.

PART I

The Cross Life of the Christian

CHAPTER 1

Christian Life

Cross or Glory?

If you are among many Christians who have burned out on the empty promises of what Martin Luther would call glory stories; or if the vibrant-feeling, glorious life in Christ has seemed to escape you; or if you just want some straight talk about the Christian life, we suggest you consider Luther's *Theology of the Cross*. Cross Theology will provide a realistic understanding of what you are experiencing in your life, will not accuse you of being a spiritually underachieving Christian, and is soundly rooted in the apostolic faith of the New Testament.

Like the Apostle Paul, Martin Luther often employed paradox to describe the mysteries of God's saving work in the cross of Christ. Many of the paradoxes of the Theology of the Cross are reflected in Luther's famous Heidelberg Theses of 1518. Our objective will be first to acquaint you with a few of these and then develop and apply them in greater detail as our discussion of various aspects of cross life unfolds.

Luther's Theology of the Cross has never been very popular in American churches, not even Lutheran ones. Cross Theology emphasizes much of the distasteful negativity of the human condition: the total depravity of sinners, vocation as a rather mundane focus on your neighbor's daily needs, and the fact that even when you "get saved" you never move beyond the cross of Christ. Such cross-centered teachings hold little appeal to those who have been nurtured on American holiness brands of Protestant thought. In addition, Cross Theology's insistence of the normalcy of spiritual distress and warfare in the Christian life runs counter to the dominant American Christian emphases on so-called victorious living and seemingly more satisfying experiences of Christ.

The contrasting point in the *theologies of glory* that dominate much of American Christianity is this: if you will just trust, surrender, persevere, and obey more, God has additional blessings for you that will transform your life in Christ into one that is much more enjoyable and rewarding. This formula has been most appealing for baby boomers of contemporary North American culture. *You can be deeply spiritual and religious; reap the bounty of God's temporal and eternal blessings; and, at the same time, continue to have a spiritual life where your efforts and commitments enable you to be in control.* What a deal! Is it any wonder that churches and religious media that market this brand of spiritual resources are immensely popular and successful!

With the nineteenth century's influence of revivalist and holiness theology proponents such as Charles Finney and Ruben Torrey, more recent men such as Charles Swindoll, Robert Schuler, and Rick Warren promise a satisfying spiritual fulfillment in the here and now. Through strategies that apply principles drawn from the Law, greater blessings from God can be obtained through a commitment to change sinful patterns of living. Through obedience to God and greater dedication to the right spiritual principles, the Christian can reap a greater measure of God's blessings and a more fulfilling experience of Christ in one's life. For some the key is the power of prayer, for others it is complete surrender and devotion to Christ, for others it is power Bible studies or the life of discipleship and evangelism.

Perhaps surprisingly to some, Luther's Cross Theology has also faced stiff opposition within the Lutheran community itself. In the nineteenth century, Samuel Simon Schmucker proposed an Americanized Lutheranism involving *new measures* designed to bring about a thorough transformation of Luther's theology by elements of Protestant Revivalism.[1] He believed that a Protestant coating of revivalist methods and atmosphere—with a diminished

---

1. See the discussion of Schmucker's *new measures* platform in *The Lutherans in North America*, ed. E. Clifford Nelson (Philadelphia: Fortress, 1980), 135–38.

presentation of distinctively Lutheran practices—would make out-reach more appealing to American religious sensibilities. His *measures* were especially directed to the sentiments of Americans whom he believed could not relate to what he deemed to be a German-Lutheran religious experience.

Today many elements of Church Growth and the Emergent Church movement continue to tempt Christians of all stripes to become zealous for a more glorious worship experience that would appeal to a broader segment of the American populous described as religious seekers. All these accents continue to be informed by the ethos of a Protestant revivalist piety. But now to the Theology of the Cross, let us invite you to give it a closer look.

Luther's Theology of the Cross

Most studies of the early Luther and the course of the Reformation in Wittenberg focus on two events: the posting of the Ninety-Five Theses on Indulgences in 1517 and the Great Leipzig Debate with John Eck in 1519. The intervening year, 1518, seems to pass in the narrative quickly, as if it were a rest period in the development of Luther's thought. Actually, 1518 is the mountain between two valleys in the development of Luther's thinking. In that year he formulated Twenty-Eight Theological Theses for a disputation in Heidelberg held as part of a triannual assembly of his Augustinian Order.[2] In these pithy, often biting theses, Luther set forth a rough outline of what it takes to become a theologian of the cross. At its core, Luther understood *Cross Theology* to be primarily a paradoxical expression of the revelation and saving work of God. It was a radical departure from the theological traditions of then current medieval theology in the West.

The medieval tradition held that God most clearly manifests Himself and carries out His saving work in analogous contexts in the world and in the lives of people. In other words, like possesses like; like manifests like; and like cooperates with like—for good and for

---

2. *Luther's Works*, ed. Jaroslav Pelikan and Helmut T. Lehmann, American ed. (Philadelphia: Fortress, 1958–), 31.42–59 (hereafter cited as *AE*). All the quotes of Luther's Heidelberg Theses that follow in our discussion are taken from this edition.

evil, for God and for the Devil. *Luther came to believe just the opposite, and he saw this most clearly in the cross of Christ.* The glory, wisdom, and righteousness of God can only be viewed rightly when perceived in the weakness, shame, and injustice of the cross of Christ. All other perspectives lead to a false view of God's glory, a false understanding of how He reveals Himself to us, and a false understanding of how He saves sinners. All other roads, avenues, or approaches offer us theologies of the Devil that Luther called *theologies of glory.*

When Luther proclaimed *the CROSS is our theology,* he implied several paradoxical elements at the core of his thinking.[3] They could be expressed in an all-embracing way in the following: "The cross is not simply the end of the journey in our quest for righteousness—not simply the destination of a happy outcome of life with God for us dead sinners; it is also the means by which the journey is made, and the experience of the journey itself."

Luther understood that the path to righteousness begins with the baptism of the sinner. Baptism unites us with Christ the crucified, where a death to sin—our sin—is both beheld and experienced (Rom. 6:3–11). The Word in the water joins us to Christ the crucified and brings simultaneously a death to sin and an emergent life now lived in the righteousness of Christ. Christian baptism is no one-and-done event. Luther emphasized that there is always a present tense of our baptism right up to the day of our final breath in this life. We can say, I was baptized, I am being baptized, and I will be baptized. The death with Christ to sin and the rising unto new life in His resurrection were singular events for our Lord. However, they are to be everyday events for us. We are daily to die to sin from our crosses and the hammering of the Law and then be raised up again and again in His life-giving watery Word—from the poverty of our sin to the riches of His grace, from repentance to faith, from death to life. Therefore, it is not simply that we *were* baptized into Christ the crucified; we *are* baptized in the cross of Christ. The sinner's progress in the path to righteousness leads both to and from the experience and inheritance of Christian Baptism.

---

3. *Dr. Martin Luthers Werke, Kritische Gestamtausgabe* (Weimarer Ausgabe) (Weimar: Hermann Bohlau, 1883–), 5.176.32–33 (hereafter cited as WA), as cited in Alister E. McGrath's *Luther's Theology of the Cross* (Oxford: Basil Blackwell, 1990), 152. The capitals are Luther's.

Baptism presents a paradox. The cross is not only our destination in the path to righteousness; it also describes the kind of experience we will have as we both approach and arrive at the cross of Christ. *This does not simply happen once, but rather it is the heartbeat of the Christian's life in the cross of Christ the crucified.* You are always arriving at the cross where you have already been. Christian Baptism at its core is a uniting with Christ in His cross, dying to sin, and a rising unto newness of life in His righteousness. In the Christian's life in Christ this happens again and again. Luther understood that as we enter the Christian life through Baptism, dying to sin and rising in Christ becomes a daily regimen that revisits the death of the old sinful self and the renewal of the new creation.[4] The old Adam is drowned. The new life in Christ arises by the killing of the Law and the raising of a new life from the Gospel. We make progress along the path to righteousness by always starting over again—dying and rising, repentance and faith worked by God in his Law and Gospel.[5] We mature as a new creation in Christ as we advance in the cross toward glory by returning again and again to our Baptism. This journey is attended also by the experience of the crosses we have been given, which can involve suffering, trials, and at times, even feelings of abandonment. These experiences are normal for all Christians.

Jesus has been raised from the dead and received His heavenly glory. He has had His Easter, but we have not. The experience of victory over sin, death, and the Devil is history for Christ. It is faith and hope for us. The cross and tomb are only empty for Jesus. At Easter we proclaim the not-so-empty tomb of Jesus, because all of us who are baptized into the death of Christ are still there awaiting

---

4.   "Thus, a Christian life is nothing else than a daily Baptism, once begun and ever continued. For we must keep at it incessantly, always purging out what pertains to the old Adam, so that whatever belongs to the new man may come forth." Martin Luther, *The Large Catechism*, 4:65, *The Book of Concord*, trans. and ed. Theodore G. Tappert (Philadelphia: Fortress, 1959), 445.

5.   It was Luther that refreshed Western Christian thinking by the rediscovery that God's Word is rightly understood and divided by distinguishing between two different words or ministries of God: Law and Gospel. The Law God uses to accuse and condemn us of our sin and work repentance. The Gospel is God's revelation and bestowal of the saving works and gifts of Christ.

our glorious, resurrected life. The Christian life has two installments, cross and glory. It is cross life for us now, and glory in the better day that is coming.

When we are finally translated into glory on the Better Day, it will be the crowning day of our baptism. It will be our best day to die to sin. We will experience then the full inheritance of the resurrected new life, freed forever from every aspect of sin and the curse of the ground. No more death, no more thorns or thistles, no more pain and suffering . . . and yes, no sweat! Every day is a good day to die to sin because every day is a good day to live with Christ. Every day is a good day to give Him our sins and to be blown away by the priceless treasure of His grace.

Paradoxes in the Law

Several of Luther's first Heidelberg Theses present a very bleak assessment of the prospects of the Law or its works advancing the sinner in righteousness. His first two theses declared the following: "The Law of God, the most salutary doctrine of life, cannot advance humans on their way to righteousness, but rather hinders them. Much less can human works, which are done over and over again with the aid of natural precepts, so to speak, lead to that end [righteousness before God]" (Theses 1–2).

The Law of Moses has often been described, as Luther did above, as the *Law of Life*. This designation, however, has created a great misunderstanding among religious people about what the Law can do for us. This misunderstanding is first seen back in Biblical history when confident Israelites were listening to the demands of the Law sitting along the banks of the Jordan, poised to enter the Promised Land. After reiterating all the demands of the Law received by Moses on Sinai, God exhorted his people through Moses to obey the Law and thereby to live and prosper (Deut. 30:16, 19–20). From this exhortation delivered through Moses, they reasoned in the still popular way that if the Law was what God expected them to do, then with His help, they could do it. God would not demand the impossible, and then promise blessings for those who would achieve it. In other words, obligation implies ability. This reasoning is both fallacious and damnable. Obligation only implies responsibility, and the purpose of the Law is to demonstrate that responsibility reveals our inability (Rom. 3:20). Since we are all unable, the Law of Life reveals our death.

There is an implicit paradox here about the Law that could be stated this way: If you pursue the Law of Life—which, of course, you simply must—you end up dying to live. If you do not pursue the Law of Life, you end up living to die. Let's explore this. An important disagreement between Cross Theology and glory theologies is over these questions: Can we do anything that the Law requires, and if we can, are we not duty-bound to do it as our little bit toward acquiring God's favor? In Luther's day, the dominant theology insisted that inherited sin has rendered all spiritually ill and sick, spiritually able to do almost nothing that God would find pleasing. Almost nothing! While there was no agreement concerning how much or just what, it was believed there was always something that sinners could do. And they were, therefore, duty-bound to do it. All must do for their salvation, as the popular expression stated, whatever was in them to do. Do what is in you to do for a beginning. Then God's grace will take over and give you resources to gradually bridge the gap between what you are and do, and what you ought to be and do, according to the demands of His righteous Law.

Luther insisted that sinners who do what is in them to do (apart from Christ), sin! And they sin necessarily. Learning from the apostle Paul, Luther held that there are only two classifications of persons before God: those who are perfectly righteous and those who are unrighteous and spiritually dead. Luther followed the apostle in Romans 5, where Paul distinguished all of humanity accordingly: those who have inherited spiritual deadness from Adam (Rom. 5:12) and those who have been made alive in the righteousness of Christ (Rom. 5:17). Therefore, you are either bound to Christ or bound to sin. You are either perfect or perfectly dead.

God uses the Law to bring us to the crushing and repentant recognition that, apart from Christ's righteousness, we must count ourselves dead to sin. We are the unrighteous, spiritually dead sons and daughters of Adam. And as we know about dead people, they are out of the running. They cannot do even *a little bit*. As Robert F. Capon remarked concerning our similarity with Lazarus in the tomb (John 11:39), all a dead person has to do is be a good corpse and God will do the rest.[6] Dead people can only stink. It is therefore silly, is it not, to encourage a corpse to do its best! Luther understood that the purpose of the Law is to show us dead sinners our true spiritual condition. Lutherans have a tradition of thinking of the Law of God in this role as a mirror that shows us our sin (Rom. 3:20). A better metaphor describes the Law's function as a spiritual autopsy, revealing to sinners the pathology of their spiritual deadness. As we know, autopsies have no therapeutic value for the dead person—not in medicine or theology.

The Law of Moses is the Law of life, but the devil seeks to entice us to adopt one of two spiritually lethal roads on how to approach it. The first is the road of semi-self-approval. It is to believe that the Law of Life does not have to be kept perfectly to receive God's favor. God will respect and honor those who put forth their best efforts to live according to its demands. No one is perfect, but if you are really making a sincere effort, He will surely accept your best. After all, God is a God of love and therefore He would never demand the impossible from us. This is deception number one. Number two is the road of rebellion. It is to rightly recognize the Law's impossible demands of perfect righteousness but say, *to hell with it all!* Let's live it up today, for tomorrow we will die, but . . . well, that's tomorrow.

Let's be clear about the only options the Law of Life provides; you can die to live or live to die. You can walk the road of the cross, which brings life out of death and repentance unto faith, or you can walk the roads of the devil grabbing to secure your own life by whatever you choose—to excel at being good or to excel at being naughty. Take your pick—either way, you die. The Law of Life is really a cross in disguise. It demands that we crucify even our best efforts and works that may tempt us to rely on them to secure God's favor. The Law accuses and reveals these works for what they are. They are self-serving; therefore, as Luther declares, they are damnable mortal sins. Whether by the working of the Holy Spirit or by the Unholy Spirit (the Devil), the Law renders sinners repentantly dying to live or rebelliously living to die. Notice how Luther wants to go further in exploring not simply the works we think evil but also the works we

---

6. Robert Farrar Capon, *Between Noon and Three—a Parable of Romance, Law, and the Outrage of Grace* (San Francisco: Harper & Row, 1982), 133.

see as very good indeed and take pride in. Further, he wants to contrast the latter with the saving works of God that appear common, ordinary, and even evil. He says, "Although the works of humans always seem attractive and good, they are nevertheless likely to be mortal sins. Although the works of God are always unattractive and appear evil, they are nevertheless really eternal merits" (Theses 3, 4). Whether on the streets or in the pews, people expect religion to produce righteous persons according to the measure of God's Law. They think that because the Law and its Commandments are holy, just, and good, they serve the job that in their minds is assigned to the Church—namely, to make people righteous. Here is the paradox: *Our works that seem to be our best are probably damnable, and God's work that seems as damnable as the Cross of Christ is in reality righteousness before God.* What appears good according to the good Law of God is not good, but rather is likely to be mortal sin. How might obeying the Law be a mortal sin? If the person lives according to the Law, doing good works and thinking he is contributing to his own righteousness, then that person sins, because such thinking is a denial of the fact that only Christ makes us righteous.

This is why St. Paul says that the Law brings about wrath (Rom. 4:15). And this is why Luther declares, although the works of humans always seem attractive and good, they are nevertheless likely to be mortal sins. The man or woman on the street, and all too often the man or woman in the pew, views the outward appearance of works as good; even so, he views the things of God as unattractive and even evil. People want a God who is impressive. They will tend even to take evil if it is impressive. Surely if humans can do such impressive things, then God's works should even be more so.

God's greatest works, however, appear lowly, unimpressive, and sometimes even downright repulsive. God brings His miraculous, faith-creating power called *Baptism* in simple, everyday water. God brings His authorized Word of both judgment and forgiveness through the mouths of mortal, sinful men chosen by Him as His spokesmen. God brings the forgiveness of sins through consecrated bread and wine and tells you that as you are eating and drinking this bread and wine, you are actually eating and drinking Christ's body and His blood. God's work is seen in the midst of blood, sweat, and tears on a wooden cross outside Jerusalem. His greatest work is the atonement for all sinners of all time, worked by the suffering and death of Christ, as He turns an ugly instrument of capital punishment into the holy redemptive cross.

Good Works: Good for What?

The works of the righteous would be mortal sins if they would not be feared as mortal sins by the righteous themselves out of pious fear of God. (Thesis 7)

The paradox in this thesis could be stated something like this: *Your trusted good works will separate you from God's favor unless God's favor separates you from your trusted good works.* All theologies of glory insist that we can keep the Law to some extent, but our problem is just that we cannot keep it perfectly. In other words, most everyone who is dedicated and spiritual can do some good and God-pleasing things, but they must look to a merciful God to make up the difference where they fall short. With such a view, Jesus becomes a part-time Savior of part-time sinners who are able to trust that at least some of their works are good and acceptable to God. This position is actually born of the deceptive cleverness of the Devil. It imagines that a third kind of individual could have entered the temple to pray along with the Pharisee and the Publican in the parable (Luke 18:9–14). He might pray: *Oh Lord, I thank you that I am not like this smug self-righteous pharisee, but I also thank you that I am a heck of a lot better than this tax collector.*

The Pharisee is always criticized because he wrongly imagined that his life was filled with nothing but good works. He thought he was incredibly righteous in his doing even without a savior from sin. By contrast there was the Publican whose whole life had been dedicated to sinful living. Everybody recognizes that he needed a savior and *God bless!* There is one who can save the likes of such wretched folks, both then and now. But many connected with the Church imagine that there is a third class of individuals: those who are looking to Jesus because they realize that while they try hard to keep the precepts of God's Law by some good clean moral living and benevolent giving, they are far from perfect. They slip up and do not always render what

God demands in his Law. These people imagine themselves as part-time sinners. They rely on the idea that they can take credit for some of their works being good; therefore, they look to Jesus to supply a make-up-the-difference kind of grace, which, along with their good works, can be trusted to win God's favor and salvation.

In Luther's day, many Christians relied upon their own fasting, self-denial, monastic exercises, and going to Mass daily in addition to the grace and merits of Christ. Today popular works would include personal commitments, surrendering to Jesus as your personal Lord in life, going to church regularly, personal evangelism activities, doing your best and striving to do better, and participation in the activities of your congregation.

Cross Theology understands that what really damns is any trust or confidence in anything other than—or in addition to—the righteousness of Christ that He bestows on us. There is no such thing as part-time sinners or those in need of a partial righteousness of Christ. There are just dead-in-their-trespasses sinners who need the life-giving, all-sufficient righteousness of Christ.

The Devil understands well that any work in which we trust to contribute something to God's favor is not a good work, but a sinful work. This is so, because a work is only good if it is for your neighbor's benefit, not yours. Luther's thesis rightly reflects the stance that all works you send to God for your own benefit are damnable sins. God is seeking a faith that simply and thankfully clings to Him and all His gifts and blessings, especially those gifts that flow from the saving work of the cross of Christ. God is God, in part because He alone saves sinners. Faith is for God, and works are for your neighbor. If you try to do some of them for yourself you make yourself into an idol, because you trust in your works as having some saving benefit in addition to those of Christ.

The Paradox of Humility

Living in Christ the crucified not only produces a growing faith and maturing in Christ; it also humbles us in the process. God intends to grow in us a self-awareness similar to St. Paul's. As a mature apostle, he saw himself as chief of sinners (1 Tim. 1:15; Rom. 7:21–25). Humility, a spiritual quality, and works that please God share the similar characteristic of invisibility. If you think you see yours, they probably are not there. Indeed, humility in all God-pleasing works flows from a focus and concern of others, serving Christ through their needs. He is producing both of these nicely in your life as you grow and mature as a new creation. At Heidelberg Luther expressed a paradox about our works this way: "Arrogance cannot be avoided or true hope be present unless the judgment of condemnation is feared in every work" (Thesis 11). Explicitly the paradox could be expressed this way: If you exalt yourself by your works, God will humble you. If you are humbled by them, God will exalt you in the works of Christ. If you can identify with St. Paul's reflection about his own works in Romans 7:21–25, he would point you to recognizing that your best efforts always seem to fall short. He confesses not simply weakness and ineptitude but also the experience of a law within (the fleshly self) that is actually working in rebellion against the Law of God. The old sinful flesh is another law waging war against the law of my mind making me captive to the law of sin (v. 23). Paul is telling you that the good you seek to do and the striving to do it actually reveal within you the old sinful self's working against such efforts and polluting them with selfish, prideful rebellion.

There really are only two possibilities for how, as a sinner, you may look inside at your works. You may either imagine you see them with a sense of self-pride or look at them through the lens of full-strength Law, written on the heart that always accuses as it is supposed to do. The purpose of the Law inside is not to reveal your good works, but rather your sin (Rom. 3:20). And in doing so, the Law would produce a sense of repentant regret where you can lament with Paul that the good you would do—you don't and you can't.

But how should you think of your works? Can you believe that any of them are ever acceptable to God? Will you ever do a truly good work that God is pleased with? The answer is certainly a confident, *yes!* As a new creation in Christ, you have become a slave to God and righteousness (Rom. 6:19, 22). But in this life our good works are an article of faith, not sight. Right now, you do not get to see these things. You just have to believe in them according to God's Word that declares we will do the works we were created to do as His workmanship because He has foreordained them (Eph. 2:10).

However, if you go inward to find them, you will be disappointed. You will either find works that create a sense of arrogant self-righteousness, which will ultimately lead to your destruction, or the old sinful flesh interjecting its own selfish pride into all that you are doing. That, in turn, will lead to an experience of the wrath and judgment of God, which will send you on your way to the cross of Christ hungering for His righteousness. You must simply cling to His Word that promises that as you abide in Him and His righteousness you will indeed (as a branch to a vine) produce much in the way of the fruit of faith. Luther maintained that ". . . speaking in this manner (the condemning voice of the Law) give cause for despair but for arousing the desire to humble oneself and seek the grace of Christ" (Thesis 17). The Law of God can bring despair that leads to Christ, but it can also bring despair that leads to ruin. The Law at full-strength impacts the lives of sinful human beings by always accusing us of our sin and revealing God's wrath and judgment. It reveals the poverty of both our doing and being. It shows that we do not what we ought to do and are not what we ought to be. It reveals that we are dead in our trespasses; not semi-righteous but unrighteous. Does this mean that everyone who sees themselves accurately in the mirror of the Law must despair of their own righteousness? Yes, it does! In addition, the more you struggle and strive to make amends, the more it will accuse and condemn. Does this mean that the Law brings every sinner to repentance? Unfortunately, such is not the case. There is a mystery here. There are actually three possibilities of what the Law at full-strength can produce: rebellion, ruin, or repentance. The first two are effects that are produced by the Devil. With some, the Law produces a destructive rebellion that pushes a sinner to greater acts of sinfulness than before. With others, the despair of the Law brings them to ruin. For example, Judas betrayed Jesus for 30 pieces of silver and the Law accused him severely and brought him to despair. Unfortunately, it was a despair that led to his ruin. After he threw the silver back at the chief priests he went out and hanged himself (Matt. 26:14–15; 27:3–5). King Saul despaired over his disfavor with God and committed suicide on the battlefield against the Philistines (1 Sam. 31:4).

As Luther notes, these are not the effects of the Law that God would produce to set a sinner on the right path that leads to righteousness. God would produce a repentant heart that desires nothing but God's favor out of pure mercy. This attitude is well reflected by the prayer of the publican in the temple: *Oh, Lord be merciful to me a poor sinful being* (Luke 18:13). It is a repentant despair that leads to a hunger for mercy. With the repentant heart, God creates a cross shaped void that can only be filled by the foolishness of the Gospel. This is exactly how the Law places the repentant sinner on the path of righteousness that leads to the bloody cross of Christ. There we join our Lord who walked up that hill that was worth dying on that included a huge pile of sins. After all, it had all yours and mine. He will die a sacrificial death to acquire that gift of grace that our despair has motivated us to seek.

Paradoxes in the Gospel

> The Law brings the wrath of God, kills, reviles, accuses, judges, and condemns everything that is not in Christ (Rom. 4:15). (Thesis 23)

It is important to note that of the Twenty-Eight Heidelberg Theses, only the last four present elements of the Gospel. The vast majority of the theses are devoted to a proper understanding of the nature and purpose of the Law over against prevalent misunderstandings that existed then and continue to exist both in and outside the Church today. This abundance of Law may strike us as odd coming from Dr. Luther, especially realizing that he considered the Gospel to be God's proper Word to us and the Law to be only a provisional, alien Word from God. Luther wrote these theses on the basis of two considerations. First, he discovered that the more he turned his attention to observing the commandments of God and the more he strove to do his best, the more he saw clearly not only his obvious shortcomings but also his inward shortcomings in what others saw as his best works. He was always discovering in himself the desire to appease God for his own self-centered good. Second, the more the Law revealed that he was not progressing very well, the more the Law accused and condemned him.

Luther realized that if the Law be a ladder, it leads only downward to Hell, not upward to Heaven. Second, Luther found that his experience paralleled both the experience *and* the inspired insight of the apostle Paul, who told the Corinthians that the Law is *the ministry of death.* It is designed to kill, not to make alive (2 Cor. 3:6– 9). It may be glorious, but it carries out *a ministry of condemnation,* not a ministry of righteousness (v. 9). The Law presents no portal to Heaven; rather, the Law presents the Highway to Hell. It is God's ministry of condemnation for all who are not in Christ.

Jacob's Ladder (Gen. 28:12), on the other hand, is rightly seen not as an instrument by which we might climb to Heaven, but rather as a portal by which the Son and the Spirit of God descend to us. We do not ascend to righteousness through our doing; rather righteousness descends to us by the grace and doing of our gracious God. The Son of God has not simply *descended* Jacob's ladder to us but *condescended* by becoming one of us. *He who lives by the Law will perish by the Law,* but the last of the Heidelberg theses are devoted to this truth: *He who lives by grace will live . . . by grace!* The Gospel predominates in the lives of sinners when it is presented as God's final Word, and in these last theses Luther wonderfully captures God's final Word to sinners in the Gospel of Christ the crucified: "He is not righteous who works much, but he who, without works, believes much in Christ" (Thesis 25). The Law of God declares what righteousness is, and it commands you to be righteous. Satan, knowing your fallen state, also urges righteousness upon you and encourages you to pursue righteousness in order to please both God and your conscience. When you fail in this pursuit—as the Scriptures testify that you will—Satan scurries to God and tattles on you while stirring up your conscience with guilt. The Devil's goal is to move you to despair and perhaps also some rebellion from being caught in the vice of the Law. Here is the paradox: *Everything you know about righteousness comes from the Law, yet by this same Law you will not be found righteous.* Instead, by the Law you will be found guilty of unrighteousness. The Law both describes and commands righteousness, but it cannot produce it.

When the Gospel is not allowed to be God's final word to sinners, its comfort for burdened consciences is compromised. When the demands of the Law are applied to sinners after the preaching of the Gospel, the Gospel is perverted by being put into the service of the Law. As Capon has expressed it, *"Jesus must not be read*

as having baited us with grace only to clobber us in the end with law.[7]
According to the Scriptures, it is the Law that is to be in the service
of the Gospel. Christ produces righteousness, and so Luther rightly
exhorts you not to do much, which produces no righteousness, but
to believe much, which gives it all to you. *You cannot become more
holy than being wrapped in the righteousness of Christ.* And you cannot become more obedient to the demands of the Law than living
with the perfect obedience of Christ. Notice how Luther contrasts
the slavery of the Law and the freedom of Grace. "The law says, 'do
this,' and it is never done. Grace says, 'believe in this,' and everything
is done already" (Thesis 26). Here is another way of expressing the
two paradoxes embedded in this wonderful thesis about the Law and
the Gospel. When all is said and done, there is always more to do. Yet
when all is believed, all is already done and there is nothing left to do.
And with that nothing . . . you get everything!

Let us explore the first paradox. It is our continually nagging
realization, is it not, that we are not the people we ought to be, nor
are we living as we ought to live? We hear from none other than God
Himself about how the people of God are to think, order their lives
and behave, and we note that in so many ways and instances we are
not, we do not, and we cannot. Alarmingly we observe that as time
passes, this realization about how we are doing does not go away, nor
do we get any sense that we are improving. We seem stuck and powerless to walk the walk, though we continue to talk the talk about how
we ought to live as would-be citizens of the Kingdom of God. The
Devil thinks that this is just wonderful. He wants us to doubt whether
we really have God's favor for the sake of Christ. He then tempts us
to deal with this insecurity in one of two ways. He wants us either to
question the inadequacy of our works or to worry whether God has
really included us in his solution in Christ. That is, he wants us to
question either whether we need *only* the righteousness of Christ or
whether we really qualify for it.

As we have noted in our discussion earlier, that to do what is in
us to do is to sin. This news is certainly bad enough to crucify us
under the curse of the Law. But neither Luther nor God's Law stops

---

7. Robert Farrar Capon, *Kingdom, Grace, Judgment: Paradox, Outrage, and Vindication
in the Parables of Jesus* (Grand Rapids: Wm. B. Eerdmans, 2002), 355.

here. There is one further curse of the Law that this paradox seeks to illuminate. Even if we did succeed to render something to God that met the dictates of the Law, and even if we were able somehow to do such a work spontaneously and selflessly, the Law and all it demands would still remain. The Law presents us with a cruel refrain similar to the old saying: *What have you done for me lately?* The Law issues demands that are not fulfilled once we are able to achieve the kind of works they require. Should we somehow achieve the standard (which is impossible), the Law still insists that we *do it again!* The Law always and forever demands *do it again and again.* And if we were to inquire, *How long do we have to keep it up?* The Law replies, *Forever! You are never done!* Even if you do it perfectly, even if you have always obeyed the Law perfectly (which you have not and you know it), *you are never done!* The Law always requires *more.*

The Law does not simply demand that we achieve or attain righteousness by works; it demands that we continue to maintain perfect works every moment of every day of our existence—yesterday, today, tomorrow, and forever. You must do them forever to be righteous. Therefore, one thing is perfectly clear: at any time before forever, we are not yet righteous and fit for the Kingdom according to the Law. If its demands to be righteous require righteous works that never come to an end—then it is impossible. *Yes!* And that is just what the depths of the Law intend to reveal. So here is Luther's point: When all is said and done—we never are! There will always be a tomorrow with the Law and its fresh set of demands that extend forever. The curse of the Law is the constant conviction of our sin—coupled with its demand: *Do it forever!* This is the paradox in the Law: *When all is said and done, there is always more to do.* Our death is both seen and experienced in the realization and impact of the magnitude of the impossibility of the demand *Do it forever!* And this cross of impossibility was planned by the God of the Law right from the start. It is this realized impossibility that He uses to take us to the other dimension of the Cross, where we discover the gracious God who freely gives all that has been demanded in the Law.

Only the crucified Christ of the Gospel can overcome this curse. He comes to the cross as our champion. He has fulfilled all the requirements of the Law, suffered, and died for the guilt of all our shortcoming and transgressions. In the cross Jesus says to us, "Now believe this: I have perfectly fulfilled the demands of the Law for you and I give all of my forever works to you. I have also atoned for all your guilt and sins. The Father declares that you are righteous yesterday, today, tomorrow, and forever for the sake of my sacrificial death on the cross. Believe this and all is already done. There is nothing left that you must do." Here is life from the cross that comes out of death—Christ's and ours. This is the life of righteousness now possessed and lived in through faith alone. Ponder for a moment the freedom you now have and all the things you do not *have to do*. You can stop all labors to please God. You can rest. You can take the obligations of the Law with all their forever demands and tear them up, give them the deep six. Trash them! It's over for the Law. There is nothing that God demands you to be or do. You are free from its curse (Gal. 3:13).

In the cross where faith receives from Christ all that is needed to secure total righteousness, favor with God, and the happy forever, there is only one thing left to do—that which you simply *want* to do. This is what Gerhard Forde has called the *hilarity* of the Gospel. It is to hear the voice of God speaking softly in the cross of Christ, asking, *What are you going to do, now that you don't "have to" do anything?*[8] Listen again to how Luther expressed it, and see if you can hear the hilarity of the Gospel. *The Law says, "Do this," and it is never done. Grace says, "Believe this," and everything is done already.*

If you can hear it, then you have arrived at the foot of the cross of Christ, which is just where you want to be in the path of righteousness—indeed, to be and to stay. Here we continually hear what we are to believe, and there is nothing left that we have to do—nothing today, nothing tomorrow, nothing forever. And when it comes to the nothing of works of the Law—*nothing* is everything!

---

8.   Gerhard O. Forde, *Justification by Faith* (Ramsey, NJ: Sigler, 1991), 56.

Chapter 2

A Parable on Law and Gospel

He stood on the porch of his ten-year-old home. He was soaked through from the downpour of rain. He had been walking for hours . . . thinking, thinking about how things could have gone so very wrong for him in his marriage. He was bewildered, disillusioned, and angered by what he had just learned about himself. It was his tenth wedding anniversary, but not what he had planned. He must tell his wife about his new discovery. But what should he tell her? Let's go back to the beginning.

There was once a young Christian man who married the woman of his dreams and was determined to be the husband that God's will obliges him to be. He joined Promise Keepers and committed himself publicly to loving his wife as his most supreme duty in life below his faith and love of God. On his first wedding anniversary, which he remembered, his actions were guided by his commitment and his awareness that his wife loved long-stemmed roses. So, on his way home from work that day he picked up a dozen beautiful long-stemmed, dew-dripping, red roses for his wife. Upon greeting his wife at the door with a warm, "Happy anniversary," he presented her with the lovely bouquet of roses. Now imagine the reaction of his wife when in the midst of her gracious thank-yous, he responded happily, in perfunctory accord with his committed duty to love her (remember, he promised), "Think nothing of it honey, I'm just doing my duty!" Instantly, an expression of angered disbelief came over her face, the roses came flying in his face, and she ran to their bedroom in tears.

What does this wife understand—and we through her eyes—that her insensitive husband does not? It certainly is the husband's duty to love his wife. Husbands should love their wives. It is an important part of God's Law and he has solemnly promised to do so. Moreover, it is also true that his commitment in this regard at Promise Keepers is certainly in keeping with this obligation. Yet the wife understands in the depths of her heart that this duty of love can never be fulfilled by mere commitments and promises to do so. Indeed, she understands, and we through her eyes, that love is a duty that can never be fulfilled out of a commitment to do one's duty. And the more committed her husband becomes in his actions to doing his duty, the farther away he will get from actually loving his wife. She just intuitively understands that all motivations by her husband to fulfill his obligation to her indicate an absence of love.

So we, and this bewildered husband, are left with a mysterious paradox. Love is the duty he has toward his wife, but it is a duty that will never be fulfilled by commitments to doing his duty. On the other hand, we all understand that if he ignores the occasion of his wedding anniversary by doing nothing, he surely falls short of his obligation to love his wife as he ought. Therefore, taking in all that we have recognized through the eyes of his wife, this husband realizes that as concerns his obligation to love his wife . . . he is damned if he does his duty and he is damned if he doesn't. And the more committed he becomes to doing his duty in all he does toward his wife, the worse off it gets for him.

> Now, ten years have passed since this couple married. Today is the occasion of the man's tenth wedding anniversary. The husband comes home to his wife at the end of the day and makes the following confession and promise: "Dear, I want you to know that for the past ten years I have been striving to love you. And I want you to know that in this coming year, I promise to redouble my efforts."

Has this husband not confessed to his wife that he does not love her? Indeed, has he not disclosed that he has not loved her for all the years of their married life together? If you were his wife, how would you respond? Perhaps . . . *please stop!* Again, what is it about love that the wife understands right to the depths of her heart, that this husband of hers does not? She understands that love is not ours from the efforts of striving. Indeed, if you are *striving* to love . . . you don't. But surely we must strive to love. What would be the wife's reaction if the husband comes home and confesses, *Dear, I want you to know that for all the ten years of our married life together, I haven't loved you . . . but I want you to know that in this coming year, I'm not even going to try?*

Now imagine that this husband has been reading this piece about him up to this point. Today is his tenth wedding anniversary, but he has not gone home to his wife yet. He reflects on what he has learned about himself from the foregoing.

> I must love my wife. It is my duty. I am committed and I promised. But, let's see now. . . . I am damned if I do my duty, and I am also damned if I don't. I am damned if I strive to love my wife. My striving to love her just reveals that I don't. But I am also damned if I don't even try. Well then, I'm out of options. I'm dead!

In the game of chess, when there are no options left by which you can keep your king out of harm's way, it is called, *checkmate!* As regards his obligation to love his wife, is it not true that this husband has recognized that he is in the moral equivalent of checkmate? This, of course, does not mean that he does not have choices. He has several choices. He can choose to do his duty, or not do his duty. He can strive to love his wife or he can choose to make no effort at all. But just as in chess where a checkmate position presents possible moves, none of the choices remove the checkmate-game's-over-condition of the player. Make any move, choose any option, the game is still over. . . . You're dead. *And so am I*, realizes the husband in a magic moment of self-discovery. He is a changed man. He can never go home to his wife as he has for the past ten years. But what will he do? What will he now say to his wife on this, his tenth wedding anniversary? Here is one possibility. Now we pick up our story from the beginning.

> The husband goes inside his house to his wife and tells her the following: "Dear, I have something to tell you. It has been quite a day for me. I have learned some things about myself during

our married life together that I never knew. Let me get to the point. I have come to the realization that for the past ten years I haven't loved you. God knows how committed I have been to doing so, and how I have striven to love you, but the fact is I don't and I can't. That's just the way it is. So . . . to hell with it and to hell with you, I'm out of here!" And he walks out on his silent wife never to return.

It was the great Danish thinker, Søren Kierkegaard, who observed the paradoxical character of love and law. "Of this we shall speak: you *shall* LOVE, for the very mark of Christian love and its distinguishing characteristic is this, that it contains the contradiction: to love is duty."[1] Love love and law have a *hide-and-seek* relationship with one another. If you see one, the other is hidden and cannot be found. *Loving God with all one's heart, mind, and soul, and one's neighbor as the self* is indeed, God's Law of Life. Do it and you will live. If you see the demand—*you must*—love is absent and nowhere to be seen. If love is a present flowing reality, then the Law has disappeared from view. Yes, love *is* the Law of Life, but love and Law can never be present together for they repel one another like oil and water. The Law of Love presents us with a moral and spiritual *catch-22*. Love is obligated by the Law, but all legal considerations and commitments to duty void and destroy love. Where there is Law, there is no love. It always reveals that we aren't, we don't, and we can't. We both understand and sympathize with the reactions of the wife in our parable. And therefore we also understand something about the mind of God as we shall explore later in this chapter.

But what if we respond like Israel, when they realized that they had transgressed God's Law and came under His wrath? *Give us another chance!* Let's explore the idea of more chances by returning to the analogy of the game of chess. Imagine that the demands of the Law of Love could be compared to the task of having to defeat the world's greatest chess player. (Actually, the demands of the Law for sinners is a far more impossible task.) You draw white and make your opening move—king's pawn two spaces forward. Now imagine

---

1.   Soren Kierkegaard, *Works of Love: Some Christian Reflections in the Form of Discourses,* transl. by Howard and Edna Hong (New York: Harper and Roe, 1962), 40.

the chess champion looks over at you and announces, *Checkmate!* You protest: *Look the game has just begun. I still have all my pieces on the board, and you have not even made a move. What do you mean, "Checkmate?"* The champion responds, *Don't you see it? Well then, play the game. You'll see it in seven moves.* And sure enough, in seven moves you see it.... Checkmate! So you say, *Give me another chance!* So another game begins with the same announcement, *checkmate!* You play the game and see it in seven moves. Now, *if you play long enough,* he tells you, *you may get good enough to see it in six moves.* And better still, perhaps you can get good enough to see it in five.

The real question for you, however, is the same as it was for Israel: How many times do you have to play the game to come to the realization that you can't win? It took our husband ten years in connection with his wife. Where there is Law there is no love. But some of us take longer to see this than others. And some never see it in a lifetime. Let's return to our parable. There is another possible scenario.

The husband goes inside his house to his wife and tells her the following: "Dear, I have something to tell you. It has been quite a day for me. I have learned some things about myself during our married life together that I never knew. Let me get to the point. I have come to the realization that for the past ten years I haven't loved you. God knows how committed I have been to doing so, and how I have striven to love you, but the fact is I don't and I can't. That's just the way it is. Now I believe that you have every right to leave me and I wouldn't blame you if you did. You deserve far better than I have ever been able to give you. But, I just want you to know how deeply sorry I am."

In this version of the parable, the wife breaks her silence and has the following astounding revelation for her husband. "Your lack of love for me may be a recent revelation to you, but it is no surprise to me. I have known it all along. But, there is something else I want you to understand. I do love you, and I always have. And as it has been in the past, that love shall be sufficient for the both of us. I'm not going anywhere; you are just fine the way you are." The husband can scarcely believe what he has heard from his wife. Tears well up in his eyes and he just goes over to her and hugs her. Now, about that hug, he did not make any commitments to hug his wife, nor did he hug her out of any

sense of duty. He did not strive to hug her. He just spontaneously
did it. It was the first loving thing he had ever done for his wife
in their life together. Indeed, she had been waiting ten years for
that hug.

How do we explain the hug? While it is true that Law cannot beget
love; love can beget love. And that is just what the wife accomplished
in her husband in the second scenario. When there is a humbling
repentance before a lover for a failure to love, love can beget love
when first it begets a faith in that love. The husband only gets up and
hugs his wife by first believing her incredible account of her own
commitment and love. Her love and trust blossomed into his returning love—something that all his commitments to duty and striving
could never produce. This is the second half of Kierkegaard's paradox: where there is love, law is nowhere to be found.

Now we must understand what an extraordinary woman this is
in our parable. She understands the Law of Love, and she also understands well something important about her own heart's desire for a
loving relationship with her husband. There would be only one way
that she could get what she wanted, but about that one way there
would be no guarantees. To gain a loving relationship with her husband he would first have to discover that he did not love her, and
for that matter, he never would by commitments to duty or striving.
Until that time, she must keep her silence. There are things that a man
must discover about his own heart on his own. She cannot *tell* him.

> Imagine his response if after five years of marriage, she breaks
> her silence and informs him that she knows that he does not
> love her. Moreover, she then declares, "That's OK. I love you
> and that is sufficient for the both of us." He would be incredibly
> offended and outraged by her comments, would he not? And he
> would say things to her like, "Where do you get off telling me
> such offensive things? After all the things that I do for you day
> in and day out, etc., etc.!"

The woman knows that she must keep her silence—a silence
without any guarantees. He may spend his whole life and not come to
a true understanding about his own heart. If so, she loses. Moreover,

even if he does discover it as in our parable, this is a magical moment. Scenario one is always a possibility; he may walk, in which case she also loses. She must hold her silence . . . even if it means forever. There is no other way and she knows it.

Thus God deals with us in His Law and Gospel. The chief purpose of the Law is not to show us where we love when we do. Nor is its purpose to enable us to love. All commitments to duty and striving destroy love. (There may be much striving in love, but never to love.) The Law's purpose is to reveal the checkmate, the dead-in-our-trespasses character of our sinful condition. It does this not by announcement, but by showing us our own heart when we engage the Law of Life in daily living . . . when we play the game. Its purpose is to take us behind God's spiritual woodshed and give the kind of thrashing that humbles us before Him. Yet as in our parable there is no guarantee of this outcome. The self-realization of moral checkmate may just as well produce rebellion and greater lovelessness as repentance. About this truth much of the contemporary church has lost its nerve and imagines other options. The ministry of the Law in the service of the Gospel is predicated on this spiritual truth: there is no other way.

In scenario two, the woman reveals the heart of God in the Gospel . . . a heart that only reveals the true self to the man of her dreams when he has been humbled before her. Perhaps she is a rather unbelievable figure of pure imagination. What woman in reality would be so lovingly committed to a husband who has no love for her? On this question there may be many different opinions. But about our God, there can be no doubt. He is just such a loving God who has designs on us loveless humans. He is a gambler, and He plays for keeps—win or lose—with all of us in Christ Jesus. But about Him, let us not get sentimental or fool ourselves. When it comes to what is necessary for a relationship with Him, through faith in His favor for the sake of Christ, there is no other way. He is the Champion who pushes the chessboard in front of us to play the game of life. The stakes are death and life. The rules are contained in the Law of Love, which is the Law of Life. Make your move.

Now lest we think that recognition of the checkmate comes by viewing the matter simply as the wife perceived her husband in the parable, it must be said that this is only half of the matter. The real hopelessness of the checkmate must be seen in the woman's eyes as she would survey her own heart. If mere commitments to duty doesn't satisfy you, honey . . . don't think they ever will with God.

CHAPTER 3

The Two-Faced God

More than reflective learned scholars have pondered the question, what is God really like? Or even more momentous questions such as, *What does He think about us and this problem of evil here on earth? Does He care? Can we bargain with Him or enlist His help in how we want to deal with it? Is He a mighty, vengeful, hard-nosed kind of God who is really not satisfied with anything less than perfection; or is He, rather, a kind, merciful sort of Deity?* From mature intellectuals to young, inquisitive children, questions such as these have been mulled over and debated in every age. At some point in our lives, perhaps we, too, have desired to take the measure of God and wondered, what would it be like to meet Him face-to-face?

The Hidden and Revealed God

Although God is always closer to us than the nose on our face, He has not taken the wraps off and given any sinful and mortal human being a full-measure, face-to-face meeting. As God told Moses who requested such a meeting, the face or full splendor of His holiness and glory would be the immediate death of any sinful human (Exod. 33:20). Our God, out of His mercy, keeps Himself on the whole under wraps, a hidden God—but not totally hidden.

He has chosen to reveal Himself at some particular times and certain places—and then only to reveal certain aspects of Himself. In early Old Testament history, God often revealed Himself as the One who is really in control of things here on earth. Again, and again He manifested His might and power in awesome ways. In the days of

Noah, it was the destructive flood. With Sodom and Gomorrah, it was fire and brimstone. In Egypt it was the plagues, the death of the firstborn, and the parting of the Red Sea. To those on Mt. Carmel it was fireballs from heaven that reduced a water drenched sacrifice and altar to powdered ash. As much as we modern-day believers sometimes think that a good exhibition by God today—as He did back then—would do wonders for the cause of true religion, these spectaculars by God never did inspire much in the way of long-term faith and devotion. For the most part, God's mighty displays in the Old Testament simply scared the daylights out of people. Even in the wilderness when God first took up a glorious presence with His people in a special tent, the children of Israel always stood outside as if saying to Moses, *You go in and see what he wants; we'll stay out here. You can tell us all about it later.* God's special way of saying *hello* in the Old Testament often necessitated the continually spoken words *Do not be afraid.* Meetings with the sovereign God back then were usually rather frightening experiences.

Mindful of our sinful frailty and desiring us to have a personal relationship with Him, God has chosen to reveal Himself to us cloaked in the mundane things of this world. Our Creator has made Himself personally known through His Word made flesh in the man Jesus, verbally in the prophetic and the apostolic Scriptures, and visibly in Baptism and the Lord's Supper. With the masks of humanity, earthly language, and the simple elements of water, bread and wine, God has not simply descended to us, but *condescended* to us. Here He continually gives us the opportunity to take Him in with all our senses in long, slow, and unalarming ways—face-to-face! God has no desire to blow us away. He wants to love and tenderly embrace us as His own. Moreover, His burning desire from creation on has been that we might respond to His love by a returning love, molding a magnificent relationship and life together. But as we know, love always complicates things for us. It complicates things for God, too. Kierkegaard illustrated God's problem well in the following:

> Suppose there was a king who loved a humble maiden. The king was like no other king. Every statesman trembled before his power. No one dared breathe a word against him, for he had the strength to

crush all opponents. And yet this mighty king was melted by love for a humble maiden.

How could he declare his love for her? In an odd sort of way, his very kingliness tied his hands. If he brought her to the palace and crowned her head with jewels and clothed her body in royal robes, she would surely not resist—no one dared resist him. But would she love him?

She would say she loved him, of course, but would she truly? Or would she live with him in fear, nursing private grief for the life she left behind? Would she be happy at his side? How could he know? If he rode to her forest cottage in his royal carriage, with an armed escort waving bright banners, that too would overwhelm her. He did not want a cringing subject. He wanted a lover, an equal. He wanted her to forget that he was a king and she a humble maiden and to let shared love cross over the gulf between them.

The king convinced he could not elevate the maiden without crushing her freedom, resolved to descend. He clothed himself as a beggar and approached her cottage incognito, with a worn cloak fluttering loosely about him. It was no mere disguise, but a new identity he took on. He renounced the throne to win her hand.[1]

As we know, the truth in Kierkegaard's parable entered human history in Jesus, the Christ. Paul eloquently summarized the historical version of the story in Philippians 2:

> Who, though he was in the form of God, did not consider equality with God a thing to be grasped, but made himself nothing, taking the form of a servant, being born in the likeness of men. And being found in human form, he humbled himself by becoming obedient to the point of death—even death on a cross!

The king cast off his regal robes and became a helpless baby, a lowly foot washer, and a shameful crossbearer. Not very scary, but that is precisely the point. God has love and courtship on His mind. In Jesus, God meets us face-to-face. But incognito! He comes humbly to win us over with a dying, sacrificial love to be His own bride

---

1. Paraphrase of Søren Kierkegaard, *Philosophical Fragments*, 31–43, by Philip Yancy, *Disappointment with God* (Grand Rapids: Zondervan, 1988), 103–4.

forever. As He conquered the forces of darkness and death, the risen and exalted Christ is still with us. Out of His loving designs, He is humbly hidden in His Gospel, cloaked in mundane human language and the common elements of water, bread and wine. Through these, Word and Sacrament, His Gospel ministry of salvific courtship with frail, sinful people continues. Only now He carries it out through common human bodies like yours and mine. We in His Church have become part of our Lord's humble disguise!

It's not very flashy or spectacular—nothing like the great Old Testament extravaganzas. Hollywood would never clamor for the screen rights, but here is God's loving face as clearly as we can receive it from Him. And it is His ministry and the way He condescends to meet us for our sake out of His mercy and love. Make no mistake about it, God was not fooling around with the Incarnation. The cross cost Him the humiliation and death of His own Son, and all for the sake of His burning love for us sinful human beings. In the Gospel we truly meet an honest-to-God *God* as He truly is—a loving and merciful God.

God's Preparatory Meeting

Face-to-face meetings between persons human or divine, however, require an honest encounter where everything significant is out in the open. Fireballs and smoke will not reveal a loving and gracious God on the divine side of the meeting, and deceitfulness and dis-honesty will not do on our side. All who think they have the spiri-tual mettle to request a face-to-face meeting with God must realize, as C. S. Lewis did, such a meeting requires that we rebellious sin-ners bring only our true face to the encounter.[2] And there is the rub that brings curiosity about divine matters within both child and learned scholar to a screeching halt. We don't have the spiritual met-tle natively within us for that. True moral self-honesty is a spiritual virtue, but we sons and daughters of Adam are spiritually dead.

---

2. See the illustrative instance of Orual's complaint against the gods in C. S. Lewis's novel *Till We Have Faces* (New York: Harcourt Brace, 1984), 290–94.

God, therefore, has another face and ministry to prepare us for the real-face-to-face meeting with Him through the Gospel. Through this preparatory meeting, He would give us a true and honest face and the humility to meet Him in His love and mercy. *You cannot meet God as He truly is until you have met up with yourself as you really are.* God will not be mocked by sham meetings with faceless human beings. We must wear our true face, and that is just what God would provide by meeting Him through His Law.

Here we see one of the most unique and distinctive features about Christianity that separate it from all the religions of man. Most religions have a moral code commended to us with the promise that through it we can all become better people. With legal enlightenment and commitment to a virtuous sense of duty, we can all make significant progress in overcoming our *perceived* moral defects. Do-ability with sufficient resolve is the hallmark of man's moral precepts. *I ought, therefore I can*, said the famous moral philosopher Immanuel Kant. He constructed a whole system of ethics based on that assumption.

But when we stand in the mirroring light of God's Law of Life, it casts a shadow of darkness and death about us that elicits the opposite confession: *I ought, therefore I don't, and I can't.* God's Law shows us that our problem is not, at its root, immorality or weak resolve. Ours is a problem of spiritual bankruptcy and death. This is the dark truth that lies tucked away deep in the soul of every sinner that must be faced with all repentant honesty before we can meet the gracious God face-to-face. Our idolatry and deceitfulness of the heart must be confronted for what they are. The gap between what we are and what we ought to be needs to be seen as the great abyss that we are unable to cross.

Jesus expressed the pith and marrow of God's Law when He approved the Deuteronomic formula; *You shall love the Lord your God with all your heart, mind and soul and your neighbor as yourself* (Luke 10:27–28). And setting Himself up as the revealed enfleshment of the Law, He commanded His disciples to *love one another even as I have loved you* (John 15:12). Love is the Law of the Spirit of Life, for God is love and God is life.

There are two elements in *full-strength* Law. The first is love, the character of God and the core purpose of human existence that

God designed for us from the beginning. Love is the foundation of the moral and spiritual environment that we inhabit, grounded in God's very being. When we love we are captivated by another with spontaneous, joyful regard. The beloved's needs, desires, and concerns become the center of attention that motivate and shape our involvement and relating to the beloved. Love's activity and concern is always other-directed and always freely given. Love seeks not for the self but for the other (1 Cor. 13:5).

The second part is *law proper*, which was added because of sin (Gal. 3:19). It is the you must—or perish. *Do it or die!* Law proper places duty and obligation before us with the threatening penalty of death, a penalty that captivates us at our very well-being, the most fundamental level of our self-love and concern. Love is demanded under penalty of death. To serve the Law is to enlist in the service of legal duty and to do so out of concern for the self, not concern for the other. Do what is required, and you shall live. In other words, your duty or your death! To be moved by legal necessity and the damning curse of the Law suffocates the freedom and spontaneity that love requires. When we are captivated and driven by the Law, there can be no love—but when we are grasped by love, the Law's demands and threats evaporate. Indeed, they can even seem silly.

Imagine strolling in a park and spotting a young couple sitting on a bench. Watching them out of the corner of your eye for several minutes it becomes obvious that they are deeply in love with one another. You can tell just by noticing how they look at one another. Now imagine going up to them and saying, *Surely you realize that you must love each other. It's the Law—do it or die!* They would look at you like you were crazy, would they not? Surely, they would wonder, How can we *must* do what we simply cannot help but do? Love's compulsion is tied to the beloved—not to legal necessity. Where there is love, the force and compulsion of legal necessity are not only absent to lovers; they seem ridiculous.

As noted in his parable, Kierkegaard understood that the two elements, love and law, have a paradoxical if-you-see-one-the-other-is-missing relationship. If you are captivated by one, the other is nowhere to be found. If you experience the demand *you must*, love is absent. Where love is a present flowing reality, then the Law has disappeared from view. Yes, love *is* the Law of life, but love and law are never experienced together. They repel one another in our experience of each, like oil and water. We are either grasped by the necessity of doing our duty for our own good or captivated by love and what is good for the beloved.

Let's explore the paradox further. It is certainly true that we are always capable of being kinder and more considerate of others than we have been and we corrupt ourselves if we do not even try. Moreover, we will never love unless we make a conscious effort. Nevertheless, deliberately striving to love people will not accomplish the goal. Love is a fruit of faith not a work of Law. Where love exists, it spontaneously carries its own burden for the beloved without strife or any sense of legal compulsion. The Law of love presents sinful humans with a paradoxical dilemma, a moral and spiritual *CATCH-22*. The paradox can be illustrated by the example of a painter who deliberately tries to become a great artist. If he does not strive, he will never become an artist, much less a great one. But since he makes genius in his craft a deliberate goal of striving, he proves he is not and never will be a genius. Great artists are such without striving. Their abilities simply unfold in their work like the petals of a rose before the sun.[3] Genius is a gift of God, not a work, and so also is love. Love blossoms from a grace-nourished faith in the Christian life as faith is exercised in our relations with others. If we do not strive to love with all that is in us, we surely condemn ourselves. But on the other hand, love is not ours for the striving. Moreover, Love is our duty, but we can never love driven by a sense of that duty.

Remember our husband on his first wedding anniversary who presented roses to his wife with the words about just doing his duty. The more committed he becomes to doing his duty, the farther his heart and life will travel from real love. Duty damns if we do it, and it damns if we don't—for both destroy love. But then also in the *Parable*, the husband confessed to his wife that he has been striving to love her for ten years and plans to redouble his efforts in the coming year. He revealed to her that he has not loved her in years, he doesn't love her now, and for that matter, he is not able. Yet as we observed,

---

3. It was Edward John Carnell who made this excellent observation about the disparity between striving and the true character of love in *Christian Commitment* (New York: Macmillan, 1957), 212–13.

he would stand self-condemned before his wife if his future intent was not even to try. This is the *CATCH-22* checkmate of the Law.

Love is not ours for the striving, nor ours for the refusal to strive. Love is our duty of the Law, but commitment to duty and all legal considerations void and destroy love. When we are captivated by the demands of the Law, there is no love. The Law always reveals where we don't, and we can't. We both understand and sympathize with the reactions of the wife in the *Parable*. Therefore, we also understand the mind of God. Love is a fruit of faith through grace where, of course, the Law has been replaced and is nowhere to be found.

The words of St. Paul in Romans 3:19–20 NASB 1977 speak to us: "Now we know that whatever the Law says, it speaks to those who are under the Law, that every mouth may be closed, and all the world may become accountable to God; because by the works of the Law no flesh will be justified in His sight; for through the Law *comes* the knowledge of sin." This is God's central purpose of the Law. He did not intend it to be a motivational tool to nurture a true loving heart from one of selfishness and pride; nor did He intend it to be an exercise guide that would enable the practitioner of some ten Bible-based principles to advance in the art of loving. When God added the Law to His creative design of love, He provided a potent diagnostic tool to set in bold relief our spiritual deadness and the impossibility of transforming ourselves back into His original plan for us in creation. Love was the constant condition of human existence in paradise, until Adam and Eve exchanged their trust in God for trust in themselves. When their trust was destroyed, the full contours of love evaporated with it. At its core, human capacity became bankrupt of the spiritual resources to center our existence on a whole-being love and trust in God. Such an existence was paradise, but Paradise was lost. The demanding duty of law proper was added to show the sons and daughters of Adam that we have no resources within ourselves to return to Paradise. *Moral necessity coupled with the threat of death will not generate either love or trust in God.* For Luther, they generated anger and hatred. Attempts to enlist the Law to please God will only generate a false self-righteousness, despair, or full-scale rebellion.

The truth about us seen in the Law at full strength is painfully hard to receive. All of our pride and sense of fleshly well-being is crushed by the verdict it pronounces. It pushes us to a level of self-honesty that we know would spell the end to all our self-made *I'm doing OK* faces. It destroys all plans and pretensions of self-justification by doing our duty. The Law condemns us! We can be easily tempted to turn away from the full impact of the Law and try to negotiate with its demands. Some popular ways include making the demands of the Law into goals as if the Law is saying, *Become the person who can love God with all heart, mind, and soul, and neighbor as self and you will live.* Another is this: *Do your best in loving God and neighbor and you will live.* And of course, there is the popular old standby: *Be more loving than most of the people you know, and you will live.*

All these pretentious evasions deny the full thrust of the Law, which proclaims that if we have not already and always been loving God with everything that is in us and other humans as ourselves, then we are dead in our trespasses already. Dead people cannot do anything; they are out of the running! This is the curse of the Law (Gal. 3:10). To finally hear this chilling truth from the God who pronounces it places the sinner under the wrath of God and at a critical juncture. The sinner will become either infuriated or broken. Either one will say from the heart, "*To Hell with the Law*" and run from God to greater levels of loveless rebellion or God will turn the individual down the crushing road of repentance. Here he would fashion the humble, honest face to meet the gracious God who saves. It is a face that recognizes the need for righteousness, love, and unconditional acceptance. And God meets these needs in the Gospel by clothing our barren and sinful condition with the righteousness of Christ and recreating our face and our whole spiritual being into a likeness of His Son. Through faith in Christ we now have a face fit not simply to meet our God, but to belong to Him in love as His bride forever.

The Chemistry of Law and Gospel

Most of us who have taken Chemistry 101 in high school or college can recall that there is an interesting polarity in chemical substances. Some are acidic to various degrees and others are alkaline in nature. Water is neutral. Perhaps we also remember what happens if we mix acid into an alkaline solution or *vice versa*. Each has the effect of weakening the strength of the other and if enough is added, eventually it will neutralize the entire strength of the solution. And water, as we know, is the universal solvent. It dilutes the strength of both. I'm no chemist, but perhaps we could say that if we need full-strength acid, alkaline solutions are *hazardous* if mixed in. They will contaminate by producing a neutralizing effect, and the same the other way around. Moreover if, for example, we need both full-strength acid and alkaline solutions, water could be considered a *contaminate* because of its effect of diluting the strength of both.

There are some useful contact points here for understanding the nature and ministry of God's Law and Gospel. I do not know who the chemist was who is responsible for discovering the duality and polarity of substances in terms of base and acid and their effects upon one another. But it was especially the insight of Luther that refreshed Western Christian thinking by the rediscovery that God's Word is rightly understood and divided by distinguishing between two different words or ministries of God: Law and Gospel. This is the central key that unlocks the true meaning of the Scriptures and enables us to hear the voice of God through them aright.

From Genesis to Revelation, God addresses us in some places with a word that is Law and other places with Gospel. And like base and acidic solutions, each has its own unique properties and characteristics that God might accomplish His purposes with us through them; yet each also has the power to contaminate and neutralize the other if mixed. Kept separate and at full strength, however, they are powerful and potent instruments that when properly applied carry out all the things that God would accomplish in our lives for our ultimate salvation.[4]

We know from our own experience and from history that the right words spoken at the right time to the right people can have amazing and powerful effects for good and ill. As the wise proverb says, *The pen is mightier than the sword.* By the right word under

---

4. C. F. W. Walther captured these points succinctly in the following: *In the second place, the Word of God is not rightly divided when the Law is not preached in its full sternness and the Gospel not in its full sweetness, when on the contrary, Gospel elements are mingled with the Law and Law elements with the Gospel* (Thesis VI); *The Proper Distinction between Law and Gospel* (St. Louis: Concordia Publishing House, 1928), 79.

the right conditions, whole nations and peoples have been moved to accomplish what was thought to have been impossible. Think of the famous words of John Paul Jones during the Revolutionary War: *I have not yet begun to fight*, or the inspiring words of Winston Churchill during the Battle of Britain: *Never have some much been owed by so many to so few.* Think of the simple words, *I love you*, magically spoken at the right time and place that transform the life of an indifferent beloved, creating a love relationship that everyone including the beloved thought impossible. The beloved sheepishly and with much chagrin confesses, *I don't know what happened, but I have fallen in love.*

We know the power of mere human words. Imagine by comparison the incredible power that God's Word must possess. The entire universe was created by it! The Lord tells us that it never returns to Him void but always accomplishes the purposes for which He sends it forth (Isa. 55:11). He has entrusted His powerful Word of Law and Gospel to us. We would be His arms, legs, and mouth to proclaim His Word of Law and Gospel through which He meets sinners face-to-face for their salvation (Matt. 28:20; John 15:27). The crucial thing, however, is that these words must be delivered unmixed and at full strength otherwise their potency is diminished, their power is neutralized, and the true face of God as He would reveal Himself to us evaporates.

Let's examine this more closely beginning with Law: God's preparatory meeting and ministry for the saving encounter through the Gospel. The Law is always preliminary and preparatory. Full-strength and pure Law is the unconditional demand first to love God with all our heart, mind, and soul. This demand, as Luther recognized, means that we *are to fear, love, and trust in God above all.*[5] Second, the Law demands that we love others when they enter our circle of nearness as we love ourselves. This fully potent Law is to be poured into the hearts and minds of complacent sinners to produce the awareness of moral and spiritual bankruptcy—the checkmate of *I must* joined to *I don't and I can't.* Remember God's purpose here is to reveal His just wrath and judgment and, in our despair

---

5. Luther's meaning to the First Commandment. See his *Small Catechism* (St. Louis: Concordia, 1943), 5.

of self-righteousness, fashion the honest face of a repentant heart. The Law exposes and condemns our false gods, our self-made plans for well-being, and our selfish, loveless treatment of God and our neighbor.

But what happens if the Law is not at full strength? What if it is contaminated by elements of the Gospel or simply watered down? What if the word we convey is a *you must*, but joined to the message that God is kind and merciful, whereby an honest, sincere effort would be considered satisfactory? Sincere, honest effort is something that we can muster through striving and a commitment to duty. Here a true encounter with the holy and righteous God is neutralized and repentance is not produced. The face of God here is a false face—it reveals neither the God Who condemns nor the God Who saves through the Christ.

Or consider the more common error of reducing the Law's demands to a simple list of moral do's and don'ts—a plan for how we ought to behave day-to-day. What happens if we present the Law just in terms of the outward dimensions of the Ten Commandments? Do we swear, lie, cheat or steal? Which of us can claim a clean slate here? Nevertheless, we have certainly watered down the Law of Love, the Law of the Spirit of life. We have reduced it to outward do-ability and the power is gone.

The Law as moral principle may indeed reveal immorality on our part, but it cannot reveal our true condition of moral bankruptcy and spiritual deadness. It may confront us with occasional or frequent *I don'ts* for which we may sense a responsibility to apologize—as we often do to one another—but mere moral principle will never bring anyone to the dead-end checkmate of *I can't*. There is room to maneuver with mere moral principles of duty on the legal plane of give and take. We know in advance that a sincere apology must be accepted, and we can always renew our commitment and hope to do better in the future.

Moralizing will never reveal the God who condemns, nor will it ever produce true repentance. We apologize for the things we have done, but we repent for the person we have been. Only full-strength Law destroys the hope of self-righteousness and lays us open to see the true depths of our spiritual poverty. The cutting edge of the Law is found in the First Commandment, the demand to reorder all our loves and concerns in life around fear, love, and trust in God.[6] It is God's checkmate that produces repentance and the honest face that recognizes the need for a gracious God. Anything less turns the Good News into ordinary news or no news at all.

Let's turn our attention now to the ministry of the Gospel. Question. What is the difference between receiving the largest, most valuable diamond in the world as a free gift—and getting it for a penny? If we look at it on the surface, the difference is not very much at all, just a mere penny. But let's look at this more closely. In the first instance we have a gift, and quite a gift at that. What do we have, however, in the second instance? Is it not true that what we have here is an incredible bargain? Notice the big difference? Great gifts are expressions and signs of great love, if indeed they are true gifts. The giving of gifts is the way persons, both human and divine, express their love for one another. Incredible bargains are different. They are usually expressions of deception, stupidity, or shrewd business enterprise at work. How many things do we get in the mail every week that trumpet incredible bargains and often with the word *FREE!* scrawled in big bold print. But as they say, let the buyer beware! We usually get what we pay for, don't we? Has experience not taught us that there is a world of difference between a bargain—no matter how great it may seem—and a true gift? Genuine gifts are expressions of love; bargains are not.

One of the most common words used to express the Gospel in the New Testament is the word *grace*. It means gift. Full-strength Gospel proclaims the Good News of a priceless gift that the gracious God who loves us has appropriated and gives to us for the sake of the saving work of His Son's death and resurrection. It is the gift of righteousness, forgiveness, reconciliation. It is the gift of secured unconditional acceptance now and forever. It is the gift of freedom, new life, and adoption into the family of God. It is the gift of well-being

---

6. The problem that sin has created is not that we can no longer love. The problem is that sin has rendered our loves hopelessly disordered. We cannot arrange all our loves around a fear and love of God. For a good discussion of this problem see Gilbert Meilaender's *Faith and Faithfulness: Basic Themes in Christian Ethics* (Notre Dame: Notre Dame Press, 1991), 69–71.

now and forever. Pure Gospel brings us face-to-face with the loving God Who, through His Son and with this grace, brings us back into the most beautiful love relationship and matures our faith and love into the full stature of His Son.

But what happens to this precious gift if Law is mixed into the Gospel or if it is diluted? What if we attach to the gift the requirement that we contribute something to Him or our neighbor—even if just *a little bit*? Why that's not asking much for such a priceless treasure as eternal life! See what has happened? The gift has evaporated, and we now have a bargain. Perhaps even a good one, but the gift is gone. Moreover, we have turned the face of our gracious loving God into a cosmic businessman or huckster out marketing His spiritual wares for a little virtue or affection. Notice also that it matters not if your little bit must come before to secure the bargain, or after to keep it. Your little bit is Law and any amount—before, during, or after, will neutralize the grace of God and diminish the power of God unto salvation. Can anyone bargain for *your* love? God's love and gifts can never be had for a bargain either.

Let's look at this also from our standpoint. In our example, the bargain of a happy forever only requires that you contribute a little bit. Will we ever have any assurance of a happy forever? How much does God think is a *little bit*? Have we provided enough yet, or is more needed? How will we ever know until, of course, it is too late? And what about the quality of our contribution? How good does it have to be? Is ours good enough? Who knows? Even a little bit of Law can rob us of all assurance and confidence that the blessings of God are truly ours. And if our happy forever is on the line, what means everything to us finally ends up depending on mere whistling in the dark. From our perspective bargains from God offer no security or peace where we need it most—our present and future well-being.

Applying Law and Gospel

Our Lord does all this by the Holy Spirit through His ministry of Law and Gospel in the Word and Sacraments. Through the Law at full strength, he would expose our fleshly self-made plans for acceptability and secure personal well-being and condemn them for the idolatrous and unworkable plans that they are. The problem here is not simply that they are wrong. Rather it is that they don't work and can't work, and those who rely and trust in such plans are not just wrong; they are dead! This is full-strength Law!

The most penetrating Law is that which is directed not to our behavior but to the core of the fleshly self, which is in the mind and heart where our selfish strategies and goals are lodged, formulated, and energized for action. It is on fleshly belief, hope, and trust that the Law must be applied. A mere behavioral application can often end up as moralizing, and the sinful self can easily adapt to a certain modicum of nice moral living. And in Christians it often does!

We need to be clear about God's objectives here as we would battle the flesh. God's ministry of Law in the life of the Christian is not to reform the fleshly self. He is out to kill it. Paul exhorts us to mortify and crucify the Flesh. Kill it! *Remember the heart and mind of the fleshly self is organized around a rebellious answer and strategy to solve the problem of existence itself—personal well-being.* What do we need to do to become secure and acceptable human beings, and what can we do to have significant meaningful impact in life? How the fleshly self in each one of us frames out answers to these strategies is ground-point zero where full-strength Law needs to be directed and applied—again and again.

What does effective ministry of the Law do for the new creation in Christ? Nothing in any direct way but it does create a powerful hunger and thirst for our Lord's bread of life and living water of the Gospel. The Law itself imparts no spiritual nutrition or power for Christian living, even when its exhortations are softened and joined with words of inspirational encouragement. Rather it is intended to be God's great appetite builder that sends us running for the Word of Life. Only through the Ministry of the Gospel does our Lord nourish the new creation to sustain and mature our faith and life in Him. Full-strength Gospel can often be the simple Gospel—*you are forgiven; God loves you and accepts you just as you are for the sake of Christ. It can even be as simple as; Jesus loves me this I know for the Bible tells me so.* For our little ones in Christ, we must take care to continually feed them with the pure milk of the Gospel. And often the simple Gospel is what we need—just the plain but full-strength words that absolve: *I forgive you all your sins.* Yet it is also true that the Gospel is *not* simple. There is more to it in its implications and applications than we will ever grasp in a lifetime.

As we grow and mature in Christ, the Lord also intends for us to feed on the "meat and potatoes," indeed the whole nine courses of the Gospel, not simply the milk and pabulum. The Spirit is working through Word and Sacrament to renew our minds and hearts to the full stature of the mind of Christ Himself. We need a mature understanding and trust of faith to handle the front lines of Christ's warfare with the powers of darkness in our lives and in the world—maturity for battle and service at the tough outposts of life. The milk and pabulum of the Gospel alone will not provide that kind of growth and equipping. With a full-orbed Gospel the new creation becomes progressively built up for a fuller and deeper flow of the love and ministry of Christ through us to those He gives us opportunity to serve.

It is important to understand how we need God's Law and Gospel in order for them to beneficially impact our walk of faith. We do not need the Law whenever, however . . . or the Gospel whenever, however. We need them balanced and rightly ordered. It was C. F. W. Walther who observed that each Word is to be addressed to sinners who are in different states of mind and attitude about their own sinful condition. The Law is to be addressed to sinners who are complacent, rebellious, or unconcerned about their sin. The Gospel is to be addressed to sinners who are despairing and repentant concerning their sinful state.[7] Becoming complacent or rebellious about one's sin just naturally occurs again and again in the Christian's life because of the fleshly self. The Law is how God fashions the repentant heart to hunger and thirst for the liberating and joyful Word of Christ's forgiveness in the Gospel. Luther expressed this relationship this way: "He who has never tasted the bitter will not remember the sweet, hunger is the best cook. As the dry earth thirsts for rain, so the Law makes the troubled heart thirst for Christ. To such hearts Christ tastes sweetest; to them He is joy, comfort and life. Only then

---

7.   See Walther's discussion of Thesis VIII: *In the fourth place, the Word of God is not rightly divided when the Law is preached to those who are already in terror on account of their sins or the Gospel to those who live securely in their sins.* C. Walther, *Proper Distinction between Law and Gospel,* 101–27.

are Christ and his work understood correctly. . . . That is, He comforts and saves those who have been vexed and troubled by the Law."[8]

The heartbeat of God's having His way with us is always the Law first, and then Gospel. But it is the Devil who gets busy when God's Word is distorted into Law/Law, Gospel/Law, or even Gospel/Gospel. An unrelenting spiritual diet of Law—even if it is watered-down doable Law—produces spiritually undernourished and discouraged sinners who are tempted either to despair of God's favor or to fool themselves with visions of self-made righteousness. When the continual refreshment of the Gospel is missing, God becomes simply a spiritual taskmaster, and we the weary workers. Moreover, the Devil will be using the Law to tempt us to believe that we are not acceptable to God because of all our failings or, on the other hand, that we *are* acceptable despite them. The Law without the Gospel leads either to despair or to self-righteousness.

Conversely, the Gospel without the Law can produce ingratitude that manifests itself as boredom at first and irritation later on. When the Gospel begins to sound like *the same old thing*, the value of grace is discounted, and faith life becomes infected with an ungrateful spirit. Actually, this is an insidious form of doubt that can afflict faith.[9] Your appreciation of the value of grace is tied to your awareness and appreciation of the magnitude of your sin. When sin becomes a small matter, so does forgiveness. If your sinful deadness apart from Christ is forgotten or discounted, your appreciation of grace will decline accordingly. Indeed, your sense of the value of grace may rise no higher than your awareness and alarm over the enormity of your sin.

From Cross to Glory (or Tacking to Glory)

Law and Gospel are the means by which we make progress in our cross life; a progress that someday will translate us into Glory. What kind of images might we employ to depict this progress? What helpful

---

8. *AE* 21, 329.

9. This and other varieties of doubt that can afflict our life of faith will be discussed in a later chapter.

metaphors could illustrate the nature of the journey, the means of transportation, and what it means to make progress? The people of God in the Church Militant have often been depicted as travelers in this world on their way to Glory. Augustine described Christians as citizens of the Kingdom of God; sojourners just passing through the lands of this world to their Heavenly Home. Others have employed the metaphor of crossing water to the other side of a river, or in the case of the poetry of Henry Wadsworth Longfellow, on a voyage traveling to a distant shore. In "The Celestial Pilot" from *Voices of the Night* (1839), Longfellow presented Dante's picture of the wings of an Angel of the Lord piloting the believer straightaway to the distant shore of heavenly bliss.

In our earlier discussion of the characteristics of Luther's Theology of the Cross, we observed that the baptismal life of the Christian involves a lifelong journey to Glory that takes place entirely in the cross of Christ. You cannot fudge Glory in this life. You get there only on the Better Day that is coming and not one day before. We noted that the cross is not simply the end of the journey in our quest for righteousness—not simply the destination of a happy outcome of life with God for us dead sinners; it is also the means by which the journey is made, and the experience of the journey itself. In other words, paradoxically, the only way we get to Glory is to be on a journey that never leaves the cross of Christ. And since this journey in all its phases is shaped by your Baptism; imagery involving water—works!

In the waters of Baptism, we unite with Christ the crucified, dying to sin and emerging forth with a New Life lived in His righteousness. However, as we have emphasized, Christian Baptism is not a one-and-done, we-move-on-from-here deal. The cross life of the Christian involves a present-tense of Baptism that continually shapes the life of faith. Dying to sin and rising in Christ is intended to be a daily regimen that produces the death of the old sinful self and the renewal of the New Creation. For this reason, Luther observed that progress toward glory involves a watery journey in the cross that always involves starting over again. The Christian's baptismal life of dying and rising, repentance and faith are to be daily accomplished by the killing of the Law and the rising unto newness of life by the Gospel.

With this understanding, we might imagine our baptismal journey to Glory as something like taking a voyage to a distant shore in a sailboat. We would be the passengers on a sailing vessel bound for Glory and piloted by our Lord Jesus. The course he takes, however, can be very puzzling to many who are not familiar with Divine sailing. From visions of the distant shore of Glory supplied by the Scriptures, it could be said that from the deck of the boat, you can see it from here. However, what may appear confusing to some is that the bow of the boat never seems to be heading toward our intended destination. We see Glory straight ahead, but Jesus is intent just to sail back and forth to the left and then to the right, as if he were always changing his mind about where he wants us to go. In sailing lingo, he insists on tacking back and forth from the port side of glory to the starboard. Tacking or coming about is a sailing maneuver by which a sailing vessel (which is sailing approximately into the wind) turns its bow into the wind through the no-go zone so that the direction from which the wind blows changes from one side to the other. To sail directly into the wind is to invite getting capsized—dead in the water. For this reason, Jesus being a savvy sailor never aims the bow of the boat straightaway at the distant shore. For some of the ignorant Christians onboard this is confusing, and they doubt that this kind of navigation is making any progress at all.

Extending this imagery, we can envision the Lord sailing us through the waters of our Baptism tacking back and forth, sending us to the Law and then the Gospel. He sails us first into full-strength Law, crucifying us and producing a repentant death to sin. But then tacking back the other way, we are raised up again unto new life in Christ and his righteousness by full-strength Gospel. Port to starboard, repentance to faith, dying and rising, back and forth, always starting over again—Jesus our pilot sails us in the waters of our Baptism tacking to Glory.

The voyage, however, is not without its dangers. The Devil is a stowaway and he is continually seeking to persuade whomever he can to mutiny. One devastating approach has been to entice Christians to leave the waters of their baptism behind and travel overland toward the bliss of Glory with the promise that you can get bits of bliss as you go if you take the right route. However, if you insist on sailing, the Devil tries to convince you that tacking back and forth will never get anyone to Glory. When sailing into the dark waters of the Law, he would have sensitive Christians refuse to tack so they might crash on the rocks of the Island of Despair. Or, when sailing into the refreshing waters of the Gospel, the Devil loves to entice us (especially Lutherans) not to tack back to the Law—*let's not get negative!* Just keep sailing onward until we are dead in the water, caught in the doldrums of complacency and ingratitude. Either way, Glory becomes just a story, and no one ever gets there.

So let the Glory story and our vision of that distant shore renew our confidence that we are on course; and with the Lord at the helm, we are going to get there! This heavenly Port O' Call we shall surely make so long as we trust in our Baptism where our Lord is continually tacking us back and forth from the Law to the Gospel. It is sin and grace, repentance and faith, dying and rising, and déjà vu all over again. Here in the ever present-tense of our Baptism, our life in Christ is truly making progress, as our Pilot knows just how to sail us where we need to go . . . *tacking to glory.*

God's Last Word

It was in the last thesis in *The Proper Distinction between Law and Gospel* that C. F. W. Walther declared that the Gospel must predominate the preaching and teaching of Servants of the Word.[10] He meant that the Gospel must predominate instead of the Law. What would that look and sound like? Well, as they say, it all depends. When servants are *teaching* the Word of God, we might expect more time or space would be spent teaching articles of faith in the Gospel than elements of Divine Law. For example, in Luther's *Large Catechism*, most of the chief parts are devoted *to teaching about* aspects of the Gospel. Only the first chief part (the Ten Commandments) teaches the demands of the Law that reveal sin and describe good works. Nevertheless, it would be a mistake to conclude that in *preaching* the Word of God, more time must be spent on the Gospel than the Law. While the content is the same, there is an important difference between *preaching* and *teaching* the Gospel.

---

10.   C. Walther, *Proper Distinction between Law and Gospel*, 403–13.

There are two different modes of discourse that convey the Gospel. The first is a *didactic* or informational mode that informs about Christ's saving work and that God forgives sinners for His sake. Here, we receive *teaching about* the Gospel usually with *him-you* language. Second, there is a *prophetic mode* or personal address of God that proclaims and bestows the saving gifts of Christ. This voice usually employs *I-you* language. As revealed information, the Gospel teaches and informs about God's forgiveness of sinners. With prophetic language, God personally addresses the sinner: "I forgive you all your sins." And what you hear is what you get![11] When preached, the Gospel does not predominate by spending more time on it. The Gospel predominates when hearers receive the saving gifts of Christ as God's *last word* to them.

We all know when we have received *the last word*. It is followed by silence. The saving gifts of the Gospel need to be delivered to sinners as God's last word. We could also think of the last word as *the bottom line*. When you get to the bottom line, you have come to the most important thing that provides right perspective on everything that has come before. It is the bottom line or last word that dominates in the proclamation of God's Word precisely because it is . . . *the last word*. Therefore, what needs to come first—what needs to be preliminary, provisional, and preparatory is God's address of Law. The Law is to serve the Gospel, never the reverse. The purpose of the Law is to prepare the heart of sinners to receive the liberating saving gifts of the Gospel.

What if the preacher spends more time on the Law? There is no problem should more time be devoted to the Law to clarify and admonish the life of faith and works and convict of sin. Sometimes more on the Law is needed. However, convicted sinners get God's *bottom line* in what follows as the Lord's gracious Word of forgiveness. When proclaimed, the Word of God that brings death to sin (Law) is always to be followed with the Saving Word (Gospel) that restores and brings life with God.

Only when the Gospel concludes with an *A-men* and delicious silence, can its life-giving freedom fully impact the heart of the

---

11. More about these two modes of Gospel discourse will be presented in chapter 4.

sinner. This is how the Gospel predominates when it is preached, and this is terribly important. What if the Servant of the Word does not shut up after delivering the Lord's forgiveness to sinners? What if he returns to the Law out of mistaken zeal to promote more or better good works (Law/Gospel/Law)? What if his bottom line presents God admonishing good works as His last Word? When the Gospel's saving gifts are not presented as God's final word, then good works are falsely construed as the bottom line of God's dealing with sinners. The forgiveness of the Gospel can easily be misconstrued as more chances to clean up your spiritual life for more good works. The goal of the Gospel is the sinner, not what the sinner can do for God. John 3:16 NKJV says, "God so loved the world [of sinners like each of us] that He gave His only begotten Son." You are the big deal to God, not what you can do for Him. So understand, listen, and thank God for Servants of the Word who let the Gospel predominate: who deliver the saving gift of the Gospel to you as *God's Last Word*, because it is.

Given then a balanced spiritual diet of the full strength of the Law and the full sweetness of the Gospel, a healthy balance of dying and rising, confession and absolution, and repentance and faith are maintained. *But the healthy balance is only maintained when the Gospel remains the bottom-line final Word and believers remember always to tach.* These in turn energize the walk and exercise of faith as we gather together around the *sacred things* and as we scatter separately in our tasks of vocation where we live, work, and play. *The cross life of the Christian is paradoxical, but then, so is the Christian himself.* The Christian is rendered by God's dual address as one whom Luther described as *simultaneously a sinner and a saint.* Examining this paradoxical identity of the Christian shall be the topic of the next chapter.

CHAPTER 4

Justification

Getting Saved, Doing Nothing

Is there anything to Christian living beyond the normal life experiences of a Christian? Understanding Christian living in the cross of Christ will help us develop a clear vision of what it means to *be* a Christian. Luther's Theology of the Cross will continue to help us sketch out an understanding of the Christian self: *who* and *what* is the *me* that God has laid claim to in Christ. Each of us is a unique person created in the image of God yet corrupted by sin inherited from the Fall of Adam. To inquire about Christian self-identity is to explore that reality in conjunction with the inheritance we have in Baptism through Christ the crucified.

The Paradox of Christian Identity

There are two basic questions anyone can ask about self-identity: *Who am I?* and *What am I? Who am I* is a question about a person's standing or status in community. *What am I?* is an inquiry into a person's own character. Our relationship to the Old Adam and the Second Adam provides the frame of reference by which the Christian's status and character can be grasped. In other words, the Christian can be viewed from two different perspectives: the Christian as God sees him in Christ and the Christian in himself apart from Christ. Each perspective reveals important elements that together create a paradoxical picture of Christian self-identity.

From these two perspectives, Luther answered the two identity questions above and described the Christian in the following way: *Thus a Christian man is righteous and a sinner at the same time, holy and profane, an enemy of God and a child of God.*[1] Therefore, the Christian can be understood as a simultaneous *sinner/saint*. This does not mean that the believer is partially a sinner, yet partially saintly. Rather, the Christian is understood to be both completely sinful and completely righteous. Let's probe the rich significance of this paradox and what it reveals about our identity as God's children living in the cross of Christ.

Who I am addresses the issue of a person's status. It is an inquiry about our place in community and what kind of standing we have. Am I a person who counts? Do I have standing? Is my place and acceptability secure and, if not, what does it take to make it secure? And more to the point of our discussion: What is my standing before God? Our God is a multipersonal God who in Himself exists in a community of personal relationship. He created us as a reflection of Himself, personal beings designed to live in significant relationship and community with Him and other similar created beings. As God is a community of love—Father, Son, and Holy Spirit—He created us to be joyfully fulfilled by community in love relationships, dependent and grounded in His infinite love. Human beings are fundamentally relational creatures reflecting the relational God who created us for Himself.

Issues about our status—our standing in community—address our need to belong significantly and securely in relationships where we may be accepted and have meaningful personal impact. As fallen image-bearers in rebellion against our Maker, we are bent upon finding or achieving acceptable status in every quarter except where it may be found. No one seeks after God, the One to whom we were made to ultimately belong. And in a sense, no wonder! He is a holy and righteous God and we are corrupted sinners who cannot stand under the demands of His Law. Moreover, our sinful self wants nothing of a dependent community under His lordship. Amazingly,

---

1.   *AE* 26, 232.

however, Christ has sought us out and made us His own. By His righteousness we have received favorable status with God.

So who am I as a Christian? Luther observed we all have the status of saints. The word *saint* literally means a *holy* or *righteous one*. All who have been brought by the Spirit into a saving faith relationship with Christ have a righteous, blameless standing before God. Covered with Christ's righteousness, Christians have become citizens of His Kingdom and adopted sons and daughters of God. God has given us full standing in the economy of His redemptive community. We have secure, favored status as saints before God because we have received God's full and complete justification through faith in Christ. We are justified because Christ has fully paid for the guilt of our sin on the cross. Though our status was that of a guilty sinner, Christ canceled our debt; therefore, God has declared us to be holy, innocent, and righteous for the sake of His payment for our guilt. Our justification is a matter of having acquired an innocent status before God for the sake of Christ.

Also, while we can say, *I am a justified child of God*, must we not admit that we often do not think, act, or feel that way? We therefore cling to our saintly status by faith, and we trust God's promise that it shall be so forever. All the while, we are worthy subjects praying each day, *Lord, I believe, help thou my unbelief*. We claim our justification in this life by faith—not by sight, and it is often a fragile faith that is in the *needs-improvement* category. Much to our own dismay and embarrassment, we Christians must admit that we often do not act very secure in Christ's righteousness. Our impoverished faith and love serve well to remind us that although our status in Christ is holy and righteous, our character is not. Apart from Christ, we are still sold as slaves to sin (Rom. 7:14). And this brings us to the other half of Luther's Christian identity paradox. *What am I?* I am a sinner. My character that I inherited from Adam remains corrupted by sin. We groan with the rest of creation awaiting the final deliverance from all the devastating effects of evil in the world and in our own lives (Rom. 8:26).

The word *sin* is a technical term that the Scriptures use to describe the problem of evil. Literally, the word means *missing the mark*. To be sinful is to miss the mark of God's creative purpose and design. Both believers and nonbelievers are quite aware of how the problem of evil afflicts the body with disease, degeneration, and eventually death. Modern medicine has done much to postpone some of these, but it is powerless to overcome them. Our hope as Christians lies in the fullness of salvation and the resurrection of the body, a certain inheritance that we see and celebrate in the resurrection of Christ. But what about the effects of sin on the spiritual or personal dimensions of human nature? How have they affected our personal capacities that reflect our Creator God? Perhaps we may gain helpful insight by reviewing the progressive character of Eve's demise in the Garden in Genesis 3.

Eve began her encounter with Satan with an unexplained faulty belief about God's will for her life. She believed that God prohibited her from touching the forbidden fruit, in addition to not eating it (Gen. 3:3). God, however, did not forbid her from touching (Gen. 2:17), but from partaking of the fruit. Inexplicably, Eve doubled the prescription leaving her with a legalistic understanding of God's will for her life. Her mind already corrupted, Satan would see if her faulty thinking could be turned into outright rebellion. At the Devil's suggestion, Eve chose to believe that she could become like God—a fully independent person in control of her own life and destiny. She believed that this was within her power and that partaking of the forbidden fruit could accomplish the goal. For this reason, the forbidden fruit was seen as good for food and able to give wisdom that would elevate her to the stature of God (Gen. 3:5–6a). No longer trusting God's warning about eating the forbidden fruit, she believed that she would not die. Her desires became depraved as she longed to be self-governed like God. Motivated by her rebellious and perverted goal, she ate the forbidden fruit. As Adam partakes with her, they both experience for the first time feelings of guilt and shame.

Notice how the fall into sin and the loss of the image of God did not begin with external behavior. It began in the mind and moved into the heart. Then the corrupted beliefs, attitudes, and motives in the inner character led to sinful external behavior. Eve's sin was rebellion against God. It flowed from a lack of trust in the mind and heart and then was acted out in external behavior. Adam acted on his own lack of trust and idolatry as he joined in Eve's rebellion. He could stand with God or his wife, but not both. Adam refused to trust in God, and in rebellion he chose to make his wife his ultimate concern.

Jesus observed that it is the same now for all sons and daughters of Adam (Matt. 15:19). Luther observed that the root of all sin is a rebellion against the First Commandment. At its core, sin is a refusal to trust and love the Creator God for well-being. From the fall of Adam and Eve, humanity has been brought into the world with a compulsive rebellious attitude against God. We would love and trust any other person or thing in life but Him for our own well-being.

Well known is that Luther championed justification as that doctrine upon which the Church stands or falls. Lose trust in the free grace of the righteousness of Christ alone, and the holiness of the Church and all in her are lost. Less understood, perhaps, is the realization that Luther only came to his rediscovery of the sufficiency of the righteousness of Christ after he realized the full extent of the problem of sin. Human depravity has rendered even the most virtuous citizen of the world, or the cloister for that matter, as not merely needing help for improvement but dead in his trespasses and therefore beyond help.

Luther's struggles to find a gracious God were motivated in part by the apostle Paul's declaration that by the one man's sin (Adam), spiritual death passed to all future generations, including him (Rom. 5:17). Continual reflection on his own life and works was in direct contradiction with what he was taught about original sin. As discussed in chapter 1, the dominant theology in Luther's day taught that original sin has made us all spiritually sick, but not dead. We are spiritually able to do almost nothing that God would find pleasing, but it was taught that there is always something that sinners can do, and they are therefore duty-bound to do it. To be worthy of God's mercy, everyone must do for their salvation whatever is in them to do. God's infused grace provides healing and power to do even more God-pleasing works that increasingly bridge the gap between our sin-sick condition and the eventual healing in righteousness that we need to be acceptable to God.

The program did not work for Luther and it will not work for you. We need to remember that the saving work and gifts of Christ in the Gospel are the solution to the full extent of the problem of sin and evil. If the problem of sin is watered down or misunderstood, the solution of God's saving work in Christ will be corrupted and missed as a matter of course. Spiritually sick people need healing and spiritually weak people need help. But as Luther came to understand, because we are dead in our trespasses, we are beyond help and all spiritual assistance even from God is of no benefit. Justification as the complete imputed righteousness of Christ only makes sense as the solution to sinners who understand that as descendants of Adam, they are dead in their trespasses; completely unrighteous, not semirighteous or in the needs-improvement category. With the fall into sin by our first parents, God's design for the crown of his creation was shattered. His curse of the ground has grounded all of us from whence we came—ashes to ashes and dust to dust. Dead people do not need assistance in order to successfully do; they need life in order to be. We do not need God's help in order to do what is righteous; we need a Savior in order to be righteous.

The consequences of sin have alienated us from secure status as the people of God. They have separated us from the center and source of all that we need: our Creator God. Sin has brought us a death characterized by alienation, loneliness, moral and spiritual bankruptcy, loss of identity, and meaningless existence. It has imprisoned us within a slavish all-consuming love of ourselves as our greatest concern and object of trust. Our sinful condition does not mean that we cannot love others or do anything right. Rather it means that we are incapable of ordering our life and loves around an all-embracing fear, love, and trust in God. Our loves have become disordered and now flow from selfish human pride that places the self at the center of reality. As Eve desired to be like God, we want to be like God also but know that we are not. Distorted love and sinful pride have imprisoned us in this kind of *spiritual death*.

Yet as the apostle Paul lamented, *Wretched man that I am. Who will deliver us from this body of death*? (Rom. 7:24). He then rejoiced, "Thanks be to God through Jesus Christ our Lord! . . . There is therefore now no condemnation for those who are in Christ Jesus" (Rom. 7:25a; 8:1 ESV). Notice how the apostle simultaneously laments and rejoices as a sinner and a saint. We too can lament our sinful character, but we can trust that we also live with God in Christ Jesus as saints without any condemnation—not now, not ever.

And so, as we continue our life of faith, we are reminded of our fundamental frailty, the death problem that reduces all of us to ashes. Awareness and appreciation of these realities comprise the path of righteousness that we take to the cross of Christ. As Luther said, the cross is our theology. We journey to it, we die on it, we live in it, and we receive our Savior and righteousness for the sake of it. So to that cross where God in Christ justifies sinners in a once-for-all atonement we must now go.

Universal Justification in the Cross of Christ

Luther regarded justification to be the central article of the Christian faith. It is important to note, however, that Luther and his fellow reformers in Wittenberg often used the term *justification* as shorthand for discussing several aspects of the saving work and gifts of Christ. Some additional biblical terms that Luther and the Lutheran fathers used as virtual synonyms include *the forgiveness of sins, the righteousness of God* (also *righteousness of Christ* and *righteousness of faith*), *the favor of God,* and *reconciliation.*[2] All these terms express the saving importance of the full and complete vicarious atonement of Christ on the cross. His sacrificial death fully satisfied the righteous wrath of God in relation to the guilt of all rebellious sinners. For the sake of Christ's atoning death our sins are forgiven, we are fully justified, and we enjoy God's favor.

These gifts are revealed in a *Godward* view of the cross. The *Godward* view shows us how Jesus offers Himself to the Father as payment for the guilt of our sins. The *Satanward view* of the cross, however, describes what Christ did to defeat the powers of sin, death, and the Devil.[3] This latter work reveals Christ as our Champion who achieved for us the decisive victory over the powers of evil. The Godward view corresponds to our sin problem as rebellious sinners alienated from God. The Satanward view reflects the problem of sin that has us in bondage to *evil powers and principalities* greater than ourselves (Eph. 6:12). With the former we are the perpetrators of sin, and with the latter we are its victims.

---

2. Just to briefly note, see Ap IV, 86; and SA III, XIII.

3. Note especially the excellent treatment of the distinction between these two perspectives of the cross of Christ in the terminology of the Epistles of Paul in James Kallas's work, *The Satanward View: A Study in Pauline Theology* (Philadelphia: Westminster, 1966), 152 pp.

Our discussion here is particularly interested in exploring the *Godward* view of the cross—the saving gifts that flow from the universal atonement that our Lord has made for all sinners. More specifically, we want to clarify important aspects of justification—the reconciliation by which sinners have restored favor with God. The justification of the sinner can best be explained by examining the biblical answer to three questions: How was this saving work accomplished and its gifts appropriated by God? Where are these gifts revealed and bestowed on individual sinners? And how does the individual sinner receive and live with them? The biblical answer to these three questions clarifies three facets of the single justification of the sinner.

The Cross of Christ: Justification Acquired

First of all, there is a universal, finished aspect of justification that is most important. Without the perspective of how justification is anchored in Christ's universal atonement, all other facets become distorted, as they often have been in the history of the Church. The cross presents justification from the perspective of its appropriation in the cross of Christ by God in eternity. In Christ's vicarious atonement, God reconciled the whole world of sinners to Himself, "not counting their trespasses against them" (2 Cor. 5:19 ESV; see also Rom. 5:6–18; Col. 2:13–14). He has declared all sinners to be innocent and righteous, forgiven for the sake of Christ's all-sufficient death for the penalty of sin.

In the cross, Christ takes our place and suffers death as alienation from God, the just penalty for the sins of the whole world. This atonement is a sacrifice that He makes in our stead. Christ takes our place becoming estranged from the Father as reflected in his agonizing words: "My God, my God, why have you forsaken me?" (Matt. 27:46 ESV). It is important to understand that this fully accomplished universal atonement did not simply make God's favorable disposed with a desire to forgive our sins under some prerequisite conditions. Rather, as our Lord declared from the cross, *It is finished!* It was! Because of his all-sufficient atonement, the Father has become reconciled to all sinners and no longer counts our trespasses against us.

God has acquired for the whole world the status of sainthood, perfect righteousness, and acceptability in Christ's saving death and resurrection. This declaration of forgiveness and reconciliation is described by Paul in 2 Corinthians 5:19 as existing in the present as a result of God saving work in Christ in the past. The forgiveness of sins means the same thing as the declaration of righteousness or innocence. God has already reconciled Himself to a world of sinners, and this reconciliation exists as a universal objective reality in Christ. Anyone and everyone, regardless of how wretched they may think they are, may look to the cross of Christ and know that they have the full forgiveness of their sins and God's complete favor now and forever.

It cannot be stressed enough that the Scriptures reveal a finished atonement and a righteousness of Christ that is universal and sufficient *for all sinners*. God's saving work and gifts in Christ exist for the whole world. He so loved the *world* that He gave his only begotten Son (John 3:16). Paul teaches that He reconciled the entire *world* of sinners to Himself, "not counting their trespasses against them" (2 Cor. 5:19 ESV). This is full atonement, justification, and reconciliation for all sinners in Christ.

Any conception of a limited atonement—contending that Jesus only died for some sinners—renders an uncertain Gospel message for everyone. A limited view of the atonement of Christ removes confidence in the forgiveness of sins not simply for some, but for every individual sinner. Such a view declares that only some are justified and turns every Gospel Word into a provisional message: God *may* have forgiven your sins because He *may* have sent Jesus to die for your sins, because he *may* have chosen you to be one of His elect.

Any conception of the Gospel that proclaims a limited atonement turns the saving work and gifts of Christ into an uncertainty for any particular sinner. Forgiveness exists only for some known only to God in the hidden realm of eternity. There is no objective Word from God that would identify to a given sinner that Christ died for him. Assurance for sinners is tied to the notion that God enlightens the hearts of His elect unto salvation when he brings them to a divinely created saving faith. By their subjective experience of faith, they are to conclude that Jesus died for their sins and they have been elected unto salvation. However, a subjective experience of one's faith is no assurance to terrified sinners who are wondering if they have a true divine faith or just wishful thinking. We will address more about what makes for assurance in the saving work of Christ according to the apostolic witness in chapter 7.

Those who insist on a limited atonement point out that there is a difference between a divinely created faith in sinners—unshakeable and flowing from God—and a mere human faith that is temporary (e.g., as represented in the parable of the *Sower and the Seed* by those who believe for a time but then fall away; Matt. 13:20–21). The problem is that such distinctions between divine faith and a temporary human faith cannot be distinguished by any objective Word from God to a terrified sinner. The wrath of God abides on all false believers, because He neither chose them in eternity nor sent His Son to die for them. God's wrath in Hell becomes the divinely chosen destiny for these sinners, giving them what they deserve.

Notice this additional key difference between a universal and a limited atonement perspective. With universal atonement God's mercy flows from His justice. The justice of God in the cross means that everybody gets what they do not deserve. With limited atonement, *mercy and justice* are understood as opposites. The elect that God has chosen to save receive God's mercy and forgiveness; all others receive His justice that condemns them to Hell. We will take up more about the relationship of God's mercy and justice as they relate to Heaven and Hell in a later chapter.

The Gospel: Justification Revealed and Bestowed

The second facet of God's justification addresses how it is revealed and bestowed on individual sinners through the proclaimed Gospel and the administered sacraments. The saving work of the cross took place over two thousand years ago, and we were not there. In addition, the atoning event whereby the Father forsook the Son— breaking fellowship as the wages of sin—took place in the hidden realms of eternity. If we had personally witnessed all the temporal events of Christ's crucifixion, we would have witnessed only the shame and agony of one dying an ugly criminal's death, seemingly forsaken by God. With the powers of reason and perception, the cross seems like another pathetic picture of the silence and abandonment of God. The great exchange (where Jesus took on our sin and we are reckoned righteous) took place on the other side of the interface with eternity. If we are to know anything about this event as the saving event that rescues us from death and destruction, God must crash into our temporal existence with such a disclosure. And in the Gospel, He has, and He does.

There are two different modes of discourse that God uses to reveal and bestow His gift of justification. The first is a *didactic* or informational mode that informs about Christ's saving work and that God forgives sinners for His sake. Second, there is a *prophetic* or personal voice that pronounces the forgiveness of sins as a personal address from God. This voice employs *I-you* language. As in Holy Absolution, God personally addresses the sinner with His declaration of righteousness. He personally bestows the forgiveness of sins *on you.*

As a personal address, the Gospel bestows what it reveals as an existing objective reality. If such saving gifts did not already exist, the Gospel could not bestow them. The good news of the Gospel is not that God *will* forgive your sins (at some future time) conditioned by some commitment you must first make to Him. This would falsely turn the Gospel into an announcement of a conditional offer, not a bestowed gift. Instead, the prophetic Word from God concerning justification is this proclamation: *I declare you righteous for the sake of the full atonement of the crucified Christ.* As revealed information, the Gospel teaches and informs about God's forgiveness of sinners. With prophetic language, God personally addresses the sinner: *I forgive you all your sins.* And what you hear is what you get!

God's justification of the sinner is a bestowal of the righteousness of Christ. Sinners have favor with God by what Luther called an *alien* righteousness. He repudiated any kind of moral reform in God's salvationing of the sinner. God's justification of the sinner does not *make* his sinful character progressively more righteous. The righteousness of Christ that brings the sinner favor with God covers the sinner with Christ's righteousness as completely as in the metaphor of *the robe of righteousness*; it does not infuse and then reform the human soul, contrary to the doctrines of Rome.

Luther championed the Apostle Paul's understanding of a forensic justification: God declares the sinner righteous for the sake of Christ, as a judicial verdict in a court of law. This understanding repudiated Augustine's moral model of grace as a divine power that progressively heals the sin-sick soul unto righteous spiritual health. Augustine's moral model of grace has dominated Rome's understanding of justification and, ironically, was appropriated by John Wesley to become Protestantism's standard understanding of a second work of grace called sanctification. In both instances, the grace of Christ is understood as a reforming power that makes the sinner's character progressively more righteous when coupled with the efforts and works of the believer.

The grace that saves always finds the saving gifts of forgiveness, righteousness, and reconciliation flowing from the cross of the crucified Christ in the Gospel. To be sure, the Word of pardon in the Gospel is powerful. It redeems us from sin, death, and the devil; it creates faith, as it also recreates us in the perfect image of Christ. It does not, however, reform anyone or anything. The New Creation is a perfect slave to God and righteousness (Rom. 6), gradually matured into the full stature of Christ (Eph. 4:15, 24), and needs no reform; however, the Old Sinful Self is a slave to sin, incapable of being reformed (Rom. 7:14ff). We will take up a discussion of sanctification in the next chapter.

The Gospel is God's power unto salvation (Rom. 1:16) because it bestows saving gifts that work faith, not because it provides helpful information or motivates good decision-making. Through the saving Word God declares sinners forgiven, holy saints, loved and accepted just as they are, on account of Christ's atonement. This declaration in the Gospel is a revelation in our space and time of what is true in eternity, and simultaneously bestows on sinners what it reveals. It does what it says and gives what it guarantees. The Gospel brings us to the cross of Christ over time and eternity. There we personally hear God's voice speaking to us: *Sinner, I declare that you are forgiven, holy, innocent, and righteous for the sake of the perfect sacrifice of my Son. I love you and accept you just as you are. You belong to me and my family as my child forever.*

The Gospel is God's announcement of his *already-existing* acceptance and forgiveness of the sinner. It is a done deal—signed, sealed, and delivered. Justification is not presented in the Gospel as a future possibility or bargain that can be ours if we will fulfill certain conditions. It is not mere information about some exciting offer that God has for us, as if we can take advantage of it by acting fast and doing something to make it a reality. In the cross of Christ, there is no fine print connected with God's forgiveness that presents the *catch* that details all the conditions we must meet. It is His pronouncement of unconditional acceptance and righteousness from and on the basis of the atonement of Christ, coming to individual sinners in every age and place.

It is a distortion of the Gospel to convey to sinners that God is simply willing to forgive them their sins at some future point if some proper conditions are met. The Gospel does not present God's gracious forgiveness as an offer about a future possibility. The Gospel is not mere information designed to motivate sinners to make a good decision to secure a happy forever. It is the Word that saves sinners by declaring them already forgiven in the finished atonement of the crucified Christ. It is a false Gospel to express that God merely *desires* to forgive, and this could happen if the sinner makes the right decision. The Gospel declares the existing forgiveness of Christ, a revelation in our space in time of what is true in eternity. And what you hear is what you get. The declaration does what it says and gives what it guarantees because this saving gift already exists. It is not some future possibility.

Thus, strictly speaking, the Gospel does not present an *offer* or possibility of forgiveness; it unconditionally proclaims it as an already-given reality and bestows it on the sinner. God says, *You are forgiven!* Period! There are no *IFs, ANDs,* or *BUTs* that first require us to do something to make it so. We do not have to make a commitment, say a sincere prayer, give our heart to Jesus, or clean up our lives. Nothing! Some might ask. *But isn't this cheap grace?* No, it is not *cheap* grace; it is absolutely, unconditionally free! Second, grace is not a matter of getting a warning instead of a ticket for your infractions. Grace is not God saying, *"No problem! Do better the next time."* Grace is not a matter of God cutting you some slack and giving you more chances and time to clean up your act. And third, Grace is not God posting credits in your heavenly account book to offset your bad deeds and provide you with a zero balance for the time being. As Capon has put it so eloquently, *Grace announces that God has torn up the books and permanently gone out of the accounting business.*

Ah! we may think. We get it now. We receive God's forgiveness and acceptance without conditions; but now that we have it, we must clean up our lives and bring forth good works to keep it. Is

that it? No! The Gospel presents God's forgiveness as an unconditional promise that He shall be gracious to us now and forever for the
sake of Christ. He will never count our trespasses against us and will
unconditionally accept us as His righteous and innocent child forever. He promises to remember our sins no more (Heb. 8:12; 10:12–
17). The Gospel announces and applies the righteousness of Christ
to us for eternity. There are no conditions attached to His forgiveness and acceptance—not now, not ever! The Gospel is the end of all
works of the Law and all conditional thinking about God.

Faith: Justification Received and Lived With

Furthermore, through the Gospel, sinners are saved by God *through*
a divinely wrought faith, not *in view of* it. We are justified *unto* faith
by the power of the Word of Christ (Rom. 10:17)[4] and thereby enter
into a reconciled, saved relationship with God. Faith receives an
objective, existing forgiveness of sin and righteousness of Christ,
whereby the reckoning of God becomes a *received* reckoning by
trust of the sinner. By the power of the Gospel, the reconciled God
reconciles sinners to Himself thereby creating a saved relationship.
Notice the saving grace of declared righteousness is not offered as a
potential reality; it is bestowed as an *existing reality*. Faith receives
the saving gifts; it does not create or cause them. We are justified by
grace *through* faith, not *because of* faith or *in view of* faith.

A scriptural understanding of saving faith and its formation
eliminates two misconceptions. First, faith is not an action we take;
rather, it is the *condition* of simple trust in the human heart that God
creates as He creates a New Self, born of the Second Adam (Christ).
Second, saving faith is the result of God's choice and commitment
to us, not our choice and commitment to Him. The grace of Christ
is the business of getting saved, doing nothing. The simple language
and grammar distinctions are important to rightly understand this.

Sometimes we hear the grace of Christ expressed as an offer
of forgiveness requiring us to ponder and hopefully decide to take

---

4.   God's justification of sinners is logically prior to faith. The declaration of righteousness or forgiveness for the sake of Christ is the *saving word of Christ* (Rom. 10:17) that
creates faith, not the other way around. This is what justified *unto* faith means.

it. However, the Word *grace* means gift; it does not mean *offer*. We are saved by grace, and strictly speaking, not by an *offer*. Gifts must already exist, and whoever possesses them makes the decision and is responsible for conveying them to others. Offers, on the other hand, describe future possibilities. They are, as they say, put on the table. You acquire what is offered by your *decision* to meet the specified conditions. Offers are *taken*, but gifts are only *received*. You cannot take a gift and you cannot receive what is only being offered. This important grammar lesson is beautifully illustrated by dialogue in the great Western, *Open Range*.

Kevin Costner plays a gunslinger who is about to head to town with his partner, played by Robert Duval, for the final shootout with the bad guys. He has this thing for the sister of the town's doctor played by Annette Bening. Coming to her door he discloses his affection for her but that he might not be coming back. She excuses herself for a moment and returns with a locket. Placing it into his hand and closing his fingers around it, she tells him that she wants him to have it. It belonged to her mother and always brought her good luck. Costner opens his hand, staring at the locket, and responds, *Oh, ma'am, I can't take your locket*. To which she curtly responds, *It's not your choice when it's a gift*. Right!

Gifts cannot be taken and no decisions are made to acquire them. It is just wrong to explain that getting saved is a matter of taking an offer of grace from God by deciding to take it and Jesus as your Savior. It gives the false impression that you are in control and your choice determines if God will forgive you or not. Or as if the Gospel teaches a decision theology where Jesus says, *Here's the deal. I am willing to forgive your sins; you contribute faith and a commitment to me. Now . . . you go first!*

The Gospel is not *potentially* saving information about an *offer* that God makes available to sinners for their decision. You do not have to make a decision for Christ or offer a sincere prayer for Him to come into your heart and be your Savior. Gifts, on the other hand, are passively received from the giver who chooses to bestow them.[5] The receiver of a gift does not make the choice. Justification by grace

---

5. Note that both offers and gifts can be refused but there is a big difference in how that is done. Offers are refused by doing nothing. Gifts are refused by actively rejecting them.

through faith answers the question: How do individuals receive and live with God's justification? By faith we receive God's bestowed gift of forgiveness when faith is created and preserved by the Holy Spirit through the Gospel (Rom. 10:17; 1 Cor. 12:3).

Through faith we personally grasp and cling to our standing of innocence and forgiveness, and we live in it. Faith does not create this status; it receives it. Faith should not be presented as a work or a virtue that God demands in order for sinners to be forgiven, as if God were saying, *I have some forgiveness for those who can muster some good believing in me. Have you got what it takes?* The Gospel proclaims God's declaration of the sinner's being righteous for the sake of Christ. The Gospel then exhorts faith, but not as a condition to be forgiven. Rather we teach that saving faith is also a gift of God, by which He enables us to live with His righteousness and be reconciled to Him. He creates the trust in your heart that now simply lives with God by the gift of his grace and forgiveness alone. About this free gift of grace, Capon well sums up where we need to be: "Trust him. And when you have done that, you are living the life of grace. No matter what happens to you in the course of that trusting—no matter how many waverings you may have, no matter how many suspicions that you have bought a poke with no pig in it, no matter how much heaviness and sadness your lapses, vices, indispositions, and bratty whining may cause you—you believe simply that Somebody Else, by his death and resurrection, has made it all right, and you just say thank you and shut up."[6]

The Paradox about Faith

Christians are often confused about what the Scriptures teach concerning saving faith and how it is received. The biblical record confronts the reader with a paradox. On the one hand, the Scriptures treat the subject of faith from the standpoint of its necessity, and they do so by commanding it. In answer to his question "What must I do to be saved?" Paul responds to the jailer at Philippi, "Believe on the Lord

---

6.   Robert Farrar Capon, *Between Noon and Three: Romance, Law and the Outrage of Grace* (Grand Rapids: William B. Eerdmans, 1997).

Jesus Christ, and you will be saved" (Acts 16:30–31 NKJV). Faith is commanded *as if* it were an obligation we could produce. Such, however, not how the Scriptures explain the creation of faith. When the question is raised about how those who believe do so, Paul explains in Ephesians 2:8–9 that it is *by grace you are saved through faith, and that* [the grace and the faith] *not of your own doing, it is a gift of God, not of works*. How do we reconcile the biblical command to believe with the gift character of faith as a blessing from God?

Some Christians erroneously conclude that since God commands us to believe, He is thereby implying some ability on our part to respond accordingly. Such reasoning does not accord with the biblical witness. In Genesis we read that God created human beings by His Word and command. This did not imply that somehow lifeless dust of the ground had an ability to become a human child of God. God did not ask a patch of dirt if it would like to become a human being, nor did He present lifeless clay with all the exciting possibilities of what life could be like as a personal being and then extend an invitation for a commitment or decision to actualize the possibility. He simply said, *Let us make man* . . . and it was so (Gen. 1:26). As it was with the old creation, so also with new life in Christ. The spiritually lifeless sinner has no more ability to self-transform into a new creation in Christ than the dust had in the beginning to become a human being. Both instances provide examples of the awesome creative power of God's Word when it is sent forth to accomplish His life-giving purposes.

God speaks to the sinner His gracious word of forgiveness and acceptance and exhorts us to believe. Indeed, He *commands it*, as if to say, *Let there be faith!* And through His Word and command, God creates what He commands when, where, and as He chooses. The Holy Spirit engenders faith through the power of His Word of forgiveness. God's saving declarations in the Gospel, together with the exhortation to believe, create the trust—the faith by which we receive and live with these proclamations. *Faith comes from hearing the message, and the message is heard through the word of Christ* (Rom. 10:17).

The Gospel either explicitly or implicitly includes the command to believe. However, it does not include such questions as, *would you like to believe it?* God never comes to us, hat in hand, seeking what

He desires. As Luther eloquently said in his Heidelberg Thesis 28, *The love of God does not find but rather creates that which is pleasing to it.* This understanding of God and His Word includes the following truths: What God commands, God creates. What God demands (as in His Law), God gives (in His Gospel). You can see as was indicated above, God's obligatory Word always implies inability.

In the very same way, He continually nourishes and builds up our trusting faith through the Gospel in Word and Sacrament as we feed on them. As with God's old creation, so also with new life in Christ. God creates and preserves through His Word. That Word is both the eternal Son of God and His creative command— *Let there be . . .* or *believe!* As with all gifts of God, they flow from His will and work, not ours. What God commands, He creates; and what He demands, He gives. He demands perfect righteousness to be His child, and He freely gives us that status in His Gospel. God commands faith in this promise, and then He creates it through His saving word.

Perhaps we can focus the paradox of faith in another way. The Gospel can be thought of as the message of God's dying love and acceptance in the cross of Christ. Through His saving word He courts rebellious sinners who are alienated from Him and His love. It's something like the old story of John and Marsha. John loves Marsha, and he is determined to have her as his wife. She, however, thinks he is an absolute nerd and will have nothing to do with him. This does not faze John in the least, and he continues to shower her with loving actions and words. Then something mysterious happens in the story as it often does in real life; she *falls in love* with him. She did not plan on this happening. Moreover, no conscious decision was made on her part. Indeed, her discovery that she now does in fact love John comes as an incredible surprise to her. She is totally dumbfounded by the whole turn of events! We are not.

We, of course, know what happened to Marsha. It was the power of love at work that transformed her. It happens every day. In the magic of interpersonal relations, love has the power to beget love. No coercion or compulsion was present, but certainly no decision was involved either. Marsha's love was nurtured and brought forth by John. Moreover, it was no surprise to him; he intended this to happen from the beginning. In the same way our Creator God, the gracious Lover of sinners, comes to rebellious humans through the Gospel and woos them with His saving work and words of dying love and forgiveness. By the mysterious power of His Spirit through His loving Word, sinners *fall in trust* with their Creator/Redeemer. A trusting faith then blossoms into a returning love. Marsha became John's wife in the story, and we rebellious sinners who have fallen into faith with the gracious God have become the bride of Christ. And as with John, our loving God intended it all from the beginning— yes, *even before the beginning. Before the foundation of the world, He chose us to be blameless in His sight* and by His predestining love He adopted us to be His children in Christ (Eph. 1:4–5).

The Tension between Faith and Experience

We are all familiar with Luther's championing of justification by faith apart from all works of the Law. This is the happy *sola fide* (faith alone). But the Theology of the Cross embraces also another distinction with *sola fide* that oftentimes is not so happy. We are justified by grace through faith alone, *apart from our experience*. Faith is to be anchored completely in the external Word of promise, not in anything that we may experience in our life in Christ. Our experience in this life continues to be punctuated by sinful wretchedness from within and without. Externally, trial and tribulation can visit us from the doing of God in this fallen world. He also hammers us with His Law internally as it has been inscribed on our hearts. *This is the cross life of the justified sinner as he lives in the cross of Christ awaiting the better day of glory.* We trust in the cross of Christ by faith alone and we bear our own crosses by experience alone. Justification renders a divine citizenship along with all of God's saving gifts and blessings of salvation *in, with, and under* our temporal citizenship and all that its fallen character can bring us. What flows from our temporal citizenship in the Devil's playground is fully given to our senses and openly experienced, but what flows from our divine citizenship is given to and apprehended only by faith.

The tension between worldly experience with all its trials and tribulations, and the saving gifts given to faith, are encountered in the daily living of the believer by moving back and forth between them. Neither the divine blessings nor the temporal trials and tribulations cancel the other out or call them into question. *Moreover, the tension between what we experience and what is given to faith will intensify as we grow and mature in Christ, and it will not come to an end until the Day of Glory arrives.* Nothing more will be added to the saving gifts than what we already have received in our Baptism and what we daily receive in absolution and the Supper. But in glory, faith will be no more, and we will enjoy all the saving gifts and blessings by rich luxuriant experience (Rev. 7:13–17). All false theologies of glory, though very attractive today, promise some experiences of glory to supplement faith in this life, if you will just perfect some law-oriented, Bible-based principles. With Luther, we champion a justification by faith alone apart from all experience in this life, confessing a cross life now, and glory only in the better day that is coming when Christ comes to gather His Bride.

Thus, we recognize one justification of a world of sinners with three facets: the cross of Christ, which acquired our righteousness before God; the Gospel, where God reveals and bestows His righteousness on individual sinners; and a Spirit-wrought faith, whereby we personally receive and live with it. It is with this last facet that we are saved—through faith *we* become reconciled to God and live in a justified, forgiven relationship with Him. And all this saving work—appropriation, revelation, bestowal and reception—is totally *monergistic*. It is all God's will and work.

The Paradox of the Righteousness of Christ

The Gospel reveals and proclaims the righteousness of Christ and forgiveness of sin that are total and complete. Nevertheless, this understanding of justification and the forgiveness of sin also includes the paradox that while the baptized Christian has received and lives with them as total and complete realities, these gifts are also continually bestowed through absolution and the Supper that the sinner needs and receives daily. In other words, *we have it all, but we always need more.*

This is the same paradox about the beloved who has the complete love of her lover. She has it all, but she always needs more. She is always in need of his love, and not just reminders. So as he continually tells her, *I love you,* he gives her more. These words are no mere reminders. What she hears is what she gets . . . more of what she already has. It is the same with the Gospel of our Lord, Jesus Christ. The Gospel reveals and proclaims an already-existing complete justification of the sinner for the sake of Christ's atonement on the cross. To be justified means to be declared righteous in the forgiveness that is ours in the crucified Christ. It is a done deal, and by faith we have it all. Nevertheless, while we live with this forgiveness and righteousness of Christ as total and complete realities, we are always in need of more.

For many Christians, justification is understood as a one-time pronouncement by God that happened when you *got saved* and began your life in Christ. The forgiveness of Christ being a done deal, the dominant focus of the Christian's life is now to be centered on how your gratitude and the power of the Spirit are to be channeled into achieving a greater life of obedience. Jesus did His part, it's now your turn. The astonishing reality that Christ pardons wretched sinners fades into the background of daily Christian concern as attention turns to absorbing Law-oriented principles for daily living and gaining a greater victory over sinful habits. Justification and forgiveness become a distant memory of something God once did because you once needed them, way back when you first got saved. For many, this understanding and program produce spiritual burnout and doubts when the weight of alarming sins are felt. Some have even wondered if they are still forgiven and imagined that perhaps they might need to *get saved* again.

Believers need to be taught otherwise about God's justification of sinners and how His continual bestowal of forgiveness feeds and builds up our life in Christ. It is not enough to be reminded of that God forgave you twelve years, three months, and five days ago when you were first saved. We need more than distant memories of a God who was, at one time, gracious to us. And reminders are not good enough. Christians remain sinners who continually sin. Because they continually sin much, they continually need to be forgiven much. Christians are saved sinners who need to receive again for the first time the Word of grace that bestows God's forgiveness. Yes, you have it all, but you always need more! Note how Luther expressed this in his *Large Catechism*: "Toward forgiveness is directed everything that is to be preached concerning the sacraments and, in short, the entire Gospel and all the duties of Christianity. Forgiveness is needed constantly, for although God's grace has been won by Christ, and holiness has been wrought by the Holy Spirit through God's Word in the unity of the Christian Church, yet because we are encumbered with our flesh we are never without sin" (Tappert, Large Catechism, Creed, 54). For this reason, while we are completely justified in our Baptism, we continually are in need of receiving God's justification so that our faith and life in Christ may not die but grow and mature. Indeed, it is the saving Word of justification that continually sanctifies the Christian as a lifelong renewing work.

As the continual love of the lover sustains and builds up the trust and love of the beloved, so also God's Word of pardon does more than just remind us that we were forgiven in Christ back when. It creates, sustains, and matures faith and life in Christ, and it empowers all our works of love that serve Christ through our neighbors. All comfort and consolation come to us from our Lord through these mysteries that have been entrusted to His Church. The Gospel of God's unconditional bestowed righteousness is His *I love you* to wretched sinners like you and me. We have it all, but we are always in need of more!

On the one hand, the notion that the forgiveness of sins understood as partial or piecemeal as Rome teaches about baptism and penance, is rejected. The Scriptures teach the forgiveness of sins as total, and the righteousness of Christ as a timeless reality. When we receive the saving gifts of Christ, we receive them all. Yet because the old creation and sin are still with us . . . we are always in need of the Gospel gifts in the Christian's life of faith, not as reminders but as realities that are continually needed and bestowed.

The *Godward* view of the cross is the answer to all we see and all we feel, as we examine ourselves or others apart from the external Word of Christ. Whenever we look inside ourselves to survey our own spiritual measure, we will never see who we are in the Godward view of the cross. We can never see ourselves wrapped in the righteousness of Christ by looking inward. Looking inside, we see only through the lens of the Law, which has been written on the human heart. This lens always renders a vision of the self without Christ's atonement for our sin, our justification, and God complete reconciliation. At full strength, the Law will show us to be lost sinners deserving of God's wrath. These saving treasures for us can only be seen in the external Word of the Gospel, which reveals the cross of Christ and the life we live in it.

Christians have received salvation and well-being in the righteousness of Christ given to faith. Secure saintly status as adopted children of God and His Kingdom is held in faith. About us and within us is still the corruption of the old fallen sinful order of paradise lost. We are saints by pronouncement and gift—a holy standing that shall be ours for eternity. But for now, we are still sinful in all aspects of our physical and personal dimensions of self. All this corruption is fully evident to all our senses and reasoning. Simultaneously sinners and saints! We hold the reality of both in tension until the final transformation in the resurrected life when our Lord returns in the fullness of His glory.

Sanctification

The Powerful Pardon

There is a saying in our success-oriented culture. *Dress for success: you are what you wear.* In other words, the clothes make the person. Imagine what this could mean if it were literally true. You take an uneducated and inexperienced man and dress him in a fine Brooks Brothers suit, a nice white button-down shirt, a power tie, and *Voilà!* He is dressed for success. Now tell him he has just become a qualified business executive, indeed, vice president of the company. Moreover, as he goes to work each day so dressed, he actually matures into a competent and successful executive. Pure foolishness?

Regardless of what we may think of this saying in the business world or in general, there is much about this that we can liken to our life in Christ. We incompetent and disqualified sinners are clothed with the righteousness of Christ, a constantly worn garment that gives us saintly status and life as God's children. With His righteousness, we are outfitted—made totally fit—for sainthood and citizenship in His Kingdom. And then miraculously, the robe of righteousness also creates and develops us on the inside into a mature image of the righteous Son of Man.

Through the Gospel, God dresses the sinner in the righteousness of Christ, which is worn and lived in through faith. Justification brought us what Luther called an *alien righteousness*.[1] To put on the

---

1. *A man is so absolved as if he had no sin, for Christ's sake.* AE 34, 153.

righteousness of Christ is to put on Christ. This holy clothing has a powerful renewing effect on us. We are regenerated into a righteous reflection of what we wear by faith in our baptism. As faith grows and matures, Christ's righteousness develops a new creation into a mature likeness of His human nature. As Jesus according to His human nature grew in wisdom and stature, so also does the new creation that has come forth in Baptism. The more we grow in Christ, the more daily living can take on a reflection of His righteousness and the fruit of faithfulness increasingly accent our life. This is what is called *sanctification*. It is a lifelong growing and maturing process of the Christian's new life in Christ that Baptism has created.

Power or Pardon?

To rightly understand God's work of sanctification, several important questions need to be considered for clarity about our life in Christ. These would include the following: How does God's work of sanctification relate to justification? Are these two separate works of God or are they simply two aspects of the same work? If God's grace is involved in sanctification (and it is!), is it the same grace by which we are justified or is it of a different sort? Does God sanctify by some power in addition to His pardon in the justifying Word of the Gospel or does the power that produces sanctification come simply from the impact of the Word of pardon? Where do the efforts of the Christian and good works fit in the sanctified life? Do they contribute anything to the work of sanctification?

As we discuss these questions, we would do well to take to heart Gerhard Forde's warning: *Talk about sanctification can be dangerous.* If we separate sanctification from justification, we may end up making sanctification a project whereby we contribute to God's plan of salvationing us.[2] His point is well-taken. It has happened frequently in the Church throughout the ages.

Much of Western Christian thought from post-Apostolic times to Luther was absorbed by a quest for personal holiness. This was

---

2. Gerhard Forde, "The Lutheran View," in *Christian Spirituality*, ed. Donald L. Alexander (Downers Grove, IL: InterVarsity, 1988), 15–16.

certainly true for St. Augustine. Even though Augustine championed salvation by grace apart from works, he understood the grace of God primarily as a divine power that progressively transforms the sinner.[3] In other words, God requires a holy and righteous life, and by grace He gradually produces what He demands. He infuses divine grace into the baptized Christian, which gradually reforms the sinful character of the believer, eventually making him righteous and fit for the coming Kingdom. Augustine worked with a *moral model* of sin and grace. The dominant element of God's work that saves the sinner was understood to be an infused grace that progressively reforms the sinner's character and produces an increasingly virtuous life.

Augustine's moral model of grace as an infused, reforming power dominated the thinking of the Western Church for the next 1,200 years. Significant changes were made however. Gradually, the believer's moral striving and meritorious works were understood to contribute to making one fit for the eternal Kingdom. God's empowering grace enables the virtues and works of the believer. And the works of the believer in turn were seen to merit additional infused grace. Grace understood as God's transforming power virtually eclipsed grace as Christ's pardon. Jesus our Savior from sin became Jesus our role model for how we ought to behave. Character reform swallowed up the forgiveness of sins and meritorious works became a requirement for acceptance into God's Kingdom.

Since Luther's rediscovery of the Gospel of Christ's free pardon, many thinkers within the Protestant world (and even some that bear the name Lutheran) returned to Augustine's understanding of grace, but now under the banner of sanctification. They have depicted sanctification as a program that gradually reforms the inner character of the sinner—an additional work of grace that follows after the justification. This second grace involves a special working of the Holy Spirit that enables the Christian to experience a progressive victory over sinful habits and achieve a growing holiness in life and works. Jesus saves the sinner in conversion by bestowing his free pardon. Then the Spirit and the committed Christian join forces to put away sinful living and bring forth a growing Christlike life of obedience.

---

3. See Gilbert Meilaender's excellent discussion of Augustine's views on grace and sanctification in *Faith and Faithfulness*, 76–78.

The former work is understood as justification, the latter as sanctification. Two different works of grace are involved. We are justified by
the grace of Christ's pardon, and then we are sanctified by the grace
of the Spirit's power that progressively reforms the Christian's sinful character, and energizes a holy obedience to the precepts of the
Law. The focus of justification is conversion, and the focus of sanctification is the Christian life that follows. As reflected in the Wesleyan
take on the old revivalist hymn, Rock of Ages, *Be of sin the double
cure, save from wrath and make me pure.* The Son saves us from the
wrath of God in conversion (justification), and then the Spirit progressively makes us pure (sanctification).

With this understanding, justification becomes simply a prelude to the dominant focus of Christian life, sanctification. The
believer's quest for holiness and obedience in daily living takes center stage after conversion. The astonishing reality that Christ pardons wretched sinners like me fades into the background of daily
Christian concern. The attention is now on greater obedience to the
Law and acquiring the Holy Spirit's resources to energize the task.
The Savior from sin and death vanishes, and the Holy Spirit takes
over to help us in the service of holiness through the works of Moses.

When the sanctifying work of the Spirit is believed to be progressing appropriately, according to this model, a significant victory
over sinful behavior takes place. Moreover, greater levels of obedience
to the Law are being achieved, and the blessings of God are increasing
in one's life. If these results are not unfolding successfully, the problem is understood to lie with the believer. The Christian is somehow
failing to do his part. The problem may be a lack of trust in the Holy
Spirit, a failure to *yield* to the Spirit, insincere repentance, or a weak
commitment to a life of obedience—any or all of the above. In any
event, the Christian has failed to do his part. Here sanctification is
depicted as a cooperative affair where the believer's role is critical for
success. Often the believer is told that to have a true God-honoring
faith, his own role must be played up, lest he become lackadaisical
and lapse into a dangerous attitude of *cheap grace.*

Is it any wonder that many of our unbelieving neighbors are
convinced (erroneously!) that Christianity is about odd folks who
somehow have an inordinate, all-fired preoccupation with becoming morally superior people? Moreover, they are puzzled about why

Christians seem convinced that belief in God and going to church are somehow pivotal to the success of the project. This is not the foolishness of the Gospel (1 Cor. 1:23) that some of our unbelieving neighbors are stumbling over, is it? Tragically missing is the perspective of the apostle Paul who saw himself as *chief of sinners* and would *know nothing* among the Corinthians "except Jesus Christ and Him crucified" (1 Tim. 1:15; 1 Cor. 2:2 ESV).

Talk about sanctification becomes dangerous when we fail to rightly understand its *nature and cause* and distinguish these from the *consequences* of sanctification in the life of the believer. What often becomes confused is the matter of good works and how they are fit into the discussion. If works are interjected into our thinking about *how sanctification occurs,* we erroneously end up with a role of contributing to our own salvation and the unconditional gift of God's grace is overturned. The New Testament always speaks of good works as a *consequence* of God's saving activity. This is what Paul emphasized in Phil. 2:13: *For it is God who works in you to will and to act according to his good purpose.* God's plan of recreating us in the image of the Second Adam for good works of faith was a part of His saving intention from the beginning as Paul explained in Ephesians 2:10: *For we are God's workmanship, created in Christ Jesus to do good works, which God prepared in advance for us to do.* We want to briefly clarify the nature and cause of sanctification relating them to justification as both are rooted in Baptism. Then we will be in a better position later in our discussion to wade into the matter of changed patterns of living and good works.

Baptism Brings a Dying to Live

To sanctify means to make holy. We miserable unholy sinners are apprehended by Christ and recreated back into the image of God in our baptism. The water and the Word where we are splashed with grace is the beginning of God's work of sanctification. We may think of Baptism as a portal through which God has His way with us, remaking us anew, and dragging us into His Kingdom. It is where God enters our space and time, sinks down into the mud of this fallen world, and makes what He desires us to be. Baptism is where God first nailed and killed us in the cross of Christ and then raised us up in faith as a new creation. We may think of Baptism as the gate to God is where He descends to us; where He deals with us according to His pleasure; and where the Savior makes Himself and His savings gifts manifest. We must take God at His Word in Romans 6:3–4. He comes to kill and bring us into a spiritual death, drowning us in a word-joined watery grave. From such a watery bath, we are brought forth as a New Creation fashioned in the image of God (Eph. 4:24).

Notice the paradox in our baptism: God kills to make alive— from death to life we have come (Rom. 6:3–11). *Christians are those who have fallen into the hands of the Heavenly Physician and they are just dying to live.* Indeed, without a death to sin, there is no life in Christ. The mighty Creator God comes to us through the simple earthly gate of ordinary human language and water. He masks Himself, hiding within these mundane opposites. He has His way with us according to His saving designs so that we might die to sin and live in Christ. Through the temporal, the common, and mundane chosen places, the extraordinary, supernatural God makes Himself manifest—and under the paradox of opposites—he takes deadly aim on us, that we might live. He rescues us from sin, death, and the Devil and creates in us a new everlasting life.

Baptism marks how God carries the Christian from the beginning of life in Christ to the fullness of salvation. Christians can actually say, *I was baptized, I am baptized, and I will be baptized.* Baptism is simultaneously a dying and rising work that is accomplished at the beginning (as the gateway to God); it is a work that God continually accomplishes in the Christian's life; and, it is what He promises to accomplish in the end. The Christian lives and grows by a dying to sin and a living and growing in Christ that returns him to his baptism again and again. Notice the radical difference here. This does not involve human choice and commitment to get more spiritual goodies from God—as if Christianity provides us with an edge for better spiritual living—*Life goes better with God!* Rather God is the whole show. We are taken into custody by Christ. He moves in on us and crucifies us to die with Him to sin—and then gives us His righteousness and life itself.

We make progress in Christian life by starting over again by God's baptismal work. We are always beginning anew—dying to sin and being made alive by His saving Word. Dying to live is Baptism's signature on the whole character of Christian life. God slays and makes alive again and again. He does not stop at the baptismal font, but His baptismal covenant is renewed in us continually through His ministry of Law and Gospel. *Dying to sin by the Law and rising again by the Gospel constitute the present-tense of Baptism for all God's children.* These words kill and make alive, rendering us sinners and saints at the same time.

God Creates What He Desires

As Luther well stated how God accomplishes His redemptive work in his Heidelberg Disputation, Thesis 28, *The love of God does not find, but creates that which is pleasing to it.*[4] The way God gets the kind of people He desires is startlingly different from how we seek to obtain desired qualities in one another. We have to start with a select number of people who show some promise—those who already are a cut above average. Then we must put them through a developmental regimen proven effective in building on the good character that is already there. The *US Marine Corps* is a good example.[5] In its recruiting promotion, the *Corps* indicates that it is looking for *a few good men*. A few good men is what it needs as the raw material to develop into *the few, the proud, the Marines*.

The message is clearly this: if you are good, the Marine Corps through its boot camp and training programs will make you even better. While this strategy—starting with the good, and making them better—has much to commend itself in military matters and perhaps others, it is not how God works to repopulate His Paradise Regained. There are two good reasons for this. First, if God had to first *find* a few good men, His plan of salvation would never have gotten get off the ground. God has already looked down from Heaven for a few good men, and His survey did not find any. *They have all fallen away, together they have become corrupt, there is none who does good, not even one* (Ps. 53:3).

---

4. *AE* 31, 41.

5. I must credit my former colleague, Rev. Robert W. Schaibley, for this wonderful contrasting illustration of the US Marine Corps.

Second, as Luther observed, it just is not His way of doing things. God's way of doing things is such that whatever He would love, desire, or prefer . . . He does not go seeking to find it. He never comes hat-in-hand, hoping we will give Him what He wants. He does not enlist with attractive pitches or motivational incentives—He simply creates what His own heart desires with whatever pleasing attributes He might want. We learn what He finds pleasing in human attributes in His holy Law. He desires righteous men and women who order their lives around a fear, love, and trust in Him—where the human spirit is a reflection of Himself. In this regard, it can be said that He still has a preference for humans just like those He made originally from dirt and Divine Breath (Gen. 2:7).

Now for us who in ourselves are dead in our trespasses, this is Good News. It means as God has His way with us, He will be doing everything that is necessary for us to become just what He wants. Throughout His ministry, our Lord provided clues about how He works to acquire recruits for His Kingdom. At the marriage feast at Cana He made wine pleasing to Himself and everyone else who was there, by simply ordering stewards to fill some jars with water and take some to the master. He served a banquet to thousands in the wilderness by distributing a few loaves of bread and a couple of fish. And in the upper room, He was pleased to distribute His own body and blood to His disciples simply by His desire to do it and saying so. He made an apostle to the Gentiles out of a Jewish persecutor of Christians. He required no help from anyone. We are examples of the same working of our gracious God. He makes us pleasing to Himself in the saving work and gifts of Christ the crucified through our baptism.

If we were to make a promotional sound bite for what He is looking for in each of us, we could perhaps say that He is looking for a few really bad, spiritually dead, men and women. All He needs from us is that we be something like Lazarus—a spiritual corpse willing to stay dead. We contribute our deadness, and He does the rest. As God worked in creation with lifeless clay and created what was pleasing to Him through His Word, so also in redemption we encounter the crucified Christ in His saving Word. He takes our spiritually lifeless clay and creates for Himself sons and daughters for His family—citizens, each of us, for His Kingdom. Meeting up with this kind of God-with-us is what we can expect to find at the foot of the cross of Christ the crucified. And this also means some things that we can expect not to find either at the cross or anywhere we encounter the gracious God in His Gospel. We will not find exhortations, motivational seminars, or enticing recruitment promotional offers to consider signing up for a program to become fit enlisted soldiers of the cross.

Rather, in His Gospel we will find our Champion Who on His cross defeats all the powers of darkness and then raises us up with Himself, making us as pleasing to the Father as His only begotten Son. God is looking for more than a *few* good men and women, boys, and girls. And by the power of His own redemption and recreation in Baptism, He has made us what we are in Christ Jesus, enlisted citizens of the Kingdom to come . . . *the few, the righteous, the children of God.*

Power in the Pardon

Paul informed the Christians in Rome that he was not ashamed of the Gospel, because it is *the power of God unto the salvation of everyone who believes* (Rom. 1:16). Moreover, he taught them that faith comes from hearing the message, and the message is heard through the Word of Christ (Rom. 10:17). By grace we are saved through faith and that not of our own doing, he told the Ephesians. It is a gift of God, not of works (Eph. 2:8–9). The apostle's perspective is that God salvations sinners through the Gospel of the grace of Christ through faith. Entirely! The power of God is the Word of Christ, the Word of God's gracious pardon. The righteousness of Christ that justifies also sanctifies—the pardon that bestows the righteousness of Christ also creates and empowers a new life in Christ. Baptism bestows the gifts of forgiveness and the Holy Spirit (Acts 2:38) and unites us with the crucified Christ's death bringing forth a new creation that is a slave to God and righteousness (Rom. 6:10–22). And make no mistake here. We become what we are in Baptism due to God's will and work not because we make a good choice or cooperate with His plan.

We do not have to look elsewhere for a second plan or word from God. The pardon of Christ's righteousness *is the power* that renews and matures us into the stature of Christ. Sanctification happens when we are grasped ever anew by the unconditional grace of

God's pardon in Christ. It happens when we are transformed by the reality that living under grace is the end of all striving to fulfill what He demands in His Law. True sanctification is the hidden secret of God that continually happens when we are captivated again and again by the free grace of Christ. Gerhard Forde has put it succinctly: *Sanctification is a matter of getting used to our justification.*[6]

This does not imply that sanctification is not the business of the Holy Spirit or the result of His power in our lives. This is certainly true and important. A problem arises, however, if we identify the work of the Spirit in sanctification apart from the power of the Gospel, which bestows the righteousness of Christ. Here is where God has chosen to do everything for our salvation. When we look for the Spirit's power separated from the saving Word of Christ, or conditioned by anything we must do or not do, we have vacated both the work of the Spirit and the Gospel's power unto salvation. Sanctification is not related to a supplemental power of God separate from, but then added to the pardoning grace by which we are justified. Rather, sanctification results from the powerful impact that God's justifying pardon has on our faith and life in Christ. *From our new life in Baptism, the Gospel pardon matures us as a new creation, frees from the slavery of sin, and empowers us to walk in the Spirit. It strengthens and develops faith.* The Holy Spirit's power in sanctification and the Gospel's power that saves sinners (justification and sanctification) are the same power!

The Gospel is essentially the revelation and bestowal of the righteousness of Christ. Luther and the reformers knew of no work of sanctification apart from the saving work of justification. As Oswald Bayer has observed in his study of Luther, "For him justification by faith alone meant that everything was said and done; living by faith is already new life. When, nevertheless, Luther speaks about 'sanctification' he simply talks about justification. Justification and sanctification are not for him two separate acts that we can distinguish, as though sanctification follows after justification, and has to do so."[7] The Word of justification is the powerful pardon through which the Holy Spirit

---

6. G. Forde, *Christian Spirituality*, 23.

7. Oswald Bayer, *Living by Faith: Justification and Sanctification*, trans. Geoffrey W. Bromiley (Grand Rapids: Wm. B. Eerdmans, 2003), 58–59.

works to effect all the blessings of life in Christ. As the Spirit works faith in the heart, we receive and live in a righteous, forgiven relationship with God. This is justification. As the Spirit works through this same Gospel message, the powerful pardon of Christ's righteousness creates a new life in Christ, matures that life, and empowers faithful living. This is sanctification. It is not a separate work of God from justification. Rather, both are simply aspects of God's saving work through the same righteousness of Christ (grace!), which is ours through faith.

In various places the Scriptures focus on our status before God and membership in His Kingdom (*who* we are in Christ). Here our attention is directed to the justifying significance of the grace of Christ's pardon. Saving grace bestows a forgiven, reconciled relationship with God through faith. Thus Paul writes in Romans 5:1-2 NIV, "Therefore, since we have been justified through faith, we have peace with God through our Lord Jesus Christ, through whom we have gained access by faith into this grace in which we now stand [before God]." Likewise, in other places, God's Word tells us how the impact of Christ's righteousness transforms us into a new creation (*what* we are in Christ) and produces changes in our daily living (faithfulness in life and works). As Paul again wrote in 2 Corinthians 5:17-18, 21, "Therefore, if anyone is in Christ, he is a new creation; the old has passed: behold, the new has come. All this is from God, who through Christ reconciled us to himself. . . . For our sake he made him to be sin who knew no sin, so that in him we might become the righteousness of God." Here Paul is simply describing the sanctifying power of the same gift. As the children of God and citizens of His Kingdom, we are what we wear! Dressed by faith in the robe of Christ, we are reckoned righteous by God (justification) and we have become a new creation in Christ fashioned in His image that grows and matures into an image of the full stature of Christ (sanctification).

Is There an Unforgiveable Sin?

Have you ever wondered if you might have sinned so much, or in such a way, that God's forgiveness in Christ Jesus would no longer apply to you? If you have, what have you turned to for confident answers? It is not uncommon for Christians who have been battling nagging sins that trouble to wonder if they might be running out of God's mercy and forgiveness. Is there an end to God's forgiveness? Can a Christian sin so persistently that God would lose His patience and withhold His forgiveness? Can we reach a point when our sinning becomes unforgivable? Indeed, is there such a thing as an unforgivable sin? Anxious sinners, who see alarming sins sticking to their lives, desperately want to know the answers to these questions. Do you know someone like this? Are you one of them?

Let's ponder what the Scriptures tell us about God's forgiveness in Christ Jesus and hold fast to what they tell us despite how we may be inclined to feel at times. Notice how comprehensively Paul describes the saving work of Christ in 2 Corinthians 5:19 CSB: "In Christ, God was reconciling the world to himself, not counting their trespasses against them." Notice how Paul describes the *who* and the *what* that are included in the saving work of Christ. The *who* is the whole world of sinners, and the *what* is described as simply their trespasses. Paul's words are categorical and provide for no exceptions. Christ forgives all the trespasses of the whole world of sinners. He does not say that *some* have their trespasses forgiven, nor does He indicate that only *some* trespasses are forgiven. It is as simple as that: all sins of everyone are forgiven through the atoning sacrifice of Christ Jesus. The same point is made with different wording by the Apostle in Romans 5, and this language may be even more helpful to those Christians who may have questions about the magnitude of their sinfulness. Paul states, "Where sin increased, Grace abounded all the more" (Rom. 5:20 ESV). Christians alarmed about their sins may take comfort in these words of the Apostle. If you see your sins abounding more and more through the accusing finger of the Law, please be assured by the Word of God that grace is abounding all that much more (Rom. 5:20)—big sins, small sins, infrequent sins, habitual sins, all sins, period. The riches of God's grace will always outstrip the magnitude of your sins.

Let's carry the matter further. Some sensitive Christians may be alarmed over the question, *Yes, Jesus forgives all my sins, but have I separated myself from His forgiveness by the way I am living my life?* Perhaps some may recall that the famous actor, George C. Scott, who won the Oscar for best actor for his portrayal of General George S. Patton in the 1970 movie, *Patton*. Perhaps, less remembered is the fact that

Scott refused the Oscar. Objectively the Oscar exists and it is his, but Scott has chosen to live separate from it. Tragically, while everyone is forgiven in Christ Jesus, many do not live with it through faith. Sinners receive and live with the forgiveness of Christ through a faith that is created and sustained by the power of the Holy Spirit through the power of the Gospel (Rom. 1:16; 10:17). Can the sinfulness of your life put your faith in Christ at risk? Perhaps. Jesus warns of blasphemy against the Holy Spirit as unforgivable (Matt. 12:31).

God makes our sinful hearts hungry and ready to receive His forgiveness and strengthen our faith again and again through the Gospel by fashioning and maintaining a repentant heart by the accusing work of His Law. It is why we need the ministry of His Law as well as the Gospel continually in our Christian walk of faith. It makes a soft heart hungry for His healing, restoring forgiveness.

Satan, however, is always about trying to turn Christ's forgiveness into a license for sin, rather than a remedy for sin (see Rom. 6:1–11). When we become uncaring about our sins; when habitual sins no longer bother us; when we no longer struggle against them; then, God's Law is blunted, our hearts become hardened, and we lose our appetite to feed on the Gospel. As a result of not feeding on God's Word of forgiveness, faith is weakened, the Holy Spirit is grieved, and we are in peril of having our trust in Christ's forgiveness snuffed out by unrepentant indifference. In this sense the Church has spoken of the *unforgivable sin*. Jesus names "blasphemy against the Holy Spirit" as the unforgiveable sin (Matt. 12:31–32 NLT). In what way is this sin against the Holy Spirit unforgiveable? The Holy Spirit has been sent to convict us of sin and righteousness (through Law and Gospel; John 16:8). He works the faith and confession of Christ in the hearts of sinners by the Word of Christ (1 Cor. 12:3; Rom. 10:17). Such faith alone is saving in that it trusts and embraces the finished reconciliation of God and forgiveness that Jesus accomplished once and for all on Calvary's cross. To blaspheme against the Holy Spirit is to reject this grace and the Spirit's working of faith. It is to *fall away*, reverting back into unfaith. Unbelief is the rejection of the perfect sacrifice, crucifying Christ again as it were, *to their own harm* and *holding him up in contempt* (see Heb. 6:5–6; Matt. 13:20–21).

But you ask, *Am I committing the unforgivable sin?* It is important to understand that *the unforgivable sin* is not the absence of forgiveness, but rather like George C. Scott and his Oscar, it is the *refusal* of forgiveness. It is not unforgivable because Christ did not die for such a sin; it is unforgivable because it is the separation of the self from His forgiveness by unbelief. Such is the condition of all who have died without faith in the forgiveness of Christ and are now in Hell. It is not that they were bigger or more despicable sinners; it is that they refused to live with Christ's forgiveness through faith.

But you want to push the matter further, right? You want to know if your nagging, habitual, nasty sins are destroying your faith and ultimately working to grieve the Holy Spirit and separate you from Christ's forgiveness. You can take your measure on this very important question in the following way. If you are bored by this topic, if you don't care about the matter of your sins and God's forgiveness, if you think that you have a great arrangement, loving to sin so much while God loves to forgive so much . . . then, the answer is Yes! You probably are in danger of committing the unforgivable sin. You need to repent of your indifference, your mocking of God, and your smugness; and then you need to feed on His forgiveness, not simply presume it. However, if you are alarmed about your sins and the threat of them choking off your faith and appetite for the forgiveness of Christ, you need not be. If you are longing to have and live with the grace of our Lord, be assured; you have it securely. If you desire the mercy of God while your sins bother you—regardless of the continuing presence of nagging sins—be assured your faith life is healthy and you, like St. Paul may gloriously consider yourself chief of sinners. If these things shape your attitudes and concerns, be assured, you are not committing the unforgivable sin.

We live by grace, not by getting rid of our sins. While we are called to smash, bash, and trash the old sinful nature in all of us, there is no ridding ourselves of that Old Adam until we enter glory. It is not the presence of persistent sin, but the absence of faith that separates us from the graciousness of God in Christ Jesus. *The forgiveness of Christ saves because it covers our sins, not because it removes them.* And let me encourage you to cling to God's objective Word of forgiveness as it comes to you through Holy Absolution, through its objective presentation to you in sermon and lesson, and through the body and blood of Jesus in His Holy Supper.

CHAPTER 6

Assurance of Salvation

Blessed assurance, Jesus is mine;
Oh, what a foretaste of glory divine!

Thus have Protestant Christians sung lustily about their salvation ever since the hymn was written by Fanny Crosby and appeared in Palmer's *Guide to Holiness and Revival Miscellany* in 1873. *Yeah, but how do you know that Jesus is yours?* queries the rude skeptic. However, more than rude skeptics have raised the question of assurance about being saved. Christians of all traditions have raised the question and often with existential angst: *What is the stuff of blessed assurance? How can I know that Jesus is mine?* And perhaps an even more important question as concerns assurance of your salvation: *How can I know that I am His?* What should Christians run to and lean on for assurance that they truly do belong to Christ and that through him they are heirs of a final glory that is for real? Christians of all communions have sought advice on these questions especially when they are in the midst of some challenging tribulations or trials of spiritual warfare.

It is important to understand that according to the apostolic Gospel, assurance of salvation does not rest on anything you can experience or realize in the subjective reaches of your heart. Assurance of salvation rests on the objective truth of the Good News and not just one element. The Gospel is multifaceted and foundationally there is no assurance of salvation unless all of them are true. There is no hope in religiously motivated wishful thinking or in prescribed spiritual experiences that just warm or excite the heart but do not pass the requirement of hard truth. Reflecting this distinction, the apostle

Peter declared, *we did not follow cunningly devised myths and fables when we made know to you his power and coming but were eyewitnesses of his majesty* (2 Pet. 1:16). The apostolic witness anchors our assurance of a gracious God on the basis that all promises of the Gospel are anchored in objective truth, truth that is hard.

Assurance Based on Hard Truth

There was a great cartoon that recently appeared in the *Wall Street Journal*. A bewildered man is depicted in Hell standing in front of a smirking Devil with the caption *How can I be here? I didn't believe any of this stuff*. The great surprise for this guy who still can't quite believe it is that *truth is hard*. What is real and true is not affected at all by what we may believe or disbelieve. The humorous depiction about the hardness of truth in the cartoon is not particularly a message about who is going to Hell. Rather it pokes fun at a prevailing sentiment today that our own personal inclinations about what is true or good are valid and viable simply because we believe them. We hear it said: *These things are true for me, so you need to respect them simply because I believe them*. We could call this *soft truth*— believing things are true simply because we believe in them.

Embracing life with soft understandings of truth has not been limited simply to disbelievers in Hell and the Devil. Christians have sometimes been susceptible to thinking that the verities of the Gospel are grounded in nothing more than the presence and strength of their faith in them. Perhaps you have heard expressions that reflect this understanding: *I know that Jesus has risen from the dead because I trust I am experiencing Him here in my heart*. In religious circles, a soft understanding of truth is sometimes called *fideism*: having faith in faith. Some years back, it was John Montgomery who warned Christians against *fideism*, asserting that faith validates neither Christianity nor affirmations of atheism.[1] A biblical faith is in tension with the fallenness of the world, but it is not in tension with hard truth. Hard truth is objective truth. This is truth that

---

1. See John Montgomery's discussion in "Is Man His Own God," in *The Suicide of Christian Theology* (Minneapolis: Bethany Fellowship, 1970), 99, 260–63.

does not rely in any sense on anyone believing it. The Apostles and Evangelists in the New Testament exhorted trust in the saving work of Christ because it is grounded in hard truth. They exhorted faith in God's forgiveness not simply because sinners needed it; but because it is anchored in the objective facticity of the saving work of Christ. Let's consider some important aspects of the Gospel that support their claim.

Jesus ministered to John the Baptist (or perhaps his disciples) with hard truth about His own identity as the Christ when his disciples asked the question, *Are you really the one to come or should we look for another?* (Matt. 11:3). This is the central truth question of the Christian faith. Who is Jesus of Nazareth? Take note of how Jesus did *not* respond. He did not instruct the disciples to tell John to pray about the matter and ask the Holy Spirit for assurance about his messianic identity. Turning to the disciples He said, *Go back and tell John of the things that you have seen and heard: the blind receive sight, the lame walk, the lepers are cleansed, the deaf hear, the dead are raised, and the good news is preached to the poor* (Matt. 11:4–5). Jesus used His actions during a day's-worth of ministry to evidence the hard truth about His true Messianic identity to shore up wavering faith commitments; theirs, John's, or ours.

Foundational to apostolic preaching of Jesus was this testimony: *Of these things we are witnesses* (Acts 2:32; 2 Pet. 1:16). Faith and God-talk in the ministry of Christ and His Apostles was grounded in objective evidence about hard truth. When we reflect on authentic Christian faith, the heart trusts in the hard truth of what the head has come to know. As Edward John Carnell described a biblical understanding: *Faith is the subjective element in warranted belief* where the heart *rests in the sufficiency of evidences.*[2]

John constructed his Gospel around seven miracles of Jesus, capping them with His resurrection appearance to the skeptic, Thomas. He then stated their purpose to the reader: *Jesus did many other signs which are not written in this book, but these are written so that you may believe that Jesus is the Christ, the Son of God, and that believing, you may have life in his name* (John 20:30–31).

---

2. Edward John Carnell, *The Case for Orthodox Theology* (Philadelphia: Westminster, 1959), 31.

The apostolic Church proclaimed God's mighty acts through Jesus as hard truth that undergirds our trust that God is gracious to us through his saving work. Indeed, John offered testimony of multisensual contact with the works of Jesus to assure us of hard truth that He is the Word of life in which we have life. *That which was from the beginning, which we have heard, which we have seen with our eyes, which we looked upon and have touched with our hands, concerning the Word of Life—the life was made manifest, and we have seen it, and testify to it and proclaim to the eternal life, which was with the Father and was made manifest to us—that which we have seen and heard we proclaim also to you* (1 John 1:1–3).

About hard truth, it works both ways. As the apostle Paul declared, *If Christ be not raised from the dead, your faith is futile, and you are still in your sins* (1 Cor. 15:17). Should this not be hard truth, it means that we also will not be raised from the dead. In which case, Paul advised believers to "eat and drink, for tomorrow we die" (v. 32 ESV). However, this is not the case. Our faith and God-talk are grounded in the corroborated multisensual testimony of the women, the Apostles, and over five hundred witnesses. Their testimony provides overwhelming evidence of the hard truth that Jesus *did* rise from the dead, and therefore so will we (1 Cor. 15:3–8, 20–22).

The other hard truth is that there is a Hell, souls in prison, and the Devil. However, because there is compelling evidence that Jesus conquered sin, death, and the Devil in His atoning death and glorious resurrection, we can have confidence that in His victory we do not have to end up like the hapless fellow in the cartoon. After defeating all the powers of darkness, Jesus took a victory lap in Hell (1 Pet. 3:19), and we former citizens of that lower region have become permanent citizens of the Kingdom of God. The Devil is not in these details. They are grounded in saving truth that is hard.

Assurance Based on the Cross

When the work is all done, when what must be accomplished is achieved, when all is finished it's time to rest. When Jesus uttered his sixth word on the cross—*It is finished*—well it was! Therefore, he spoke his final word: "Father, into your hands I commit my spirit" (Luke 23:46 ESV). The logic of these words joined together is that when all things for the atonement of our sin were accomplished, it was time to rest. That is the significance of our Lord's last words on the cross. Having completed his work of redemption, he does as he did in creation (Gen. 2:3; John 1:3); he takes a rest. Perhaps we could even express his final words in today's street vernacular: *Father, I am outta here.*

We should recall that Jesus went to the cross as the willing, humble *Suffering Servant* (Phil. 2:2–8). He told His disciples when arrested in the Garden that the angels would be standing down (Matt. 26:53). He would now go it alone. We usually think that the greater the numbers—especially when facing daunting opposition— the better the chance of holding fast and holding out. You know the saying: *We can hang together, or we can hang separately.*[3] We think that should our side come down to the last man standing, our cause is certainly lost. And should the last one die, all will just become a bitter memory of great intentions, but dashed hope. Not so, with the passion of our Lord. Where he went, he went alone. But where he went, he proceeded not just as the *Suffering Servant* but also as our *Champion.*

As the *Second Adam*, Jesus faced off against the powers of sin, death, and the *Unholy Spirit*. On the cross he defeated them all with nothing in His hands but nails and blood. When it comes to biblical champions, we often think of the face-off that David had with Goliath and others like it. After the trash talking, it's time to get down to the conflict at hand. And we always think that if our man dies, we lose. Not so with our Lord Jesus. It was not in his standing, but rather in his dying that we win. The powers of darkness were defeated by his death, and by *that* death, we get life. With the final words of our Lord on the cross it was a done deal, and so it was time for a *Sabbath's* rest.

Father into your hands I commend my Spirit. As the Son commended his spirit to the Father, he commends ours as well. We get to rest. They took our Lord's dead body off the cross and laid it into the donated tomb of Joseph of Arimathea (Matt. 27:57–60). How fitting! The Sabbath day of rest was about to begin (Luke 23:54) and the body of Jesus was put into the earth and laid to rest. The earth

---

3. A clever turn on words attributed to Benjamin Franklin as representatives at the Continental Congress of 1776 considered signing the Declaration of Independence.

is the designated place to rest from the death to sin (Gen. 3:19). With his body, the body of our sins was also laid to rest in that dark cold tomb. As the Apostle has taught us, our old Adam was crucified and buried with Him in our baptism and we can therefore reckon ourselves dead to sin permanently (Rom. 6:3–4, 11). The death he died, he died once for all. So with this hard truth you may rest, totally free from the penalty of your sins forever.

On Good Friday, our sinful self and all our sins were put to rest with Jesus in His tomb. Our transgressions are fully atoned. Our enslavement to the Law has been overcome. God has become completely reconciled to us, just as we are. We rest in these amazing realities as we have been joined to the crucified, dead, and buried Jesus through our baptism. We must understand that for Jesus, however, this was just a short nap. He was not long for this tomb. Very soon thereafter, he proclaimed the Hell of it all to the Devil and all the souls in prison (1 Pet. 3:18–19). But for our old sinful self and our sins, they will remain buried in His tomb forever. They are finished, and we may rest assured on that.

Assurance Based on the Empty Tomb

Job was no stranger to cross life. For the sake of a wager, God allowed Satan to have his way with Job. He could do anything to him short of killing him. So he did. Satan turned his wealth into poverty; he turned his good name into scorn; he took the lives of his children, and he inflicted on him every manner of disease and physical suffering. Job's wife told him to curse God and die. His friends tried to persuade him that his afflictions were all the result of God punishing him for his sins. Job would not hear of such things. Even though he was never told about the wager, he nevertheless anchored his hope in God, his Redeemer. He stubbornly believed that one day, perhaps even after he has departed this life, he would be raised up in the flesh and behold him face-to-face. His lot of suffering and even his death would not have the final say. Job knew his Redeemer lives (Job 19:25).

Hundreds of years later, we behold another spectacle of One delivered over to Satan for cross life but also a cross death. God laid down another wager with Satan that he was determined to win.

However, this time there would be no holds barred. Jesus could be killed; and He was. It was all about being the Savior and taking our place. We are sin-sick cases, dead in our trespasses. We do not need to get a grip; we need to get a life. And that is just what would-be saviors must provide; provided they first get one for themselves. Job bore his cross and he eventually died. Jesus bore His cross and He also died. Does the parallel with Job stop here?

Between Job's hope and our Lord's cross, our happy forever hangs in the balance. He was named Jesus because He was to save us from our sins.[4] His death on the cross was to be a payment for our sins. But how can we be assured this is true? He said, *it is finished,* but was it truly? How can we know that Job's faith was not simply the pious wish of a poor misguided, suffering soul? We need more than a pious faith in faith. We need more than a blind hope. We need the assurance that comes from hard truth. Here is the bottom line about our redemption from sin, death, and the powers of evil. If the tomb of Jesus is not empty, then the promises of the cross are. If the resurrection of Jesus is not a fact, then our Happy Forever is a fiction.

It has been customary for the Church to gather on Easter morning and race with Peter and John to the tomb of Jesus upon hearing the report of the women that the tomb was empty. And while the Church's proclamation always echoes joyously this report of the women, let's reflect about its complete accuracy. Should we consider the tomb of Jesus completely empty, or just *somewhat* empty? Such a question might seem to hedge the great Easter message of the glorious resurrection of our Lord, but it is not. We are simply suggesting that a more careful reflection about Jesus' tomb take place.

On a sensory level, the apostolic witness indicates that while the body of Jesus was no longer in the tomb, the burial linen cloths and the napkin that was about His head were folded up nicely (John 20:5–7). They remained in the tomb. The big point, however, was that the body of Jesus was no longer wrapped in them. The hard truth of Easter is that when you go to the tomb of Jesus, there is blessed assurance that what you don't see is what you get. This is the one place where the real absence of the true body of Christ is joyously affirmed

---

4. The name Jesus means the Lord is salvation.

as Great News. *It is finished* on the cross gets verified by the One who is no longer there. It is the negative space that captures the blessed assurance and great joy of Easter.

But not so fast about the tomb being completely empty! We need to consider what the apostle Paul declares about our baptismal union with the crucified Christ. Second, we need to remember that the Easter victory proclaims now and not-yet dimensions that need to be taken into account when we consider the tomb of Jesus after He left. Admittedly, this is not our central focus when we are singing, *"Jesus Christ is risen today"* but it is important for understanding how and when we receive the saving gifts of our Lord's death and resurrection. In Romans 6 Paul informs us that Baptism unites sinners by water and the Word to Christ the crucified. There in his death, he takes all our sins and gives us all his righteousness as we are then buried with him.

> Do you not know that all of us who have been baptized into Christ Jesus were baptized into his death? We *were buried therefore with him* in baptism into death. . . . For if we have been united with him in a death like his, we shall certainly be united with him in a resurrection like his. (Rom. 6:3–5; emphasis mine)

Just ponder what this means. All baptized sinners through the ages are joined to Christ the crucified, dead to sin, but are now still tucked away in His tomb! It is a pretty crowded place in here, is it not? The existential question about Easter therefore is this: Does the Apostle's final promise to baptized Christians hold water? Do we the baptized—crucified, buried with him, and dead to sin—do we also get to live? (Rom. 6:5). This question is not; do we get to die to sin with Jesus and rest in his tomb. The question is, Do we get to get out?

Today's culture wants to propose the stupid idea that the cycle in nature of death to new life offers some good news about *our* problem of death. What silliness! When Adam and Eve were tossed out of the garden, the ground was not rested; it was cursed. As Adam's body came from the dirt he walked on, it then returned to it. The wages of sin is death, not recycling. The dead stay dead. The women came to the tomb of Jesus to anoint a dead body out of respect for the departed Jesus, not to prepare for some cycle of return. They came looking for a dead Jesus. There is no cyclical springtime for sinful humans under the curse. Even the most unreligious farmer today knows the difference between a fallow field and a graveyard. Corn cycles, humans don't. Because of sin there is death. And because of death, there are graveyards. And because there are graveyards, there are loved ones who visit to pay their respects and grieve those who are dead and buried.

This brings our discussion back to tombs. As the baptized, we receive and bet on our Happy Forever based on the Easter victory, by faith. Again, echoing the words of Paul; *In fact, Christ has been raised from the dead, the firstfruits of those who have fallen asleep* (1 Cor. 15:20). This element of negative space from the tomb of Jesus makes all the difference in the world about graveyards and those who are buried there. According to Romans 6:5 ESV, "For if we have been united with him in a death like his, we shall certainly be united with him in a resurrection like his." Christ's resurrection guarantees ours. We get to get out! Concerning this promise, the only options are living through faith in this not-yet or living with a not-at-all. The victory over the grave is now for Jesus, not yet for those baptized now living in his tomb, and not-at-all for the rest. Nobody gets recycled.

As we died to sin and were buried with Christ; we for now remain in his tomb. *Jesus Christ is risen today!* But as old sinful saints, we are still hunkered down in the dark space. For all of what we and our neighbors see while there—our weaknesses, our sinful habits, our frailties, and all our imperfections—we live still buried in the tomb with his righteousness where his victory over the grave anticipates our own. About all this we the Church of Christ can make book. We can make very certain book; for behold the somewhat-empty tomb of Jesus.

Yes, like Jesus on the way to his cross, we are not much to look at. We can look in the mirror and say to ourselves, *Not much glory to behold here!* But in the crucified and risen Christ, we have assurance that we *have* received his glory. We are already righteous saints, recreated in the image of Christ. However, no one can see our halos just yet. We are forgiven, wrapped in the robe of righteousness but we appear to others (and to ourselves in the mirror of God's Law) with all our flaws, imperfections, and weaknesses; and many of them are glaring. Yes, we wear the King's clothes, but we wear them so transparently! We may wonder at times, *My God, is this robe of righteousness real?* Our poverty and sinful nakedness can put our faith to the test, and we can have our doubts at times. We have the promise of the Better Day coming when all our imperfections will pass away. But the question is, Can you see it from here?

We would like to have just a glimpse of the *Glory Story*. We want assurance based on hard truth that this is not simply *pie-in-the-sky by-and-by*. When you need assurance, go and gaze long and hard at the empty space of the tomb of Jesus. Listen to the parade of witnesses and appearances of the risen Christ. As He went from death to life, here is your down payment and guarantee that you also shall be raised to a newness of life. Cross life was provisional for Jesus, and it is provisional for us. When you die to sin, you rise to God, you rise to righteousness, and you rise to a certain hope in the New Day coming when all sin and suffering will come to an end. Christ has been pleased to rise and therefore so will you. All other would-be saviors are dead—Jesus lives.

God the Father put a wager on Job, and He won. The joy of the empty tomb is that He also put a wager on Jesus, and we all have won. We also know that our Redeemer Lives! That is our assurance. His resurrection is *the Trailer* that has already been projected on the big screen of human history; our resurrection is the coming *Main Feature*. Decked out in the robe of righteousness, we are the holy, innocent and spotless bride of Christ awaiting His return to take us home. When the Church of Christ has her Easter, we will all come forth and shout, *We are risen!* And our Lord will shout back to us with a big smile, *You are risen indeed!*

Assurance without a Doubt

The Gospel narratives that relate our Lord's glorious resurrection are accented with several occasions of believable skepticism. Not for a moment did anyone anticipate a farfetched eighth-day miracle. The women went to the tomb to continue anointing a dear friend's dead body. Discovering that the tomb was empty, Mary Magdalene confidently informed Peter and the other disciples that someone had stolen the body. Returning to the tomb she tearfully repeated her reasonable conclusion to a couple of angels sitting inside. Then taking the risen Christ to be the gardener and possible culprit, she pleaded with him to give back the body (John 20:1–2, 11–15). We should not think of Mary's reactions and conclusions as unusual. Even before the age of modern science, first-century Jews were confident that dead people stay dead. When Jesus then appeared to his disciples in the upper room, they thought they were seeing a ghost. Luke records that even after He showed them the nail prints on his hands and feet, they still "disbelieved for joy" (Luke 24:40–41 ESV).

John's recording of this appearance of Jesus to his disciples makes the point that Thomas was not with them and having received their testimony he remained unconvinced. For many generations of English-speaking Christians, Thomas has been known as a "doubter" of the resurrection. Upon inviting him to see and touch his nail and spear prints in his second appearance to his disciples in the upper room, Jesus exhorts him in the KJV: *Do not doubt but believe* (John 20:27). Hence, he has been popularly known as, "doubting Thomas." This implies to many in our time that Thomas at this point thought the resurrection may or may not have happened. He was uncertain.

But as noted in chapter 6, Thomas was without a doubt a skeptic. And he was a skeptic without a doubt. He didn't merely harbor reservations about the resurrection reports. He flat out refused to believe that Jesus had risen from the grave despite the corroborated eyewitness testimony of ten of his best friends. The KJV rendering, *do not doubt but believe* (John 20:27), is a faulty translation. A more accurate rendering of Jesus' words from the Greek would be "Do not disbelieve, but believe" (ESV). Thomas moved from unbelief to faith through his encounter with the risen Christ. In both instances— before his inspection of the risen Christ and after—he was without a doubt.

Jesus said to Thomas, "Have you believed because you have seen me? Blessed are those who have not seen and yet have believed" (John 20:29 ESV). Some Christians have understood His words to disparage Thomas for insisting on some objective evidence to ground his faith but extolling those who would believe without any evidence at all. This is a faulty understanding that ignores the New Testament stress on the importance of eyewitness testimony. Thomas should be understood as a skeptic, without a doubt. He had the benefit of overwhelming evidence that Christ had risen from the dead based on corroborated eyewitness testimony from his closest friends (John 20:25). Despite this solid evidence, he would not believe. Our Lord's words to him should be interpreted to mean; blessed assurance comes to those who rest their faith commitment in the sufficiency of eyewitness testimony.[5]

Until matters of fact are justified by sufficient evidence, there is always room for healthy skepticism. But a resurrection skeptic like Thomas disbelieves not based on the weight of evidence but despite it. Jesus told his disciples (soon to be apostles) at his first meeting in the upper room that His personal appearance was to qualify them to be His witnesses (Luke 24:46–48). His appearance to Thomas was for the same reason. Apostolic firsthand witness enables our assurance of the risen Christ to rest on very sufficient evidence. The apostles understood the importance of the eyewitness character of their proclamation of Christ. On Pentecost Peter declared, *This Jesus God raised up, and of that we are witnesses* (Acts 2:32). The New Testament writers provide a strong objective foundation for us to anchor our knowledge and trust in the risen Lord. Therefore, with assurance we can also say, He is risen indeed, *without a doubt!*

Assurance Based on Being Included

Perhaps in your darker moments of not feeling very righteous or close to God, you have entertained some doubts about being included in God's plan of salvation. Am I really included in John's testimony that God so loved the *world* that he gave his only begotten Son? (John 3:16). Am I really included in the Apostle Paul's declaration that "in Christ, God was reconciling the world to himself, not counting their trespasses against them"? (2 Cor. 5:19 CSB). Could there be something about me or about God that would exclude me from the saving work of Christ on the cross?

Some Christians have thought that it could possibly be so. They do not believe that Jesus atoned for the sins of everyone. Therefore,

---

5. For further explanation and discussion of this text and the importance of apostolic eyewitness testimony for grounding the facticity of the resurrection of Christ see my *You Can Give an Answer: A Study in Christian Apologetics* (Irvine, CA: 1517 Publishing, 2018), 12ff.

it is theoretically possible that Jesus did not die for me, or you. This possibility is predicated on an interpretation that the word *world* in the above two New Testament passages should be understood to mean the full number of those God has chosen to save.[6] In other words, Jesus did not suffer and die for those who are finally lost. This conclusion is based in part on the thinking that it would be beneath God to send his Son to atone for the sins of those who would end up in Hell. Hence Jesus just atoned for the sins of some sinners; those whom God chose to save. With this understanding, the question *Am I Really Included?* can be very troubling indeed.

As observed in our previous discussion about the atonement in chapter 4, if Jesus only died for some sinners, the Gospel becomes an uncertain message for everyone. It turns every Gospel Word into a provisional message: God *may* have forgiven your sins, because He *may* have sent Jesus to die for your sins, because he *may* have chosen to save you. This limited view of Christ's atonement removes confidence in the forgiveness of sins not simply for some, but for every individual sinner. It makes the question about Christ's atonement and forgiveness—*Am I Really Included?*—a relevant question for all sinners.

If Jesus only died for the sins of those God chose to save, maybe that includes you; but then again, maybe it doesn't. Given this classic Calvinist understanding of the cross of Christ, it was popular in early American Reformed history to anchor an existential quest for blessed assurance in the conviction that God takes care of His elect in this life. He grants them eternal and temporal blessings, which in the words of Crosby can be taken by the sinner as *a foretaste of glory divine.* Thus what Max Weber coined, *the protestant work ethic* motivated many within this tradition to lives of hard work, discipline, and frugality to work out their salvation with fear and trembling and the desire to acquire the blessed assurance that glory divine is in their future. But some are dirt poor, and others have had tragic events punctuate their life. How about you?

---

6.   For a rather thorough presentation of the Reformed view, see Wayne Gruden, *Systematic Theology* (Grand Rapids: Zondervan, 2000), 594–600.

If we allow God to interpret His own Word, how should we understand *world* in John 3:16 and 2 Corinthians 5:19?[7] Can I know if I am really included? Does the term *world* above mean that only some have their sins forgiven, or should it be understood to include *all* sinners, including you? Notice how those included in Christ's atonement are described by the writer to the Hebrews. Christ entered *once for all into the holy places, and by his blood*, secured *an eternal redemption* (Heb. 9:12; emphasis mine). And "he has appeared once for *all* at the end of the ages to put away sin by the sacrifice of himself" (Heb. 9:26 ESV; emphasis mine). He described this redemption as accomplished by the *offering of the body of Christ once for all* (Heb. 10:10; emphasis mine). From these passages, all sinners can understand confidently that the word *world* means *all*. God so loved all that by his only begotten Son, He reconciled all to himself not counting their trespasses against them. All is everyone and that includes you and me!

God has acquired for everyone perfect righteousness and acceptability in Christ's universal atonement. This means that the declaration of forgiveness and reconciliation presented by Paul in 2 Corinthians 5:19 exists already in the present because of God's saving work in Christ in the past. The forgiveness of sins means the same thing as the declaration of righteousness or innocence. God has already reconciled Himself to a world of sinners once for all, and that means everyone including you and me. Anyone and everyone, regardless of how wretched you may think you are, may look to the cross of Christ and be assured that you have the full forgiveness of your sins and God's complete favor now and forever.

Assurance Based on Good Answers to Good Questions

A good question has at least one answer that can be true. A bad question has no answer that can be true. Imagine a loving husband being asked the question, When did you stop beating your wife? This is a

---

7. For God so loved the world that he gave his only begotten son, that whoever believes in him should not perish but have eternal life (John 3:16) All this from God, who through Christ reconciled us to himself and gave us the ministry of reconciliation—that is, "In Christ God was reconciling the world to himself, not counting their trespasses against them, and entrusting to us the message of reconciliation" (2 Cor. 5:18–19 ESV).

bad question. Any answer carries the damning assumption that this husband is guilty of mistreating his wife. Since the assumption is false, no answer to the question is possible. No answer can reflect the truth of how this husband lovingly treats his wife. While the unanswerable character of this question is easy to spot, there is a question related to the outcome of being saved or not that is often raised by Christians and even some theologians that is equally unanswerable. *Why are some saved, and others are lost?* While it might seem to be a good question, it is not. Let's examine it more closely with the use of another illustrative example.

John loves Marsha and is committed to winning her heart.[8] Alas, however, all his advances and efforts to woo her prove fruitless. Marsha spurns all his affections and rejects all his gifts. The closer he gets just makes her skin crawl. On one occasion, however, John came calling when Marsha was not at home, but her roommate was. Her name is Mary. Upon opening the door, Mary took one look at John and fell madly in love with him. John and Mary became quite a number, and a wonderful love relationship developed. At night Mary and Marsha often shared a meal together and their conversation invariably would turn to John. Marsha would explain how she could never accept John and rejected all his advances. Her explanations all began with the word *I*. I can't stand the sight of John. I could never have him in my life. I want nothing to do with him—I, I, I. Mary's explanations of her love for John always began with the word, *John*. John swept me off my feet. John captured my heart—John, John, John.

Why are John and Mary a loving couple but John and Marsha are not? This is a bad question. It erroneously assumes that a single reason can explain Mary and Marsha's relationship to John. However, if we ask, *How* is it that Mary has a loving relationship with John but Marsha does not? This is a good question and the explanation that each woman offered the other provides the answers. Notice their words described causes not some abstract reason. Marsha explained that she is the cause of having no relationship with John. She would have nothing to do with him and said so. Conversely, Mary credits John for capturing her heart, nurturing a returning love. Both women spoke the truth.

---

8. A different John and Marsha from the example in chapter 5.

With this insight, let us return to our question: *Why are some saved, and others are not?* Notice the same assumption is embedded in this question as above. Both assume that a single reason can explain relationships that are created and those that are not. This is a false assumption. It renders the question unanswerable and therefore a bad question. However, if we ask, How is it that some come to faith in Christ and are saved while others do not and are lost? This *how* question assumes that causes are involved, not some singular reason. It is a good question and one that the Scriptures readily answer. It is also the most existentially important issue that gets at what each of us is concerned about: *Am I included and if so, how is this so?*

The Scriptures are crystal clear on these two related how questions. First, God alone is the cause of the saved being saved. The Apostle Paul explained that the Holy Spirit creates faith by the power of the saving word of Christ (Rom. 10:17; 1 Cor. 12:3). The grace by which sinners are saved through faith is the doing of God, not the sinner, lest anyone take credit (Eph. 2:8–9). Second, concerning the lost, Jesus offered both tears and blame. For instance, he wept over a disbelieving Jerusalem, crying out, *Jerusalem, how I longed to gather you, but you were not willing* (Matt. 23:37). As Marsha was unwilling to have John, unbelievers are unwilling to have Jesus. And as Mary with John, it is God who has swept us off our spiritual feet and saved us by the power of His Gospel (Rom. 1:16).

Yes, but in light of some of the great challenges you must face from the world, the flesh, and the Devil, you may well ask at times with some anxiety, *Am I going to be able to persevere in my faith and ultimately receive the crown of glory?* This is a related good question. First, Jesus addressed the concern. *He who perseveres to the end will be saved* (Matt. 24:13). *Many are called but few are chosen* (Matt. 22:14). Second, the Apostle Paul declared *No one and nothing can separate believers from the love of God in Christ Jesus* (Rom. 8:31–39).

The assurance he offers of this security is based on the reality that those whom he called and justified by the Gospel, he foreknew and predestined them also to be glorified (Rom. 8:29–30). So being one whom he has called by the Gospel and justified through faith, the Lord through his apostle provides you a comforting answer to your incredibly good question. Can you be confident that this is God's blessed assurance to you? Absolutely! Paul elaborated on this assurance when he declared that God chose you to be his own before the foundations of the world, having predestined you to be holy and blameless according to the riches of his grace (Eph. 1:4–7). As you may at times be anxious about holding up under the stress and perhaps suffering from elements of spiritual warfare in your life, this is your blessed assurance that you shall always belong to Jesus.

Assurance Based on the External Word

As noted in chapter 5, some have mistakenly held that forgiveness and salvation come to sinners not as a gift bestowed, but as an offer for personal decision. Blessed assurance is portrayed to be based on a sincere commitment to Christ as one's personal Lord and Savior. If that commitment wanes or grows weak, then so does your assurance. Often the formula to recover a blessed assurance has directed alarmed doubting Christians to recommit their lives to Jesus. Sincerity of your commitment is, of course, requisite. But how do you know if your sincerity about your commitment is sufficient? Some have thought that the Holy Spirit will assist in the matter of sincerity. Others have pointed to one's zeal to put away carnal patterns of life and live obedient to the precepts of God holy law.

Following Luther, the Reformation in Wittenberg always pointed to the external Word of Christ as the source of blessed assurance. It is the objective Word of Christ's universal atonement that proclaims to all sinners that they are forgiven, and God *is not counting their trespasses against them* (2 Cor. 5:19). Blessed assurance is found in the cross of Christ as the Gospel reveals it and bestows its saving gifts. *But I do not feel forgiven*; many Christians have confessed. However, when it comes to matters of assurance of salvation, *your feelings be hanged!* Do not look inside for that assurance. God wrote His Law on the human heart and for all of us sinners its purpose is to reveal our sin (Rom. 3:19) not our salvation. It just keeps accusing us of our wretchedness—convicting us of sinful lives and anemic faith. That is what it is supposed to do.

Nevertheless, there is a message going around these days that many Christians are missing out on significant blessings of Christ because of insufficient tapping into power of his indwelling presence. This message goes something like this. You must make an important distinction between *Christ-for-you* and *Christ-in-you*. The former references the finished work of Christ on the cross and His forgiveness of your sin when you accepted him as your personal Lord and Savior. The blessings of *Christ-for-you* are well and good, but they are past blessings. Christ-in-you, on the other hand, has more riches to bestow in your here-and-now daily life. Christians need to appreciate and connect with Christ on the inside. The experience of Jesus within provides divine power and strength to meet the challenges of everyday life. Our union with Christ taps his power, peace, and joy that deliver us from the fears, hurts, and disappointments that come from living in this fallen world. The key to rising above all that the sinful world unleashes against us is becoming aware and celebrating the riches of our union of Christ within. The message is enticing. If you are not feeling enough joy, excitement, and a fulfilling life of faith; be assured that by connecting with Christ-in-you, these uplifting experiences can be yours.

Certainly, the New Testament and especially the writings of Paul teach believers that Christ and the Holy Spirit dwell within them. Paul reminded the Corinthians to appreciate this reality: "Do you not know that you are God's temple and that God's Spirit dwells in you?" (1 Cor. 3:16 ESV) and "Do you not realize this about yourselves, that Jesus Christ is in you?" (2 Cor. 13:5 ESV). The preposition *in* is the common translation of the Greek word *EIS*. More accurately, however, *eis* means *into*. Our connection with Christ is not casual; it is an intimate union. Forget for a moment our modern sense of being *into* something or someone. Paul teaches that baptism brings about a profound union with Christ-the-crucified. Baptism unites us with Christ in his death to sin on the cross with the inheritance of his glorious resurrection (Rom. 6:3–11). From this union, the baptized are *into* Christ and Christ is *into* us. Being so united to the crucified Christ, Paul declares that we should reckon ourselves dead to sin, alive to God, and slaves of righteousness (Rom. 6:11, 18).

Let us return to the issue of our experience of faith life in daily living and the matter of assurance. Perhaps you have secretly longed for a more fulfilling experience of your life with Christ. Should you think that connecting with Christ-in-you will provide a greater measure of his power, comfort, and peace? Should you buy into the message that experiencing Christ-in-you is the way to receive more blessings in your walk of faith? I think not and neither did the Apostle Paul.

It is meaningful to distinguish between the finished saving work of Christ on the cross (e.g., full atonement for our sins) and his saving work through the Gospel (e.g., bestowing his saving gifts). However, the distinction between Christ-for-you and Christ-in-you presents a misleading dichotomy by assuming that our Lord provides additional blessings by connecting subjectively with his presence in our hearts. When Paul instructs us about receiving the saving work and gifts of Christ, however, he does not direct us to connect with Christ on the inside. Rather, he directs the reader only to the preaching of the cross of Christ. He would know nothing among the Corinthians except a Gospel that proclaimed, *Jesus Christ and Him crucified* (1 Cor. 1:17; 2:2). He declared to the Romans that he was not ashamed of this Gospel because *it is the power of God for salvation for all who believe* (Rom. 1:16). The power of the Gospel is the proclaimed *word of Christ* used by the Spirit to connect us to Christ by faith (Rom. 10:17). The Gospel proclaims the saving work and gifts of Christ then and now.

Christ carries out his saving work and bestows his saving gifts on sinners from the outside. Through the external proclaimed Word and sacraments, our Lord creates and nurtures faith, hope, and love on the inside. Christ-for-you bestows the blessings of salvation from outside you and plants them by faith along with his dwelling in you. Will Christ-in-you eliminate or diminish the anguish and turmoil that comes from living in this fallen world? No, and often quite the reverse.

For now, believers are consigned to groan along with this fallen world because we have just the first fruits of our Lord's final victory (Rom. 8:23). The *all things* that God will work for our good (Rom. 8:28) are especially the rotten, tragic, disappointing, and fear-producing things that so often befall us. Paul stresses that while tribulation, distress, persecution, nakedness, peril, and sword can be expected in this life, they cannot *separate us from the love of God through Christ Jesus* (Rom. 8:35–39). For now, standard Christian living includes spiritual warfare and the anguish that goes with it. Part of the battlefield is within us, for there the enemy is also present. The Reformers never appeal to Christ in you as a source of strength or comfort in the face of spiritual warfare. Indeed, Luther could refer to the heart as the *devil's playground*. Satan uses God's Law written on our hearts (Rom. 2:15) to convince us that our works are either so righteous that we do not need the saving work of Christ or so wretched and numerous that we do not qualify for it. Self-righteousness or despair is his victory and our defeat. There is no blessed assurance to be found by searching for our gracious God on the inside.

The fruit of the spirit: love, joy, peace, patience, and so on (Gal. 5:22) certainly counter the disappointments, fears, anxiety, and turmoil of spiritual warfare, but they do not replace them. At his baptism, Jesus was filled with the Holy Spirit (Matt. 3:16; John 1:32–33). Nevertheless, it is silly to think that if Jesus would have experienced more of the Spirit within, he would not have experienced so much turmoil in the Garden of Gethsemane that He sweat drops of blood. An angel came and ministered to our Lord during his agony; he did not receive comfort by connecting with the Spirit within (see Luke 22:43–44). And it would be a mistake to think that if the Apostle Paul connected more with Christ-in-you, he could have experienced less turmoil about his fleshly self's slavery to sin (see Rom. 7:14–24).

Christ promises to continue his saving work for you from the outside in his external Word. This is where all the power of the Gospel comes to you for your salvation. Take heart! While your life may continue to have its hurts, disappointments, fears, and discouragements, Christ-for-you promises to give you a peace that will pass all understanding. Ironically, this means that while you may become progressively more disturbed about yourself and the rotten things in your life, you can sleep really well.

Assurance Based on an Outrageous Parable

> And the son said to him; "Father, I have sinned against heaven and before you. I am no longer worthy to be called your son."
>
> —(Luke 15:21)

The *Parable of the Prodigal Son* (Luke 15:11–32) reflects some of the most outrageous aspects of the grace of God. Blessed assurance is knowing that wretched living cannot void it and its giftedness never assumes a shred of individual merit or virtue. Even the most offen-sive behaviors on our part cannot cancel or diminish God's desire to treat us with nothing but pure grace. Moreover, while you can walk away from his covenant of grace to live rebelliously separated from it, His grace remains secure, awaiting your return.

We could perhaps rename this the *Parable of the Ungrateful Brothers*. The younger brother seeks to cash in his inheritance and his older brother resents that this did not lead to a permanent loss of sonship. We all know the story. The younger of two sons has become progressively disenchanted with life in their father's household. He demands his inheritance to find a more fulfilling life on his own indulging in sinful worldly pleasures. After becoming destitute and discovering that the pigs he must feed have a better life, he realizes that in his current state, he is as good as dead. His remedy is to go back home, eat humble pie, and beg his father to become the household's slave. His father will have no such thing. He is joyous over the return of his lost son and considers it a great occasion to party. The older son, however, does not see things that way at all. He is put out by his father's joy and celebration. He resents the restoration of his return-ing rebellious brother and considers his own continued service to the household more deserving of a good party.

Exemplified here are two misunderstandings about assurance and the graciousness of God among some Christians. The first is very popular and is represented by the younger son. It is the belief that the sufficient prevalence and the magnitude of your sin can cancel or void God's grace. The younger son is convinced that his sins have forfeited his sonship and father's favor and therefore negotiating for slavery is his best option. *Yes*, tragically you can walk away from the inheritance of God's righteousness and baptismal covenant, but *no*, you cannot cancel them. The second faulty understanding is reflected in the reactions of the older brother. Lifelong Christians who have served the Lord through thick and thin are not more deserving of God's favor and commendation than wretched sinners who leave the fold like this guy's younger brother.[9]

---

9. Note the same kind of thinking by the daylong laborers in the vineyard (Matt. 20:11–12).

Lurking behind the reactions of both brothers when the younger returns home is the faulty understanding that God's grace is offered to make up for our weaknesses and failings. It is there to fill the gap between the flawed people we are and the people we ought to be. However, if a person decides to turn his back on doing his best at godly service, then all bets are off. If we are not going to do our part, we forfeit God doing His part. God's grace covers a multitude of sins, but it does not cover a lack of good effort on our part to avoid them. Both brothers are operating with this same misunderstanding of how to remain a son in the household. They must be as faithful as they can in order to *retain* their inheritance. The prodigal believes he cashed in that inheritance when he left to make his own way in the world and his older brother thought the same. They both were wrong, and it is the father who sets them straight—much to the joy of the younger and the indignation of the older.

The parable has a happy ending for the younger brother. He learns that life itself is what flows from living in the father's household. This life exists only by the utter outrageous grace of God in Christ Jesus. You do nothing to get it and do nothing to *retain* it. Your good works do not preserve this grace, and your sins do not void it. You can tragically walk away from it and Hell is the final exile if you refuse to return. But blessed assurance is in this: What *you do* can never change its reality. God has and always will reckon you as forgiven and righteous for the sake of the saving work of Christ. The objective hard truth of this forgiveness is in the cross of Christ and its verification is in the empty tomb. They provide our assurance that you will always have a gracious Heavenly Father. That is the outrageousness of God's grace represented by the father in the parable. If you are a return-back-home child of God, this is your assurance, and you can celebrate this reality. And if you are a stay-at-home child of God, this is also your assurance that you can celebrate. In any case, it is always a reason to party in the Kingdom of God for God's grace has been, is, and always will be sufficient for you. Of that, we all can be assured.

The Experience of Living in the Cross

Part II

The Experiences of Living in the Nursing Home

CHAPTER 7

The War within Life

The past few decades have witnessed a veritable explosion in the production of books that promise a vibrant, joy-filled and exciting adventure in Christian living. Such promises are attractive to ordinary saints who realize that their Christian living leaves a good bit to be desired. Our experience of living the Christian life often feels like one step forward and two steps back. Wouldn't it be heavenly to rise above the sin, afflictions, and trials of life or have them removed altogether by God's mighty power? If these are blessings that God would grant us right here and now and they could be ours if we will just devote ourselves to some outlined Bible-based program, who would not jump at the opportunity? Perhaps you have already jumped, but achieved less than the desired results.

Living as a Fragmented Self

The New Testament paints a quite different picture of what we should expect from life in Christ in this present fallen world. If we do not read beyond Romans 6, the raised-up life through Baptism can seem singularly victorious. Romans 7, however, provides sobering insight into our Christian character. Here with the apostle Paul, we must lament that we still have a *fleshly self* in which *nothing good dwells* because it is *sold as a slave to sin* (Rom. 7:14, 18). Therefore, like the Apostle, we must also say, "I do not do the good I want, but the evil I do not want is what I keep on doing" (Rom. 7:19 ESV).

In chapter 7, the apostle seems to contradict his chapter 6 statements where he assures us that in our baptism, we are dead to sin, alive to God, and slaves to righteousness (Rom. 6:11, 18). But there is no contradiction here. Both portraits of the Christian in Romans 6 and 7 are true. As a new creation in Christ, the Christian has died to sin, entered into full union with Christ, been filled with the Holy Spirit, and this has totally transformed him or her in all aspects of the human character into a slave of righteousness. But since the Christian is still tied to this old fallen creation, he or she is also *Old Self*, or what Paul often refers to as *flesh*. Such bondage to sin, death, and the devil pervades all aspects of the functioning human character.

Many Christians have reflected on their Christian experience and confessed, with much bewilderment, that they really want to serve Christ, but then again they don't. They really think and trust that they are fully acceptable to God in Christ's justification, but then again they think their acceptance and security is in their own hands to acquire by their own doing. They really want to respond to God's love with a returning love, but so often selfish and rebellious interests get in the way. Duplicity, ambiguity, confusion, and often exasperation are commonly experienced. *I just do not in any way feel all together in my Christian life*, is often the unspoken confession of the Christian's heart. *There must be something terribly wrong with me.* Well, there is!

We must remember that Christian life is lived totally in the cross of Christ. We continually live by grace or we don't live at all. Justification is not some past event that the Christian moves on from, but rather a constant reality in which all aspects of life with God are focused and grounded. We walk by that faith or we lose our way and stumble. In Romans 7, Paul, writing by the Spirit, confesses a wretched sinful state of affairs in his own life.[1] But then, pointing to the cross, he can say, *But thanks be to God through Christ Jesus our Lord. . . . For there is now no condemnation* (Rom. 7:25–8:1).

---

1. While some want to ascribe Paul's confession of his struggle against his sinful fleshly life to be a description of his former life as a Pharisee, it is important to note his use of the present tense to describe his experience in Rom. 7:14–25. For an excellent discussion and defense of the understanding that Paul is describing his life after the impact of redemption and not before, see Michael Middendorf, *The "I" in the Storm: A Study of Romans 7* (St. Louis: Concordia Academic, 1997), 185–225.

Because the fleshly self is still a part of us, we are and continually remain sinners in this life. This is both what is terribly wrong with us and at the same time a part of normal Christian character and experience in this life. We are simultaneously a new creation in Christ and an Old Sinful Self. They are continually battling one another in our thinking, our desires, and our motivation for behavior. The Christian life involves fighting a war that rages inside all believers. The New Self lives in Christ by the Spirit as a slave to righteousness and the Old Sinful Self is tied to this old fallen creation, in bondage to sin, death, and the devil. In Galatians 5:17, Paul tells us that they are in conflict with one another. Let's make no mistake about it. This is no small-time skirmish in which we engage.

The New Testament paints a picture of a cosmic struggle between Christ and Satan. The decisive confrontation has already been won by Christ in His redemptive death and victorious resurrection, but the battle still rages in this fallen creation. What Paul indicates in Romans 8:18–25 is that our war within is simply a part of this larger cosmic battle that will be brought to a climactic end when Christ returns. Then He will usher the fullness of His victory in the resurrected new life.

Is it any wonder that we as Christians experience turmoil, suffering, and conflict as part of our Christian experience? Right now, we have just the first fruits of this final victory. Tribulation, distress, persecution, nakedness, peril, and sword we are told can be anticipated as part of the Christian's lot for now (Rom. 8:35). Deeply embedded in Christian living is participation in a cosmic war. Part of the battlefield is within us, for there the enemy is present. Our joy and peace in Christian living comes from trust and hope that is anchored in the promises that God will work all of it together for our good and none of this suffering and turmoil can rob us of His love, which is ours through Christ Jesus (Rom. 8:35–39).

How wonderful it would be to have things calm and peaceful inside and a real victory over our sinful thoughts, desires and behavior. It would be such a relief if our often-impoverished worship, love, and service to Christ could be fully transformed into the likeness of Christ! Do we not long to be free of the sorrows, suffering, and confusion that often plague our lives? While the New Testament promises these blessings to us, they are now hidden in the risen and ascended Christ. We shall not taste them in all their fullness until the final fruits of our resurrected life in glory.

There are no spiritual exercises for us to perfect that then promise a bargaining God to shower blessings upon us in this life. To fall prey to such thinking is to place us back under the Law, which only kills, and to desert living under grace by faith. We must beware of those who promise heaven on earth in the here and now. Jesus tells us to hitch up our cross and follow Him. He goes to battle in our lives against the powers of sin, death, and the Devil and He bids us as a new creation to join in the fray. This is not a detour to real Christian living. It is a vital part of what the sanctified life is really all about.

The War Within

Let's expand on the insight we have gained from Paul's description of the Christian's character in Romans 6–8. In chapter 4, *Justification: Getting Saved, Doing Nothing*, we explored spiritual or personal dimensions of human nature as we described the progressive corruption of Eve in the fall into sin. We want to explore now how these personal dimensions relate to the Christian's character, which is simultaneously a regenerated New Self and Old Sinful Self.

The Central Issue: Personal Well-Being

If the Christian life of sanctification involves a war between the new creation in Christ and the Old Adam, where are the strategic battlefields and how does this conflict play out in our lives? We remember that Satan's temptation of Eve preyed on her natural interest and commitment to her own personal well-being. The key to her downfall was the chosen but false belief that she could be like God with His divine status and power. She believed the forbidden fruit would accomplish the goal. Her self-love made Satan's lie immediately engaging.

God created us with a dignity that is anchored in the majesty of being a divine image-bearer. We humans have great worth as the crown of God's creation. The love of self flows from this reality. Because of that love, the individual who prefers his own lack or loss of personal well-being is a contradiction in terms. The Law commands us to love our neighbor *as* ourselves not instead of ourselves. Self-love is simply presumed in the Bible. If there is anything that is shared by both our New Self and the fleshly self, it is a commitment to our own well-being that flows from a natural and healthy love of ourselves.

From this point, however, all similarity between the two ends. The New Self is grounded in the faith conviction that all life and well-being flows dependently from the grace and blessings that are ours in the Gospel of Christ. Christ is our only salvation. To have the love of God and the life He has for us in Christ is to be well now and forever. The Old Self, however, is committed to strategies for securing personal well-being independent of God and the Lordship of Christ; and, if necessary, even at the expense of others. Sin has produced a rebellion against God and a perverted self-love that would place all other persons and concerns in the service of it. The flesh would love and serve the self above all. The new creation would serve and love God above all; and flowing from that, the love of neighbor and self.

Is the nature of the battlefield within ourselves beginning to come into focus? From a common commitment of the heart for self-well-being, the New Self and the flesh clash over the deepest convictions and yearnings of the human spirit about what we need for well-being. The New Self lives in the mind of Christ, assured that well-being is an everlasting reality in the righteousness of Christ. Justification is the continual spiritual heartbeat of life itself. His life empowers ours through His Word to significant loving service in our vocation. But then, in complete rebellion against God, the sinful self exists with a mind of its own. Bound to this fallen age and Satan's own rebellion, it strives to have us interpret experience and establish goals that are intended to secure a status and meaningful impact for life independent of the grace and Lordship of Christ. The Old Adam is convinced that personal well-being must be achieved by our own initiative through some strategy that will enable us to remain in charge and in control. A sense of self-made doable law rules the flesh in all of us. I simply must do this and achieve that according to my own self-made plan of personal achievement. If one plan does not seem to be working, the flesh will either rethink strategy and redouble efforts or adopt a new plan. Any plan is a potential candidate so long as we think it might work, especially if it promises us that the self will be capable and in control.

Fragmented Priorities

In a sense, the Christian's character in this life is the most fragmented among all people on earth. The non-Christian is unified in head, hand, and heart to deal with the problems that sin poses for human existence—being alienated from his Creator God. But we who have been called by the Gospel live according to two mind-sets, two conflicting and contradictory plans for personal security and meaningful impact in living. Both plans function within the deepest levels of our assumed beliefs about ourselves and the nature of reality. Here we mold our sense of self-identity and interpret the events and experiences of everyday life.

Is it any wonder that life can often seem confusing and we Christians sense ourselves at the heart of it? If we are honest, must we not admit with the Apostle Paul in Romans 7 that many times we really do not understand ourselves and what we are doing? When faced with the problems and challenges of everyday living, we sense our security and freedom in the Gospel. The opportunity to let Christ shine in our involvement with others is relished for the sheer joy of it. We are free and secure to love! And then right in the next breath we find ourselves thinking about what we need to do to be OK and what we must demand or take from others so we can feel significant and important, safe or happy.

Conscious thought begins in the mind of Christ and with lightning speed the fleshly mind is talking up a storm of self-centered rebellion in our heads. The same battle occurs in our subconscious stream of thought as well. The mind of Christ and the fleshly mind slug it out to reign in our thought life—the slave of righteousness against the slave to sin, death, and the Devil. At the bottom of it all, the key issue remains the same. What do we really need in the face of our problem with evil; and what can we do that will bring us meaningful significance and security?

The war within, however, does not just take place in the evaluative thought of our minds. The heart is also a strategic battleground exerting great influence over how we relate to others and choose to

THE WAR WITHIN LIFE

live. We pray with David in our liturgy: *Create in me a clean heart, oh God, and renew a right spirit within me* (Ps. 51:10). The thought world of the mind or spirit and the desires of the heart are intimately related and God created them to function as one. What we believe is true and good for us, we desire. What we desire, we believe is true and good for us. Because Eve thought she could be like God and it would be good for her, she longed for divinity and desired the forbidden fruit. Head and heart functioned together in depravity to frame out her rebellious goal.

But what do we Christians long for and desire? Don't we sometimes get the feeling that we really do not know what we want? Our desires often seem to be jumbled, confused, and even downright contradictory. But perhaps, if we thought about what we *really* wanted, we might say with a real sense of togetherness in the heart, *We want to be happy, just like everyone else.* We know only too well from our brief sojourn on planet Earth that there is much here that seems to make us unhappy. We long for health and physical prosperity, but often experience disease, death, and want or realize we may experience these at any time in the future. The heart yearns for quality relationships within our families and among our friends and fellow workers, but we often experience disappointment and pain. We are not loved or accepted by others as we were meant to be. We can be betrayed. Those we love and can be disloyal and fail us. We can even be victimized physically and mentally.

Our heart's longings for personal health, prosperity and satisfying human relationships are legitimate desires. We pray for them generally and specifically in our personal prayer life and at corporate worship. Yet even the fulfillment of these desires is not enough to fully satisfy the human heart. The human spirit cries out for more. As the preacher in Ecclesiastes 3 confesses, *God has set eternity in our heart,* for we were ultimately created for God Himself. St Augustine well observed that the human heart remains restless until it ultimately rests in Him.

There is a deep thirst in our hearts that only God can satisfy. David recognized this thirst in Psalm 42:1: *As the deer pants for the water streams, so my soul pants for thee, O God. My soul thirsts for God, for the living God.* Jesus speaks to us in response to David's confession: "If anyone is thirsty, let him come to me and drink" (John 7:37 CSB).

The New Self is filled with the living water of Christ and through faith is satisfied in the deepest recesses of the heart. God's infinite and eternal love for which we were created to enjoy is secured now and forever. We have become His sons and daughters who have tasted the living water of His gracious compassion and acceptance. Only through Christ is the dry heart that has been parched by sin truly filled. As we are joined to Christ and drink from His love and grace, living water flows from our own hearts to others as we share the cross of Christ.

The realities of the war within, however, mean that we drink from Christ's living water always with a shovel in our hands. For right with our drinking, the flesh has us busy digging wells of our own. The fleshly heart will have nothing to do with the living water that flows from bleeding charity. Pride demands that we secure our happiness and contentment in life the old fashioned way, by earning it! The war within has placed us right with Saint Paul: the good we would do is what we don't, and the thing we hate is what we often do. The hand is moved by the head and the heart. Behavior is goal-oriented—that is, driven by what we think is good and by what we desire. We see the outward signs of this war in our behavior as we see ourselves either walking in the Spirit or walking in the flesh, but the real struggle is going on inside.

The battle with our fleshly self is a lifelong struggle that shall not be over until we meet Christ in our heavenly home or when He returns in glory to usher in the fullness of His Kingdom. In the meantime, how do we experience this battle as we grow in Christ? Will the Old Self hoist the white flag of surrender or begin to give up when greater levels of sanctification are achieved? Unfortunately, no. As we grow in Christ, the war within will actually seem to intensify. We will be able to identify with Paul in Romans 7 even more than we do now.

Life in the Combat Zone

Remember what it was like to tackle some of those word problems in mathematics when you were first introduced to them in grade school? How about your first attempts to sound out an unfamiliar word phonetically in reading class? It was kind of tough, wasn't it?

We really struggled back then to master very basic learning skills that we now use every day without so much as a thought. The world of a child has its share of struggles and challenges, and perhaps we can look back on some of ours and smile. They seem so trivial compared to the challenges now face as adults. But then again, our adult world is much larger and more complex. As we grew and matured, our world expanded to include more complex problems and tasks. Life became increasingly more difficult as we (hopefully!) have become more mature and better equipped to handle it.

There are parallels here to help us understand our life and growth in Christ. When we emerged as a new creation in Baptism, we did not come forth all spiritually grown up. Regardless of our age, we all entered the Kingdom of God as little children (Matt. 18:3). *Babes* in Christ is a favorite expression that Paul often used in his letters to describe young, immature Christians (1 Cor. 3:1; Eph. 4:14). As a New Self in Christ's resurrection, we have indeed received a renewed character fashioned in the image of Christ. However, just as Jesus had to grow in wisdom and stature from a small babe (according to His human nature), so also must we.

Sanctification as we have noted, in a strict sense, involves God's work of developing and maturing our New Self in Christ through the Gospel. As faith matures, we grow in wisdom and stature. However, the more we grow in Christ, the closer He moves us to the front lines of His war with the forces of evil that feed our old fleshly self. Jesus faced His greatest temptations in Gethsemane and on Golgotha, not at the age of twelve when He was dialoging in the temple. And when He was just a babe, the Father had others keeping Him safe from the war, instructing Joseph to pack Him off to the safety of Egypt when Herod's soldiers threatened His life.

It is the fresh babes in Christ that our Lord keeps tucked close in His tender care, shielding them from major confrontations with the Prince of Darkness. Jesus nurtures simple childlike trust (*Jesus loves me this I know, for the Bible tells me so*) in newly baptized small children. Behavior is often where the young child begins to do battle with the fleshly self. The powers for inner self-examination into the mind and heart are still under development. Not usually until adolescence are self-reflective powers developed enough to see the realities of the sinful inner character. God expands our world and the challenges of living in His Son as we grow and mature in Him. Nevertheless, should we face temptations beyond our maturity, He promises His strength to endure them or a way of escape (1 Cor. 10:13). Our Lord knows His own, and He will not allow any situation or power to wrench His children from His loving hand (John 10:27–28).

It is always a joy to talk to new adult converts. They have a special enthusiasm and sense of gratitude about the Gospel that is fresh and uplifting. Their backgrounds often provide them with a special awareness of what life is really like in this fallen creation when lived apart from the grace and freedom of the Gospel. Many of them know only too well what the *Prodigal Son* in the parable learned only after he left home. Many of us *lifers* who can't remember not living in the blessings of the Father's house can learn much from them.

Sometimes, however, they express their new, anticipated walk in Christ as if they will have it almost perfected with just a few more prayers and Bible studies. As green untested soldiers, they have yet to really taste battle with the enemy within and without. That will soon change as the New Self empowered by the Spirit stretches to stand and then walk in the newness of life. As faith seeks to be fruitful, the new Christian soon discovers that many old sinful habits remain and the struggle begins.

As the new creation interprets all of life from the security and finality of cross of Christ, it clashes with the flesh and its plan in the mind to acquire personal well-being. As the heart desires to exercise its freedom and love in the righteousness of Christ, it collides with the Old Self's desire to get what you pay for but take what you can. Mixed motives and erratic behavior follow. Arguments in the mind take place on how we ought to see things: the mind of Christ or the world's perspective. We really want to serve, but then we want to be served. To Christ be the glory, to the self be the glory. Duplicity, anguish, ambiguity, and confusion! These are the Romans 7 experiences of the Christian in the spiritual combat zones of daily living.

We must realize that we face a very formidable enemy. As a child, we face the fleshly self of a child. As we grow and develop in this fallen creation, the Old Self just naturally matures. The well-educated and sophisticated adult will have a well-educated and sophisticated Old Sinful Self. The deceitfulness of a mature sinful mind and heart is not easy to see. It has been nurtured by the guile and cunning of the Evil One. In an older form of the confessional service for Holy Communion, there is the confession of sin: *not only by outward transgressions but also by secret thoughts and desires, which I do not fully understand but which are all known unto thee.* There is more to our sinfulness than we will ever know.

The Experience of Maturity

The more the New Self grows into the maturity of the full stature of Christ, the more intense our spiritual warfare. Christ sees our corrupt colors perfectly and hates them with a righteous hatred. The more we grow in the mind and heart of Christ, the more we will see of the depths of our sinfulness and hate them. This has a profound effect on how we experience growth in Christ.

The experience of Christian maturity is not unlike growing in knowledge. The more we know, the more through that knowledge we are able to see the vast horizons of our ignorance. The smarter we get, the dumber we feel. Real growth in knowledge brings a sense of humility produced by a greater vision and experience of the magnitude of our ignorance. We all realize that the know-it-all has much to learn. Growth and maturity in the grace of Christ brings with it a parallel experience. The more we grow and live in the righteousness of Christ, the better we see our own sinfulness. It is with this expanded vision and experience that St. Paul could confess that he was chief of sinners. It is exactly how he felt. Moreover, this is precisely the awareness that God also seeks to produce in us. Here is the dry bones vision that brings a thirst for the Word of God that we might live (Ezek. 37:4). And it sends us back again and again to drink the living water that flows from the Gospel in Word and Sacrament.

The fruit of the Spirit grows in our hearts from that living water: love, joy, peace, patience, and all the others that Paul mentions in Galatians 5:22–23. The experience of these in Christian life does not remove the turmoil of Romans 7. Rather, they exist in, with, and under it. God blesses us with a peace that passes all our awareness of this turmoil, but it does not replace it. *Christians are those who become progressively more disturbed about themselves, but they sleep real well.* We walk by faith and we rest in grace.

We shall indeed win some battles, but they will only bring us greater and more challenging ones to fight. The fleshly self will be a part of us throughout our earthly life. It will not surrender and it cannot be reformed. It must be beaten down and ultimately killed. Moreover, we need to remember that we are not simply contending with flesh and blood; but, as Paul explained, with the powers and principalities of Satan himself (Eph. 6:12). There is no final victory or triumph for us in human history except what we claim in faith and hope in the cross and resurrection of Christ.

Beware of those who promise a sweet, calm, tranquility in this life from God by perfecting your commitment to spiritual exercises. They did not work for Luther in the monastery and they will not work for us. Do not believe that we can reach a lofty level of sanctification where we can be free of the battles that rage in our minds and hearts in this life. We walk by faith and hope for the better day that is coming when eternity blesses us with the full fruits of Christ's victory at His Heavenly Banquet. For now, we join Christ in His battle against the powers of darkness within and without as very much a junior partner. This is His mission and ministry. His resources and work have come packaged to us in the form of two ministries, Law and Gospel. Through these, His work of sanctification in us and the extension of His Kingdom through us in the world are carried out.

Holy Anguish: Ministering to Doubts

One of the challenges that Christians can experience in their faith life is to be plagued by doubt. Not much has been written on the subject, but there was a very insightful treatment written some years ago entitled *In Two Minds: The Dilemma of Doubt and How to Resolve It* by Os Guinness.[2] In this work, Guinness provides a wonderful discussion about the nature of doubt and how it should be understood as symptomatic of a problem with faith. Doubts can arise when faith is either malformed or malnourished. His work discusses several varieties of doubt and the problems of faith that correspond to each.

---

2. Os Guinness, *In Two Minds: The Dilemma of Doubt and How to Resolve It* (Downers Grove, IL: InterVarsity, 1976), 299 pp.

The following discussion is based on his analysis of three of the most common kinds of doubt that Christians experience. It will describe the experience of each type of doubt, the problem with faith that each reflects, and how God would minister to doubt with His Word.

Before we describe what doubt is, we need to understand better what doubt is not. First, doubt is not a more casual way of describing unbelief. Due to a poor translation of the text in John 20:27 (*do not doubt but believe*), we have pinned the label, *doubting Thomas* on Jesus' disciple. Thomas was not a doubter of the resurrection prior to the dramatic scene in the upper room. He just flat disbelieved it. A more accurate rendering of Jesus' words would be this: *Do not disbelieve, but believe*. Neither the word nor the idea of doubt is in the text.

Anatomy of Doubt

Our word *doubt* comes from the Latin word, *dubitare*. It means to be *double-minded*, or to be *in two minds* about something. Belief and unbelief are single-minded perspectives; yes and no. We can think of doubt as equivalent to a simultaneous *yes and no*. There is an uncomfortable tension about doubt. The more important the issues involved, the greater the tension. It is like standing with one foot in one rowboat and one foot in another. Doubt over things that matter presses us to resolve the tension into either belief or unbelief. Thomas moved from unbelief to faith through his encounter with the risen Christ. But doubt was never involved.

Second, doubt is not something that is intrinsic to faith, as if faith in a biblical sense were simply an inferior, uncertain substitute for knowing something. Faith is not affirmation with doubt or uncertainty. Rather, faith incorporates knowledge with trust and confidence. We experience doubt in our Christian walk not because it is inherent in faith, but rather because our faith is either malformed or malnourished. In such condition, it is vulnerable to either too much or too little tension between our experience or understanding of sin and what we believe to be true about God's mercy.

As our awareness and expression of faith can suffer from a variety of problems, we must recognize that doubt that can assault our faith comes in different forms. We are suggesting that doubt should be viewed as a symptom: something is wrong with faith. Different problems that faith can experience are manifested by different kinds of doubt. Doubt needs to be seen by the Christian as both threat and opportunity. If ignored and neglected, doubt has the potential to destroy faith. Yet if understood and tended to properly by God's Word, faith can be matured and strengthened dramatically.

Doubt from Ingratitude

We want to briefly survey three common varieties of doubt and the problems of faith that they manifest. The first type of doubt is perhaps the most insidious and destructive because it is rarely seen as a form of doubt. It springs from a slow growing ambivalence about the value of our inheritance in Christ. Its most recognizable manifestation is an attitude of ungratefulness. Here the Christian walk of faith is not encountering too much tension with the experiences of fallen existence. Rather, there is too little, or perhaps, none at all.

This subversive kind of doubt is well exemplified by the two sons in the parable of the Prodigal Son (Luke 15:11–32). Both sons had lived their whole lives in the father's house, enjoying the fullness of its blessings. Progressively, the Prodigal Son becomes discontent with a growing conviction that life would be better lived, out in the exciting world. Believing to have cashed in his inheritance, he leaves for the glitter of the world, but there receives a new vision. He comes to the startling realization that slavery in his father's house would be preferable to the despair of his present existence, starving in the company of pigs. Returning home with his new vision, he is surprised at the welcome and overwhelmed with gratitude to live again as a son in his father's house. Interestingly, we can also see in the complaint of his brother the same ungrateful attitude, but not quite in as advanced a stage.

Christians who have grown up in the household of faith and have lived in strong Christian homes are prone to this kind of doubt. It is so easy to take all the saving gifts of Christ for granted. Many silently suffer an impoverished faith, lacking a vision of the magnitude and stark contrast between sin and grace. It is not that grace has been in short supply. Indeed, as in the parable, all the comforts of the Gospel have been present since before one can remember. But our vision of the abundance and scope of grace is, however, closely linked to our vision of the pervasiveness and depths of sin. What is in short supply is a full-orbed awareness of the depths of one's sin and the extent of depravity in the old world. In the absence of full-strength Law and sheltered living, the vision of our fallenness can become vague and shallow. Thus the immensity of grace is missed, and its value discounted. Seeing little in what has always been there, faith is in danger of being cashed in for whatever fallen commitment may seem to offer more.

In such a state, one is not overwhelmed by a despair over personal sinfulness. Rather little holy anguish is experienced at all. This is *doubt from ingratitude*. It is the failure to appreciate the tension between being simultaneously a sinner and a saint. Absent is any sense of *but by the grace of God go I*. Moreover, the incredible joy from hearing *once you were no people but now you have become God's people* (1 Pet. 2:10) is missing. The first symptom of doubt from an ungrateful spirit is boredom. More advanced symptoms include indifference and then, perhaps, outright irritation toward the blessings of the Gospel and the means by which they come to us.

What is so destructive about this form of doubt is that Christians who suffer from it are rarely aware of its presence or even that it is a form of doubt. There is no experience of crisis to sound the alarm, just calm complacency. Perhaps many whom we count as dying or *dead wood* in our congregations are silent sufferers of doubt from ingratitude. Maybe we can even perceive shades of an ungrateful spirit in ourselves as well.

What is needed, of course, is to be taken behind God's spiritual woodshed and given a good thrashing. The hammer of fallen existence and the piercing blade of the Law need to come crashing down on our self-confidence and complacency, exposing our ingratitude for what it is. Shaken by the magnitude of our helpless sinful condition and in holy anguish, we need to be chased into the waiting outstretched arms of a gracious Father. He will again for the first time, wrap us in the precious robe of righteousness bought and paid for by His only begotten Son. Now with a healthy tension between sin and grace restored, we hear God's call anew, and gratefully take up life again in the cross of Christ.

Doubt from a Faulty Picture of God

If doubt can assail us from too little tension, it can surface from too much as well. We may think about faith in two senses. There is the faith *by which* we believe (trust), and there is the faith *that* we believe. The faith that we believe and express and confess as a child of God is often a somewhat distorted and incomplete sampling of the faith described in the Scriptures. To be sure, the faith of Christ's Church is but one faith and it is none other than the faith of the prophetic and apostolic Word. But our awareness of that faith is always limited and sometimes, unknowingly, we just get it wrong. Our incomplete and perhaps faulty picture of God is, nevertheless, what shapes *our* awareness and frames out *our* expectations of God and His promises for daily living. If our fallen existence brings experiences and challenges that contradict our expectations of God and His promises, then the tension between faith (what we actually believe about God) and our experiences of life can become excruciatingly painful, and a real crisis of doubt can result. Guinness calls this, *doubt from a faulty picture of God.*[3]

This second type of doubt can often be manifested by a real crisis of trust. Expecting God to act in ways that He does not, or not act in ways He does, can shake our confidence and produce a whole range of faulty conclusions about what He must really be like. Recall how long it took the disciples to recognize of Jesus as the incarnate Son of God. Their picture of Jesus was incomplete and sometimes faulty. For instance, seeing the Lord sleeping in the back of the boat during a fierce storm, the disciples doubted His concern about their welfare (Matt. 8:23–27). What can even a great prophet know or do during such perilous circumstances if He is sacked out and asleep in the back of the boat? You can imagine them bailing water while experiencing a twofold crisis of confidence: one in the worthiness of their boat and the other in the worthiness of their Lord. The disciples suffered doubt from a faulty and incomplete picture of Jesus.

Likewise, if our storms of life or conscience are not balanced off with an adequate picture of our Lord (His power and His

---

3.   O. Guinness, 83–100.

promises), then we too can suffer a real crisis in confidence. For example, imagine the frightened and anxious mother who trusts in the power of prayer and implores the Lord to heal her cancer-stricken daughter. However, the daughter dies and the mother bitterly declares that she can no longer trust in any of God's promises. She does not understand that God makes no blanket promises to heal our diseased children. The father who's 16-year-old daughter is killed behind the wheel in a horrible auto accident cannot forgive himself for giving her the keys to the family car. His stricken conscience also seriously doubts that God has forgiven him either. The father suffers from false guilt. He does not understand that he did not cause his daughter's accident and is not responsible for her death.

Trust, however, is not the root of the problem. The problem is in *what* is believed, not in *how much*. Indeed, the greater the trust in a faulty picture, the greater the crisis. Admonishments to *just trust the Lord* by well-meaning friends will simply make matters worse. It would be like pouring salt on an open wound. What we need is the wise counsel of one well-schooled in the Scriptures, such as our pastor. As we patiently examine our picture of God, learned instruction from God's Word can correct our faulty understanding and fill in serious voids. When the defective area of our picture is remedied, our crisis of doubt will dissipate as quickly as it began. Faith is significantly matured and a healthy balance of the tension between our experience of sin and the saving gifts and promises given to faith is created.

Our discussion above describes a happy conclusion. Nevertheless, there is cause for sober reflection. How many people baptized in the Lord have walked away from the fellowship of faith in bitter anguish, nursing the conviction that God, at some crucial point in their lives, simply did not come through for them? With faith, they neither got it right nor were set right. Their awareness of God and His promises did not correlate with their experience of the fallenness in life. The tension with trust was too great, so they walked. How many in our midst who have *not* walked are nevertheless silently nursing the wounds of doubt from an anemic understanding of the Lord and His promises? We see the importance of catechesis in the Church, of getting our lessons, and getting them right.

Doubt from Weak or Nonexistent Foundations

A biblical faith is in tension with the fallenness of the world, but it is not in tension with the truth. John constructed his Gospel around seven miracles of Jesus, ending then with the resurrection appearance to the skeptic, Thomas. He then stated the purpose of his Gospel to the reader: *These things were written that you might know that Jesus is the Christ, the Son of God, and that believing, you might have life in his name* (John 20:31). The apostolic Church proclaimed God's mighty acts through Jesus as powerful evidences that undergird the promise of grace.

If faith is to stand the intellectual challenges that our world can raise, then it must have a firm foundation. If our reasons for faith are weak, doubt can plague us when its truthfulness is rigorously questioned by the reasoned arguments of unbelief. We call this third variety, *doubt from weak foundations.*[4] Perhaps this was the problem with John the Baptist (or some of his disciples) when he was in Herod's prison. He sent his disciples to Jesus with the question, *Are you really the one to come or should we look for another?* (Matt. 11:3). This is the central truth question of the Christian faith. Who is Jesus of Nazareth?

It is instructive to note how Jesus ministered to these doubts. He simply went about a day's-worth of ministry and then turned to the disciples and said, *Go back and tell John of the things that you have seen and heard: the blind receive sight, the lame walk, the lepers are cleansed, the deaf hear, the dead are raised and the good news is preached to the poor* (Matt. 11:4–5). Foundational to the apostolic preaching of Jesus was this testimony: *And of these things we are witnesses* (Acts 2:32).

Many a Christian parent has said silent prayers as their children packed off to *Secular University* fearing that their faith might crumble. The fear in some instances is well-founded. Our confident trust needs more than just accuracy in the *whats* of faith. It also needs a firm foundation in the *whys* of faith—that is, why it should be regarded as true. If we do not know the *why* undergirding the Gospel and the Christian world view, then we do not know the *why*

---

4.   O. Guinness, 101–20.

not hidden beneath some substitute. The tragedy is that many a Christian has graduated from the Church's confession while studying to graduate from *Secular U.* Unaided intellectual doubt can be resolved into unbelief.

The Church and its educational ministry need to take seriously the apostle Peter's imperative: *Always be prepared to give a defense for the hope that is in you when called upon* (1 Pet. 3:15). We cannot answer that call and make that defense to the unbeliever until we have first made it to ourselves. The Church needs to educate in the *whys* along with the *whats* of faith. But we may ask, How firm a foundation is needed? Our goal should be an intellectual foundation that matches our intellectual development and the sophistication of the challenges to our faith that our world brings. With such a foundation, intellectual doubts will fade and a confident expression of faith can replace timidity.

† † †

Our discussion here of the experience of cross life has focused on the battle against the powers of darkness inside the Christian. It is a struggle that takes place inside the mind and the heart. The major conflict is not primarily over issues of morality. Rather, it is over the new creation's understanding that self-well-being is anchored in the saving work of Christ over against the commitments of the fleshly self to go it alone. This war within, however, is just one spiritual battleground for the Christian. Paul declared that we are contending not just *with flesh and blood but against the rulers, against the authorities, against the cosmic powers over against this present darkness, against the spiritual forces of evil in the heavenly places* (Eph. 6:12). The cross life of the Christian presses the Christian into not only a war within but also a *war without.* Spiritual warfare also entails a battle against the forces of evil *outside* the Christian that can bring experiences of temptation, trial, and tribulation. It is to this aspect of life in the cross that our discussion must now turn.

CHAPTER 8
Tentatio

Tentatio is a Latin term that means several related things; all of them rather negative. A *tentatio* is temptation in the sense of a trial or tribulation. The term also can double for such uncomfortable things as suffering, ordeal, and affliction. While not particularly pleasant, *tentatio* is part of the standard regimen in the Church of Christ and especially beneficial for its theologians. Luther believed that three things are necessary to make a theologian: prayer, meditation and tribulation. Prayer and meditation are what we visit upon God as we are filled with His Word of grace. *Tentatio* (tribulation), however, is what He allows Satan to visit upon us. The former flow, in part, from the latter. In the midst of trials and tribulations, we scream to God and are directed to take refuge in His gracious Word and meditate on His saving promises. In this way, the theologian is molded to see God's Word aright with the eyes of humility and faith. Theologians are not alone, however. Luther reminded the Church in his Large Catechism that Satan assails and vexes all Christians through temptation. His explanation of the sixth petition in the Lord's Prayer (and lead us not into temptation) promised the Christian no exemption from trials and temptations. Rather, Luther maintained no one can escape temptations and allurements as long as we live in the flesh and have the Devil prowling about us. We cannot help but suffer tribulation, and even be entangled in them, but we pray here that we may not fall into them and be overwhelmed by them.[1]

---

1. Luther's *Large Catechism*, III, 106, as cited in *Book of Concord* (hereafter cited as LC).

Heiko Oberman in his magnificent treatment, *Luther: Man between God and the Devil*, captured the legacy of Luther who taught the Church something startlingly new, something radical and perhaps unsettling: spiritual distress is not simply the lot of marginal Christians and occasional crazy monks in monasteries. It is the common inheritance of all believers.[2] Luther's discovery that the just shall live by faith alone included the recognition that faith will not be left alone in the Christian life. Faith will be assaulted by attacks and tribulations of the Unholy Spirit. Christian life is found in the cross of Christ and that means we shall also be living with one of our own. Cross life for the New Creation that emerges from Baptism not only has us contending with the Old Adam and a fallen world; it also brings us turmoil and affliction from the powers and principalities of the Prince of Darkness (Rom. 8:22; Gal. 5:17; Eph. 6:11–12). Peace with God brings conflict and adversity with the world, the flesh, and the Devil.

This new evaluation of spiritual distress by Luther leads to twin conclusions both of which are rather unsettling. First, tribulations are not a disease, so there is no cure for them. Second, only firm faith in God's unalterable promise enables spiritual crises to be withstood—not overcome.[3] God's Law reveals with brutal lucidity what has become of all of us. Each one of us is exposed in our unworthiness and spiritual bankruptcy. The Devil is on a relentless campaign to replace the Joyous Exchange of the cross with the demands of the Law for morality, godliness, and good works. God's holy Commandments are co-opted by the Devil to concoct a seeming air-tight case that for us, there is no salvation! Only when we get to this point does it become clear that the mercy of God in the divine foolishness of the Gospel is our only refuge. Many past mystics, observes Oberman, called this experience groaning and rapture. Luther thought of this as something like the agony and the ecstasy of the cross.

Tribulation and mystical ascent, diabolical remoteness from God and joyous union with God, are no longer typical of the spiritually ill and the spiritual elite, two marginal Christian groups. All

---

2. Heiko Oberman, *Luther: Man between God and the Devil*, trans. Eileen Walliser-Schwarzbart (New York: Doubleday, 1992), 184.

3. H. Oberman, 178–79.

parts of the true Church suffer spiritual distress and are at the same time united with God.[4]

The Church as the community of the faithful is and must remain in this life, the community of those afflicted by the Devil.

Ordinary Christian Experience

What follows will sketch an outline of the multifaceted character of *tentatio* as it relates first to ordinary saints in everyday living.[5] It will draw heavily on the insight of Luther whose sharp awareness and understanding of the trials and tribulations of the Evil One are most instructive. Luther's insights are especially needed today among Christians who are increasingly obsessed with finding ways to escape the fallenness of daily human existence. In the second part, we will examine Luther's insight into a special *tentatio* that Satan has reserved for the spiritually mature and would-be theologians. In this latter discussion, God's use of tribulations and spiritual attacks of the Devil to mold faithful servants of the Word will be explored with some modest applications for those who would shepherd the Church today.

Our discussion of *tentatio* is framed by the conviction that normal Christian living cannot honestly be described as something gloriously nice, inspirational, and cozy. It does not come with promises that if you will just commit to some Bible-based principles for daily living, things will go better with God. Many of the best-seller books and slick media evangelists who tout law-conditioned triumphal promises for Christian living do not tell the truth. Becoming a Christian will not make navigating the affairs of earthly living more tranquil and trouble-free. Quite the reverse! A new life in Christ transforms the sinner's life into a battleground with the unholy triad—the world, the flesh, and the devil (Rom. 8:38–39; Eph. 6:10–12). While it is certainly true that the inheritance of glory and an exalted life with

---

4. H. Oberman, 184–85; see also my essay "Overcoming Our Doubts," *Lutheran Education* 129, no. 5 (May/June, 1994): 277.

5. This essay is a revision of a presentation on *Tentatio* delivered at the North American Lutheran Campus Ministry Staff Conference held at the Queen of Apostles Renewal Center, Toronto, Ontario, July 10–13, 1997.

God have been given to the Christian in Baptism, this inheritance is lived within this fallen age only by faith. Christians place their hope in a future experience of glory. Life in Christ through Baptism has joined the believer to Christ the crucified (Rom. 6:3). Christian life is cross life. Jesus has been raised from the dead, ascended into heaven and exalted in glory by the Father, but we have not! The Christian still lives in the cross with the inheritance of glory as a not yet. Jesus has had His Easter, but we are still waiting on the cross and in His tomb (Rom. 6:4). This means that for now we live in a fallen creation ruled by the Evil One who is on a campaign to separate us from our baptismal inheritance. He is cunning, powerful, and a consummate liar. Experiencing him as he would prowl the Church inflicting casualties is standard provisional Christian living. And for now we are all consigned to a temporary fallen existence as we await our final deliverance from the powers of darkness and our promised glory. It is not dominated by triumph, tranquility, and spiritual bliss, but rather characterized by cross, trials, and affliction. *Tentatio* is ordinary run-of-the-mill Christian experience.

Holy Anguish

Tentatio occupies one of two aspects that constitute a fundamental paradox in the way the believer lives in Christ and makes progress to his heavenly home. These aspects reflect twin, but conflicting realities, of what it means for the Christian to be simultaneously a sinful citizen of this fallen world, and yet also a righteous member of the Kingdom of God. Flowing from this dual citizenship are the elements of cross and comfort as normative and pervasive aspects of Christian living. *Tentatio*, not sweet glorious rapture, is the common lot of all believers. The drama of the cross of Christ is the basis and paradigm of this polarity. God's supreme call of his Son to the cross presents us a vision with a tension between what is received by experience and what must be grasped by faith. In the cross of Christ, God worked out but hid his righteousness and pardon of sinners in the wretched shame, agony and injustice of a Roman crucifixion. Through the experience of our senses we apprehend all the worldly and fallen aspects of the passion of our Lord, but only by the eyes of faith can we see the glory of God and our righteousness acquired. This duality is also present for Christians living in God's call as his adopted sons and daughters. Christian life in the old creation is God's call to the full range of possible experiences one can encounter from being in the fallen world under the Prince of Darkness. Here *tentatio* may visit the Christian in his journey as a common and frequent companion. But then, on the other hand, the Christian travels in this life joined to Christ Who through the sacred things showers him with God's favor and peace and indeed, the full inheritance of God's salvation. All this is, as noted previously, given to and lived in by faith. In these things we receive joy, peace, and comfort. But neither cross nor tribulation nor any experience of our fallen existence cancel out the blessings of Christ given to faith. We live with a Spirit-wrought peace that passes the awareness and experiences of *tentatio*, but it does not replace them (Rom. 7:14, 24; Gal. 5:22). As faith matures and we grow in Christ, the tension between these realities will not diminish, it will increase.

Perhaps Luther's fellow reformer Philip Melanchthon's *in, with,* and *under* language would be helpful here. Christians possess their divine citizenship and all God's blessings of salvation *in, with,* and *under* our temporal citizenship and all that its fallen character can bring us. What flows from our temporal citizenship in the Devil's playground is fully given to our senses and openly experienced, but what flows from our divine citizenship is given to and apprehended only by faith. The tension between the life of worldly experience with all its trials and tribulations, and the saving gifts given to faith, is encountered in the daily living of the believer by traversing back and forth between them. Sometimes we are captivated by *tentatio* (the impact of living as citizens of this fallen world with all its trials and temptations) only then to be thrown back onto the promises of faith in the saving Word that bring peace and comfort.

How does this play itself out for ordinary saints in everyday life? Perhaps, something like this . . . We grow up in ordinary homes, reflecting the ethos of our time and place, and they make their mark on us. We become fully participating citizens of the here and now. We struggle with our sexuality and loneliness, and perhaps we marry. A new household is formed with babies' spilt milk and messy bedrooms. Our teenagers can walk out the door and we know that almost anything can happen to them, and often it does. We experience joys and sorrows with our spouse, our children, and our circle of friends. Quarrels and misunderstandings punctuate our relationships with loved ones as well as good times had by all. Our work life moves like the tide between excitement and boredom, success and failure. We can be hired, fired, promoted, and forgotten. People who matter to us suffer injury, addiction, and disease. So can we. They will get better or they will die. So will we. And more often than we would like, we sense compelling evidence that our government, our economy, and our church denomination are going to the dogs.

We experience life as bitter/sweet: our cup is somewhere between half empty and half full. We long for much more than our daily living provides. For that reason, the voice within can hammer us with a painful conclusion: the life we are living falls woefully short of our longings for what it ought to be for would-be citizens of the Kingdom of God. But this is only half of it. We also experience our slice of life as it has passed through the grim reaper of the Law that is lodged in our hearts. And perhaps for many of us schooled in the Scriptures, the cutting edge of that Law is razor sharp. The voice of the Law is continually telling us that we are falling short of the vision as well. If we are called to a life of fear, love, and trust in God; if we are called to a faith that expresses itself in a life of service with reordered loves; then the Law cuts us with its bitter verdict: we aren't, we don't, and we can't.

Experiences such as these, while they are ordinary and should be expected, can drive us to a state of helplessness and hopelessness. It is just like taking in Christ on the cross with all our senses. There is the hammer of our fallen world that beats on our sense of membership in the family of God and the blade of the Law that assaults our righteousness through faith. Here *tentatio* brings doubt and despair as unwelcome companions. Luther called this helplessness and hopelessness, *Anfechtung*. *Anfechtung* is a profound anguish. It is an assault upon us by the world, the flesh, and the Devil that can often reduce us to a state of doubt about who and what we are in Christ. It tempts us to despair of God's promises, it challenges our confidence, and it puts our faith to the test.[6]

---

6. See especially Alister McGrath's fine discussion of Luther concerning *Anfechtung* and the polarity of faith and experience in Luther's theology of the cross. He aptly noted

Yet as Luther also recognized, this is a holy anguish, an instrument of the gracious God, and part and parcel of living in the cross of Christ. God is the one behind our anguish, and He uses it to crucify our fleshly complacency and self-confidence. Then He uses it to send us running back the other way to the security and confidence of His Word of promise that is given to faith. From faith, we see the righteousness of Christ that is ours; and from faith, hope is renewed in the coming glory of the Kingdom. With faith's vision made ever new in the Gospel promise again and again, faith is strengthened, the New Creation is renewed, and the call of the Christian's vocation is revitalized. Here is the central heartbeat of Christian living: the experience of life in the old world that produces a holy anguish from the Devil's *tentatio* and the transforming power of faith fed by the Gospel. In tension, tacking back and forth between them, Luther believed this to be a common inheritance for all Christians baptized into the cross of Christ.

The Afflicted Shall Live by Faith

One of the most comforting passages of the New Testament for Luther was Paul's introductory theme in Romans 1:17 ESV: "The righteous shall live by faith." It is a quote by Paul from Habakkuk 2:4. The emphasis in Romans is on, shall live before God by faith alone. Luther recognized that the text has a slightly different slant, however, in Habakkuk. Here it is not so much a comfort as a challenge. Its focus is not so much our faith before God, as it is the righteous shall live by faith before the world. *Tentatio* brings the cross to the Christian, and it often involves suffering tribulations and unjust trials at the hands of a fallen world. Habakkuk captured the pathos of it all for believers in every age, for Israel and the Church of Christ.

---

that the Christian life is characterized by the unending tension between faith and experience. For Luther, experience can only stand in contradiction to faith, in that revealed truth must be revealed under its opposite form. This dialectic between experienced perception and hidden revelation inevitably leads to radical questioning and doubt on the part of the believer with what he experiences. A. McGrath, *Luther's Theology of the Cross*, 168–69. Luther's best discussion of this tension and *Anfechtung* is found in the "Operationes in Psalmos" (WA 5) and Luther's "Commentary on the First Twenty-Two Psalms," trans. John Nicholas Lenker (Sunbury, PN: Lutherans in All Lands, 1903).

Habakkuk was also a prophet who would fit well into the thought of our modern age. He had a complaint to lodge with the God of Israel and he delivered it with why questions. Why is it that the righteous people of God always become the cannon fodder for every godless and blood-thirsty empire that arrives on the scene? And why do they prosper in their idolatry and wickedness while we the people of God must suffer every form of deprivation and injustice at their hands? Why does God, Who loves righteousness and hates wickedness, simply sit by and do nothing?[7] Why? Habakkuk was really a man after our own hearts.

Amazingly, God not only favored Habakkuk with a reply; He was quick to deliver it. Habakkuk had a vision of the righteous suffering at the hands of the unrighteous. God did not question that vision but offered one of His own. The day is coming soon, says the Lord, when all the unrighteous will have their undoing. God will have His day of justice and all that is wrong will be made right.[8] But for now, for Habakkuk and for us, the righteous shall live by faith.

Luther recognized that both visions (Habakkuk's and God's) were climaxed in the cross of Christ. Indeed, the cross is the essence of Habakkuk's vision. But joined to his vision is the vision God provided. The one God handed over as His undoing of the unrighteous, was His own righteous Son. The day of the Lord's justice was Good Friday. The unrighteous become righteous and live by faith in a Great Exchange. The innocent Jesus takes our sins upon Himself and gives to us His righteousness. Nevertheless, the contemporary Church of Christ knows that Habakkuk's vision has not gone away. The experience of suffering and injustice at the hands of a fallen world is still with the people of God. *Tentatio* in the form of being victimized by injustice is still a part of the existence of the Christian walk of faith in this life. Moreover, the key question of the prophet remains unanswered. Why do the people of God have to experience injustice, trials, and tribulations? Why does God so often seem to just sit by and allow the righteous to suffer unjustly?

---

7. Paraphrase of Hab. 1:1–4; 1:12–2:1.

8. Paraphrase of Hab. 1:5–11; 2:2–4.

This perplexing question has absorbed our modern age and the Old Testament shares our contemporary concern with it. Perhaps the quintessential Old Testament expression of unjust tribulation and suffering is found in the book of Job. Job's plight and the unacceptable explanations by his friends bring the question of unjust suffering into as sharp of focus as any modern statement of the question. The reader has to struggle for understanding a God who would put Job through all his suffering and tragedy for the sake of a wager (Job 1:9–12; 2:4–6).[9] Job, however, doesn't even get that much. He was never told about the wager. God's response to his question of why was met in a whirlwind of thunder and lightning. He did not explain; He exploded. Rather than deal with Job's questions, God flattened him for his whining and his audacity to question how He runs the universe (Job 38–40). Job was humbled to repentance, restored in health and possessions, and died a happy man. But God never answered his question why.

In the Old Testament writings, there is no mistaking the character of the God of Abraham, Isaac, and Jacob. He was just and He was merciful, but He most assuredly was not nice. He played spiritual hardball and was out to win at any cost. *Tentatio* helps instruct Christians why we were never taught to pray; Our Grandfather who art in Heaven. And about paying the price, the world would see to what ends He would go to accomplish His saving will with the incarnation and cross of His Son.

What is a curious thing is that the question of injustice and why so often raised in the Old Testament is not voiced at all in the New Testament. The apostles suffered much for the faith, but never seem to be bothered by the question why. Neither raising the question nor providing an answer, they were concerned with the issues of what God does through suffering and affliction and how it will all come out in the end. They understood Christian living as an expression of our union with Christ. They were captivated by a vision of God's call to live in the cross of Christ with crosses of their own. The key question for them was this: How should we view our suffering and affliction in light of the suffering of Christ? Vision is everything here,

---

9. For a fine overview on the unfairness and silence of God in His treatment of Job, see P. Yancy's *Disappointment with God*, 177–91.

but it is not the same thing as sight. Our vision is the sense of what we make of the things we see and experience by the reality of those things we do not see, but are given to faith. Faith molds vision. So from faith to faith, the apostolic Word has instructed the Church of every age in proper vision.

The apostles were captivated by a vision that the struggle against the forces of evil in time and eternity came down to one final wager with Satan that God was determined to win. And in a Job-like confrontation, He wagered His own Son, who without complaint, wins a world of sinners from the Devil's claim. When they looked at the cross and considered the matter of justice, it was clear to them that God plays by different rules. The righteous suffered for the unrighteous. Therefore, as Jesus suffered and died to sin, we who are joined to Christ suffer and die to sin. As His life and death included suffering the injustice of the world, so also does ours. Our cross is fashioned after His, and for this we may glorify and thank God for the privilege to share in the sufferings of Christ (1 Pet. 4:12–13).

This does not mean that the apostles saw something intrinsically virtuous in pain and suffering. These things are evil, and they come from the Evil One. God takes no pleasure in the suffering of His people. But the New Testament vision is that God will either alleviate it or use it. And at that, He tends to do the latter with the mature in faith. Jesus healed many, but Paul was told that his thorn in the flesh would remain to keep him humble and to remind him that God's grace was sufficient for him (1 Cor. 12:7–8). Pain and suffering bring us into contact with our frailty and weakness, and surprisingly, it is Paul who instructs us that God's strength is made perfect in our weakness (2 Cor. 12:9). As the country singer sang; some of God's greatest gifts are unanswered prayers.[10] Living in the cross with one of our own is God's way of accomplishing His purpose of bringing our whole life into conformity with an image of Christ (1 Pet. 1:6–9).

One key question remains. How is it that the apostles and the New Testament Church could have such an unwavering commitment

---

10.   The song is called *Unanswered Prayers* by Garth Brooks.

to this vision of the cross in the face of all the trials and suffering they endured? When we page through the Psalms and elsewhere in the Old Testament, we constantly meet the people of God sending up urgent petitions for God to vindicate them before their enemies. In Psalm 35:1–2, David cried, "Contend, O Lord, with those who contend with me; fight against those who fight against me. Take hold of shield and buckler, and rise for my help!" And in anticipation that the Lord would honor his cry, he sang, "Then my soul will rejoice in the Lord, exulting in his salvation" (v. 9). The apostles were convinced that they had personally seen David's vindication and the vindication of all weary and afflicted subjects of the Lord. The empty tomb and hands on contact with the risen Lord was the vindication of God and His people against all the enemies of darkness.

The vision of living in the cross of Christ with one of our own is a privilege and a sharing in the glory of the Lord. But we see the glory and the triumph of the cross in the empty tomb. Moreover, the resurrection was God's manifestation that His triumph and our salvation would not be consigned to simply the spiritual and heavenly dimensions of existence. A flesh and blood resurrection signals the end to every manner of earthly affliction that sin can mete out against us in the old creation. If our vision of the cross is that Jesus paid the price for our heavenly mansions, it is the resurrection that certified that we shall inhabit them in flesh and blood. His bodily resurrection guarantees ours.

Living in the cross with a cross is provisional Christian existence. It is only the big picture of the here and now, which of course, is but a blip on the big screen of forever. The days of trouble and half-empty cups are limited. The resurrected life with the new heaven and the new earth is hastening to dawn. This was not simply vision for the apostles. The down payment was given to their experience. They took in the risen Lord with all their senses (1 John 1:1–4; Acts 2:32). Good Friday and Easter are just preface in the never-ending story of God's salvation. The life we have now been called to live as the people of God is somewhere between the preface and chapter 1. For this place in the drama with our experiences of *tentatio*, we can think of nothing better to mold our vision than the Lord's words to Habakkuk: *The righteous shall live by faith.*

Spiritual Warfare, Children, and the Challenges of Fatherhood

While the disciples thought them a distraction, Jesus set them straight about how little children centrally focus what is required to enter the Kingdom of God (Matt 19:14). Then also, from the Lord's perspective, newborn babes are not cute. They are enemies of God, slaves to sin, and citizens of Hell. Reborn children, however, are another story. Jesus explained that all enter the Kingdom as little children (Matt. 18:3)—children who get crucified with Him—dying to sin but raised up as a New Creation (Rom. 6:3ff). It all happens when they are splashed with grace by a deluge of water and the Word in their Baptism. Parents often have a sense of got-that-base-covered when their children are baptized. The baptismal garment, the sponsors, attending relatives, and the ham dinner afterward are traditional trappings that signal and celebrate a sense of a done deal. The kid's Happy Forever has now been assured. Well . . . maybe.

Often not taught or explained to parents, especially to fathers, is that their child's Baptism has landed her in a spiritual war zone where the Devil relentlessly prowls to get her back. The often unspoken truth is that the Baptism of our kids has landed them in a lifelong spiritual war with the Devil. Jesus taught; he who endures to the end, will be saved (Matt. 24:13). With his close allies—the fallen world (say, youth culture) and the Sinful Self—Satan is working to see that your child is not one of them. They are out to make her collateral damage in the Kingdom of God. Let me say it plainly: Fathers, the Devil is out to kill your kid! You have suffered your daughter to come unto Jesus; but fathers, don't let her die! You have suffered your son to come unto Jesus; but fathers, don't let him die!

Luther understood that the chief vocation of fathers is the spiritual nurture of their household—to care for their children by teaching them the faith into which they are baptized. As Scott Keith explained, "The mother supplies the physical nurture to the child, whereas the father supplies the spiritual nurturance."[11] His observation follows Luther's understanding of the father's primary spiritual

---

11. Scott Keith, *Being Dad—Father as a Picture of God's Grace* (Irvine, CA: NPR, 2015), 77.

vocation. It was to assist fathers in this work that he wrote his Shorter Catechism. Luther began each Chief Part with the words: as the head of the family should teach it in a simple way to his household. It was Luther's conviction that fathers had the primary responsibility to provide the basic nurture of the grace of Christ to their children. Unfortunately, his efforts to instill this sense of fatherly responsibility failed. Indeed, from Luther's day until now among Lutherans, fathers have largely demurred and ceded this primary responsibility to pastors, schoolmasters, and their wives. And about this misplacement of primary spiritual responsibility, all three have been more than complicit.

Today when our children look at their fathers exercising leadership in Christ's Church, they mostly observe them making sure the congregation's parking lot is in good repair; the receipts from the Sunday offering are rightly recorded and deposited; everyone is seated with a worship folder; and they receive a timely cue of when to come forward for Communion. The one they usually observe engaging their spiritual nurture (when not the pastor) is either Mom, or assorted volunteer rent-a-moms. Moreover, often missing by Christian parents is any awareness that their children are living in the midst of intense spiritual warfare where life and death are in the balance. And yet, when the lives of their children are understood to be in jeopardy, what father does not remove all other priorities and sacrifice whatever to see that what their children need is provided—by blood, sweat, and tears if necessary? What father tells the oncologist of their cancer-stricken child that they will not make their next appointment because it conflicts with her soccer game? And yet, recent statistics suggest that many of our children baptized as infants joined many a soccer league, but never made it to their confirmation as adolescents.

When it comes to wars that must be fought, real men have always understood that their place is not hiding behind their wives. They are to be adequately equipped and moved to the front lines for battle. Real fathers understand that when the lives of their children are at stake from deadly spiritual warfare, they need to be there to protect and equip them to survive the onslaughts of the forces of evil out to destroy them. Real flowing testosterone needs to move our Fathers to rule their children with grace; fit them with the breastplate of righteousness; defend them with the shield of faith; teach them how to take it to the Devil with the sword of the Word of Christ; so that in the end . . . they stand (Eph. 6:13–17). Suffer the little children to come unto me . . . but fathers, don't let them die.

The Cross, the Devil, and the Mature Believer

While Luther realized trials and temptations to be the common lot of all Christians, he understood them as diverse in character and intensity depending on age and one's level of Christian maturity.[12] He wrote in his Large Catechism, "We must all feel it, though not all to same degree, some have more frequent and severe temptations than others. Youths, for example, are tempted chiefly by the flesh, older people are tempted by the world. Others, who are concerned with spiritual matters (i.e., strong Christians), are tempted by the Devil. . . . When one attack ceases, new ones always arise."[13]

The Way of the Cross

Our discussion about *tentatio* now turns to mature Christians— including those who are concerned with spiritual matters like theologians and servants of the Word. From the earliest days of his momentous discoveries in the Psalms and the epistles of Paul, Luther believed that the cross describes the contours of both a true evangelical theology and a true theologian of the Church. In his lecturing on the Psalms, Luther could boldly write: the CROSS is our theology.[14] In the most popular and oft-quoted of his "Heidelberg Theses," he asserted, "19. The man who looks upon the invisible things of God as they are perceived in created things does not deserve to be called a theologian. . . . 20. The man who perceives the visible rearward parts

---

12. Luther observed that in this life are many different degrees of tribulations, as there are different persons. Had another had the tribulations that I have suffered, he would long since have died; while I could not have endured the buffetings that St. Paul did, nor St. Paul the tribulations that Christ suffered. Martin Luther, *Table Talk*, trans. William Hazlett (London: HarperCollins, 1995), 306.

13. LC, III, 107, 109.

14. WA 5.176.32–33. The capitals are Luther's.

of God [posteriora Dei] as seen in suffering and the cross does, however, deserve, to be called a theologian."[15] Luther advanced a theology of revelation that simultaneously described something important
about God and the would-be theologian. God's revelation is indi-
rect and concealed. The visible rearward parts (to translate *posteri-
ora* politely!) are an allusion to God's revelation of Himself to Moses
(Exod. 33:18–23). Because of our sinfulness, we are denied direct
knowledge of God or a direct view of the splendor of His glorious
face. As seen in suffering and the cross (which reveals God's rearward
parts) is a dual reference referring to both the passion and suffering of
Christ and the passion and suffering of the Servant of the Word or the
mature believer. Concealed beneath the humility and shame of
the cross lie the omnipotence and full glory of God. God reveals
Himself under or within forms that appear to us as opposite.
Humility and shame function as masks that simultaneously conceal and reveal the true God. Cross theology is not merely that God
is known through suffering [Christ's or the individual's], but that
God makes himself known through suffering.[16] God is active in
this matter. Suffering is what Luther understood as an alien work of
God in bringing sinners to Himself—that is, both Christ's suffering
and ours. The Devil is God's instrument who performs this task.
Suffering and affliction are not nonsensical intrusions into the world.
Rather, trials and tribulations signal the revelation and working out
of our salvation by our loving and merciful God.

Many contemporary religious writers speculate about an empathetic deity who enters into solidarity with people who are victimized by injustice and who suffer all manner of want and affliction.
This is certainly not the God of the Scriptures. The God of Abraham,
Isaac, and Jacob sent His innocent Son to the suffering and tribulation of the cross and there forsook Him! He is also the One Who
is behind the afflictions that faithful Servants of the Word must
endure. By embracing a Theology of the Cross, we must accept the
fact that God plays by different rules. In man's justice, everybody
gets what they deserve. This is reasonable. In God's justice, however

---

15.   *AE* 31, 52.
16.   A. McGrath, *Luther's Theology of the Cross*, 150–51.

(as we have noted previously), it is just the reverse. Only in the cross of Christ can this be seen and embraced. Is God unfair, silent, and hidden? . . . Generally, yes. What divine foolishness! Only through the eyes of faith can we realize that because God so loved the world, He gave his Son over to suffering and the cross. God condemned His righteous Son and pardons His human enemies, each and every one of us (Rom. 5:10). As with the Word made flesh, so then with all who are in Christ. Unfairness rules the Kingdom of God.

The saving work of God in Christ is masked—hidden under the forms of what appears to us as opposites. To understand these mysteries, you must resort to paradox and stretch it. Think for a moment about the old American folk hero the Lone Ranger, the Masked Man. What you do not see is what you get. Hidden under the appearance of a desperado was just the opposite. The Lone Ranger was the warrior for truth, justice, and the American way!

In the same way God's justice and omnipotence are hidden under the opposite. They are manifested and made perfect in the shame and weakness of the cross. Apart from his mask, of course, the Lone Ranger just disappears from sight. And apart from the crucified Christ, you cannot find the just and gracious God at all. The cross of Christ also exemplifies how God is at work in the world and in our lives—under the mask of opposites. We will further clarify this paradoxical method of God's redemptive method as salvific worldliness in chapter 9 on vocation.

The cross does not imply God's empathetic solidarity with the sinner; it is his attack upon the sinner—an attack for life. Gerhard Forde wonderfully expressed Luther's thinking here: the Cross is the doing of God to us.[17] Before the sinner can be raised to life, he must first be forced to descend to the depths of death. Before he can be elevated by God, he must first be humiliated. Before he can be saved, he must first be damned, and before he can live in the spirit, he must first be put to death in the flesh. God condemns us that He may justify us, He condemns us as sinners that He may make us righteous, He slays that He may make alive.

---

17.   Gerhard O. Forde, *On Being a Theologian of the Cross (Grand Rapids, Wm. B. Eerd-manns, 1997)*, 4.

Let's keep in mind, it is God who does all these things. Nothing flows from our decisions, commitments, choices, or actions. Suffering and tribulation are never to become a program promoted in the Church for Christians to implement. We suffer divine action! Luther rightly thought it morbid for Christians to search for crosses on which to nail themselves. God shall give us our crosses when, where, and as we need them. Of that we may be confident. Sometimes we are afflicted from within, sometimes from without. Job was stricken from without, Luther from within. In either case, God accomplishes a humiliation of the heart, not of action. God is interested in producing a humble heart, not in coaxing moralistic self-denying behavior out of us. God demands in Philippians 2:5 the attitude of the Suffering Servant. The believer acquires the heart of Christ Jesus in Philippians 2 by God's alien work of crushing with the Law. Jesus said, *He who humbles himself will be exalted* (Matt. 23:12), but we wretched sinners have no spiritual resources to accomplish this. Humility is the one precondition for grace. God commands it and He creates it.[18] It is God Who humbles us by His Law, and it is He Who exalts us in His Gospel.

The Roles of the Devil

Luther was convinced that the Church on earth is living in the last days when Satan has been unleashed. The Devil is Lord in the world in these End Times. For now, God's omnipotence operates under its opposite—it is perceived in weakness, in cross, suffering, and seeming defeat. Luther was convinced that reformation will not come to the believer or the Church until the Better Day. Said Luther, that God is omnipotent is proved by faith alone.[19] For now, for our senses and experiential life—Satan rules all we can see.

Christ as Victor is an end times manifestation in which we confidently hope. The revealed God to us seems not to be an omnipotent

---

18. By the term *precondition*, we do not mean to imply any condition of merit on our part. Nor do we mean to imply that grace is only a future possibility not a present actuality. The term is meant to describe only what is needed for repentant receptivity of God's present and unconditional grace—something that He himself effects.

19. Heiko Oberman, "Between the Middle Ages and Modern Times," in *The Reformation—Roots and Ramifications Transl. Andrew Colin Gow* (Grand Rapids: Wm. B. Eerdmans, 1994), 67.

God. From the baby Jesus to Christ crucified and all points in between, the revealed God is humble, suffers, and dies to sin. The revealed God is tempted and vexed by the Devil, as are we. The tribulations of Christ are our inheritance in Baptism where we become both participant and part of the battlefield in the cosmic struggle that is not yet finished. Things do not go better with God. Sometimes they can get downright wretched. The battle enjoins us now. Our baptismal inheritance has given us all that belongs to Christ: His battle, His cause, and His adversary. For all who live in the cross, this also means that time is short. The need is great for us to get our lessons, and get them right. The Lord is coming soon, and His question is not will He find reform, renewal, or record numbers, but will He find faith (Luke 18:8)?

Luther could refer to the Devil as the Master of the conscience. He insisted that the Christian conscience be tied to the saving Word of Christ. Let it thereby be imprisoned by God. The alternative to this "prison of God," notes Oberman about Luther, is not "freedom of conscience" but rather "conscience imprisoned by the Devil," because the conscience—and this is terrifying even unbearable for the modern ear—is the natural kingdom of the Devil.[20] The greatest affliction and suffering in matters of conscience challenge Christ's Word of grace by questioning either that we have it or that we need it. When we become Christians, we become temples of the Holy Spirit and are joined to Christ. Nevertheless, it is the Devil who takes up residence in the conscience as its Master. The mirror of the Law is the Devil's tool. He would keep it either ever from you or ever before you. Self-righteousness or despair is a game he will always win; either because you can do what your conscience dictates or because you cannot. The Master of the conscience would make grace either unnecessary or unavailable.

The human conscience is the Devil's lethal playground. Tie your sense of God's favor to matters of the heart, conscience, and what can be experienced from within, and you are flirting with spiritual disaster. This is the Hound of Hell's home turf. It is not the allures of the flesh with which Satan launches his greatest assaults; it is in

20. H. Oberman, 65.

the conscience where he is most devastating. With the Law written on the heart, Satan works from the inside. With Christ it is the opposite. He works from the outside through His Gospel Word that comes to us externally. Let your conscience be your guide in spiritual matters—the cheerful song of polite civil religion—is Satan's victory either by self-righteous smugness, or bottomless, dark despair. The Law written on the human heart and sweet reason—with or without smug human pride—will damn us all.

The root of the conflict with the Devil is the Gospel. The Devil, in Luther's view, is more adept with the Word of God than Luther himself was. Notice, here the brute authority of Scripture is of no use. The Bible has words that will damn us all and the Devil knows just what they are and how to apply them. But, maintained Luther, the Devil is overcome by the gracious Word of the Gospel. Where the Gospel has free course, there the Devil is surely most present and active, yet overcome. The sacred things of the Gospel (Baptism, Absolution, and the Supper) bring God's favor and righteousness as a gift from the outside to be possessed. Here Christ is present in the midst of our turmoil with visible, tangible props making it possible for us to resist the Devil with His threats and promises. Infant Baptism performs the Joyful Exchange for the empty-handed and the ignorant. Here, together with the proclaimed Gospel and the Supper, is where God may be found by us. These are the gateways to Heaven where we meet not the omnipotence of God, but His graciousness, not a mighty display of His power, but a generous display of His saving gifts. Fellowship with the gracious God is from the heart, but always at the same time, outside of ourselves in His appointed means.

Luther had another strange title for the Devil. He called him the Doctor of Consolation—an honorary title usually attributed to the Holy Spirit. Doctor Devil comes to us and makes his case in the conscience that by rights, we belong to him. The Hound of Hell . . . has three throats—sin, the law, and death.[21] Our sinfulness, in word and deed, has erected a wall between us and God, and we are imprisoned behind it. But it is precisely at this point that we have

---

21. M. Luther, *Table Talk*, 296.

proof of Christ's presence and His righteousness. Here we have the unmistakable sign of being the elect of God—justified and joined to Christ by faith. The Devil is not interested in the unbeliever—he has all of them already. His battle is with those who belong to his Enemy, where the Gospel lives in the heart and where the Word of Christ rules the conscience by faith. Here is our experiential assurance, and the Devil provides it—that we really belong to Christ. What comfort! said Luther; the fact that the Devil presses us so hard shows that we are on the right side.[22] Satan attacks in the conscience and afflicts the heart and soul, pointing out our spiritual poverty; our wretchedness, cowardice, and weakness in fear, love, and trust. But then, these are the consolations and comforting signs that we most assuredly belong to Christ.

God enlists the Devil to assure the Christian of His own election by experiences of the sickness unto death. Luther understood well that dying to sin is requisite to a daily rising unto new life in Christ as we daily live in our baptism. As the Devil assists in this, the joke is on him. "For thus God advances his purpose through his strange work and with marvelous wisdom he knows that through death the devil can affect nothing else but life, so that while he does his utmost against the action of God, he is by his characteristic effort actually working for the divine cause against his own."[23] Never before has there been such a depiction of Satan as one pressed into God's service of providing comfort and assurance to Christians. This is a real role reversal, comfort by affliction! It is not the temptation to sin, but rather torment of God's judgment of sin and wrath according to His holy Law. Satan comes not to ravage the lost and condemned, but the faithful and righteous, offering them comfort that they do indeed belong to Christ. This is not a popular picture of the Devil most churches portray, a fearsome instigator of moral offenses, and the one who entraps the ungodly by tempted naughtiness.

God employs the wiles of the Devil in this work. Satan has a special care for strong Christians and shepherds of the soul. His temptations in this regard do not center so much on the allures of

22.   As cited in H. Oberman, "Between the Middle Ages and Modern Times," 64.
23.   WA 57.128.

the flesh, as on terrors of the conscience. This kind of tribulation keeps grace alone and faith alone from becoming obscured or transformed into dry abstract principles. It can keep them concrete and salvific. Only in the face of sin, death, and damnation does Christ and Him crucified make any sense. Without such negative thought, the Divine foolishness is just . . . foolishness. The Devil sees to it that we really understand that we do not live by a stability born of our own resources. Rather as we have noted already, we live by grace or we don't live at all. Satan, as dangerous as he is, does not have a free hand. He is set to work in God's service schooling Christians in a faith that lays hold of nothing but grace alone.

It is through experiencing the wrath of God that one becomes a true believer in the theology of the cross. It is to discover the power of negative thinking. It is through the alien work of God using the Devil that we are driven to despair. Yet in this way through delicious despair and the power of negative thinking, we learn to trust Christ alone. Everything else is taken away but God and His grace, and thus, we are brought closer to Him. Through cross, suffering, and Hell—*tentatio*—true theology, knowledge, and fellowship with God are obtained, forever.

PART III

Faithful Life in the Cross

CHAPTER 9

Good Works

The Fruit of Faith

Are good works really necessary? Do we *have to* do them? What if a believer doesn't do them, what then? These questions have been raised repeatedly in classes I have taught on Christian faith and life. I must confess, I have grown to dislike them. I fear that to give an answer—any coherent answer—is to miss the truth. There is no single response that would always be appropriate in the economy of God's Word as Law and Gospel. Perhaps Robert Kolb's insightful return question must be the first response: *Why do you want to know?*[1] If a complacent sinner is asking the question for added spiritual slumber, then I suppose the answer should be something like this:

> Of course good works are necessary! Just because you have become a Christian does not mean that the Ten Commandments have turned into the "Ten Suggestions." So get with it! Faith without works is dead and those who do not do them completely and perfectly will not enter the Kingdom of God. As Jesus said, "Anyone who breaks one of the least of these commandments and teaches others to do the same will be called least in the kingdom of heaven . . . unless your righteousness surpasses that of the Pharisees and the teachers of the law, you will certainly not enter the kingdom of heaven." (Matt. 5:19–20; James 2:14–17)

---

1. Dr. Robert Kolb, retired professor at Concordia Seminary, St. Louis, has shared this helpful question to many over the years.

However, the above answer would never do if the questioner is burdened in conscience and loaded down with guilt. Then the appropriate response should be quite the opposite: "Why no, they are not necessary at all! The Gospel has spelled the end of all works of the Law. Christ is your righteousness and, as you have put Him on through faith, you have all His works which are a perfect fulfillment of all that God will ever require. Rest in this faith alone, apart from works, and do not worry about a thing. The Son has set you free from the necessity of all works, and therefore, you are free indeed" (Rom. 10:4–9). It has been the burden of the doctrinal tradition of the Church to explain the matter about good works in the sanctified life of the Christian in such a way that, on the one hand, it makes some kind of coherent sense; yet, on the other hand, it does not violate the appropriate tension between Law and Gospel. This is a tall order to accomplish, especially when questions like the above are raised. The Lutheran tradition following Luther endeavored to tackle the issue this way: Good works are not necessary for salvation in the sense that they play no role in our acceptance by God and the gift of eternal life. It is by the grace of Christ alone apart from all human endeavor that any and all are saved through faith. Nonetheless, good works are necessary in the Christian life of faith in the sense that God commands them and faith without works is dead. It is also maintained that good works are the consequence of an alive faith empowered by the Holy Spirit through the Gospel.[2]

If all of the above takes care of your questions as you read this, well and good. But if you would like to respond at this point by asking, *Yes, OK, but now what does this mean? Do I have to do something, or don't I?* Perhaps the only response I can make is this: *I don't know; don't you want to?*

Good Works: The Impact of the Gospel

Let's change our focus. What are good works and how are they produced? For some people the term *good works* conjures up images of extraordinary deeds one takes time out in life to perform. For

---

2. See especially the *Formula of Concord Solid Declaration* IV, 14–22.

others the Boy Scout slogan *do a good turn daily* comes to mind. Still others may think of some sort of compulsive *do-goodism*. The New Testament tradition is not comfortable with any of these images. It describes good works as the fruit of faith. Good works and how they fit into the Christian life are conceptualized according to what some have called the *botanical model*. Jesus said He is the vine and we are the branches, and if we abide in him we will bear much fruit (John 15:1–5). Fruit as we know are simply the by-product of a healthy growing fruit tree or vine. Fruit just appear on the branches spontaneously and effortlessly as a consequence of being alive, according to the type of branch that God created. It is just the nature of grape vines to produce grapes, apple trees to produce apples, and so on. It is as simple as that. Reflect on what this means for a moment. The vineyards are silent at night, are they not? There is no grunting or groaning as the fruit matures—and no whining questions (*Do we have to produce grapes? How many?*). They just silently do it!

There is insight here about good works in the Christian's life in Christ. To live in Christ is simply to bring forth the works of Christ. These are works that He produces simply by being who He is through each of us by virtue of who we are. As we live in Christ and His righteousness through faith, our faith is just naturally and spontaneously fruitful in works of loving service. It is what faith does. As an indicative statement, faith *is* active in love. Moreover, God is love. He created and redeemed us from sin to love. It is not a matter of legal compulsion or coercion, as if works of love were something foreign to our recreated nature. *The grace by which we live and grow in Christ is the grace that empowers and engenders a fruitful faith.* Works of love are how faith expresses itself in daily living. They are spontaneous and seemingly effortless, without calculation or self-concern. As Jesus described the loving heart that gives, *the right hand does not know what the left hand is doing* (Matt. 6:3). The object of our love and his needs at the moment captivate our attention. Little Suzy fell down and skinned her knees. Her loving mother picked her up, comforted her, and tended to her wounds. Now should we be so silly as to ask the mother why she did this, or if she thought she *had to*, she would surely think we were crazy. Works of love may have a compulsion about them as one is captivated by the needs of a beloved, but legal considerations of duty and calculation have no place. Does not everyone know this in his heart?

Works of loving service just happen as we are grasped again and again by the astonishing reality that the grace and righteousness of Christ are the end of all legal requirements. We are free from the demanding works of the Law, and we are free to turn love outward, to focus on the needs of others as our love and trust in Christ liberates us from preoccupied self-concern. The Gospel is the end of all calculated striving to please, to become acceptable, or to perform to become fit and worthy. We are finally and forever secure in His love to abandon self-concern and burst forth our bottled-up love outward to God and others. By sheer grace alone we have forever become secure as the children of God, citizens of the Kingdom of God, and the bride of Christ. This is the incredible power of the Gospel that energizes the sanctified life with the fruit of loving works. The pardon is powerful! The Christian walk through life is continually meeting the incredible surprise of grace—the hilarity of the Gospel freedom—that cannot help bursting forth in expressions of joyful love. It is just our nature as a new creation in Christ. He is the vine, we are the branches—we do as we are in Christ. It is as simple as that.

To be grasped by the freedom of the Gospel is to face a new question: *What would you like to do now that Christ has done everything required?* The freedom of the Gospel creates a whole new agenda that arises from finally being grasped by the reality that we do not *have to* do anything and thus are free to be and do what we are in Christ. As a new creation in Christ, the necessity of good works is beside the point! Gerhard Forde has a marvelous illustration of the meaninglessness of *have to* questions about good works in this context. Imagine the joyful expectation of their wedding night by a pair of just-married lovers. Now try to imagine the groom asking his bride, *Do I have to do something tonight?*[3] If you were his bride, how would you answer his question? What would you say? The question is just crazy! Perhaps if we thought about it for a while, we might think the best reply would be something similar to what was shared above: *I don't know, don't you want to?*

---

3.   G. Forde, *Justification by Faith*, 56.

Good Works: God's Secret

During the 70s there was a popular hum-and-strum ditty among Christian youth that reflects just a bit of self-congratulation. In a repetitive refrain: the pious works of the Christian are extolled in a warm, self-flattering way—touting proof to the world of a genuine faith in Christ: *They will know we are Christians by our love.* Ironically however, there was also a thought-provoking question about your Christian living that is not so warmhearted and it caused many to squirm: *If you were on trial having been accused of being a Christian, would there be enough evidence to convict you?* How should we evaluate the song's refrain and this question? Will they know you are indeed a true believer (not some hypocrite) by your love? Second, do you have the right stuff that you could parade at some court proceeding to prove that you belong to Christ? Just how should we think about our own good works in the Christian life of faith as we live that life before others . . . and before God?

Painful as it might sound, a thorough understanding of good works that ultimately serve Christ do have a hidden or invisible side to them, and therefore we affirm them as an article of faith, not a conclusion or evaluation by others around us. Yes, the good works of the Christian do have a very visible quality that everyone can see. The visible quality is in the outward godly actions and words about which we are to understand our Lord in Matthew 5:16: *Let your light shine before others, so that they may see your good works and give glory to your Father who is in Heaven.* When we see such works by professing Christians, let's have them shining so, indeed, others see them and give glory to God. However, evidencing true saving faith in the heart of the one doing the works is another matter.

What distinguishes good works in God's sight from civil righteousness is the obedience of faith. Saving faith just passively received and clings to the saving gifts of Christ. At the same time, however, it is active producing good works. According to Luther, works are the *doing with faith.* Listen to Luther: "In theology, therefore, 'doing' necessarily requires faith itself as a precondition. . . . Therefore 'doing' is always understood in theology as doing with faith, so that doing with faith is another sphere and a new realm, so to speak, and that is different from moral doing.

When we theologians speak about 'doing' therefore, it is necessary that we speak about doing with faith, because in theology we have not right reason and good will except faith."[4] Works of the Christian that serve Christ through the neighbor only spring from true saving faith (Rom. 14:23) that is the well-spring in the New Creation that performs them out of fear, love, and trust in God.[5] For this reason, good works have an invisible quality about them and therefore, we affirm them as an article of faith in the Gospel. By faith, we believe that the New Creation from Baptism is a slave of God and righteousness (Rom. 6:18, 22); a branch grafted into the vine that is Christ for the inevitable production of fruit (John 15:5); and that God has foreordained the good works that we walk in (Eph. 2:10).

We believe we are indeed producing good works as Christ has his way with us through the impact of the Gospel. Good works that are done out of fear, love, and trust in God are not a conclusion reached by others examining any given work by the outward standards of the Commandments as Luther expounded their meaning in his Catechisms. The Law will show us what a good work is (one done out of fear, love and trust in God and in accord with the other Commandments), but it will not reveal which of our outward works are actually generated out of fear, love, and trust in God. These heart-centered elements are hidden; they cannot be perceived by those who observe how we are living our lives and they cannot be submitted as evidence before some court of law.

The Law written on the heart will expose the sinful, fleshly sentiments within the Christian that are there also in all his works, but these corrupt elements are covered by the righteousness of Christ. In this sense, works that flow from faith are God's secret to be revealed for everyone to see on Judgment Day. Then and only then when the Lord holds His Court will evidence of our saving faith be provided to prove we are Christians by our love of both our neighbor and our Lord. So trash the song and resist all who would seek to put your faith on trial. Just trust the Lord's words about your Baptism; trust His Word about how your works have been foreordained and

---

4. *AE* 36, 262–63.

5. The First Commandment that Luther understood in his catechisms is embedded in all the others.

anticipate listening to Him extol your works of faith on Judgment Day at the Great Honors Banquet to come.

Our discussion about good works and faithfulness in Christian living is hardly comprehensive. There are other important issues to consider about them, not least of which is how our vocational stations in life shape and particularize our works and our neighbors. We will address these matters in the next chapter. Our concern here has been to note how they are produced by the impact of the Gospel as a consequence of our life and growth in Christ. In addition, we have stressed that how we should respond to the questions about the necessity of good works depends on a person's disposition toward them: *Why do you want to know?* This is a very personal question. God addresses us differently in his Word according to our disposition. To self-righteous and complacent sinners, His word of Law commands works to the fullest extent of purity and number. He does this not to produce any good works from us. The Law does not energize or empower the fruit of faith; instead, it crushes. God drives us to repentance over our barren complacency and produces a hunger and thirst for the Gospel blessings. But for sinners who are burdened in conscience with guilt and despair, he sets before us nothing but the righteous gifts of Christ that are ours through faith. *Christ is the end of the law so that there may be righteousness for everyone who believes* (Rom. 10:4).

In addition, we have indicated that the true ethos of good works lies in the free, spontaneous response of love to the hilarity of the Gospel's freedom. When we are clothed by the righteousness of Christ through faith, we die to sin and emerge as a new self, fashioned in the image of Christ. For the New Creation, works of faith flow spontaneously in this freedom as the self grows and becomes *lost* in loving concern for the other.

Exhortations of the Law in the New Testament

But our discussion about good works and how they are produced needs further clarification. Some have argued that the matter of works and their production in the Christian life should be viewed on a *practical, down-to-earth* level as aided by exhortations of the Law. Some have suggested that the New Testament exhortations for godly living should in part be seen as positive, encouraging, and persuasive *Gospel-based exhortations*. They believe that Jesus' words to the woman caught in adultery, *Go and sin no more* (John 8:11 NKJV), should be seen in this way.[6] They suggest that the exhortations of the Law found in the middle and ending chapters of Romans (6, 8, 12–16) should be understood partially as encouragement for positive decision-making by Christians in choosing their works. For instance, Paul writes:

> Beloved, never avenge yourselves, but leave it to the wrath of God, for it is written, "Vengeance is mine, I will repay says the Lord." To the contrary, "if your enemy is hungry, feed him; if he is thirsty, give him something to drink." . . . Do not be overcome by evil, but overcome evil with good. (Rom. 12:19–21)

According to these views, the hortatory material in Romans treats Christians *as if they are a third party standing between two powers, sin and the Spirit*, as if the Christian were a *charioteer* with a bad horse and a good horse. Using this analogy, the apostle Paul uses the Law to urge the individual *to let the good horse lead and resist the bad horse*. Their argument is that the Spirit indeed empowers the Christian life and produces sanctification, but only in a *deeper, theoretical and ontological* sense. On the more practical level, they understand Paul advancing positive and negative arguments with the Law to encourage sanctified living. All this is done not on the deeper theoretical level where the Gospel operates but rather in terms of the practical everyday life of Christians *as concrete, down-to-earth human beings.*[7] Should we embrace this understanding of Law in the New Testament? Yes and No.

There are two basic things that should be kept in mind when considering the Law. First, the Law was added because of sin (Gal. 3:19). God uses His Law to deal with sinful humans, spiritually and temporally, but each in quite different ways. *Spiritually, He prepares sinners for*

---

6. For a more detailed discussion of this view, see Paul R. Raabe and James W. Voelz's "Why Exhort a Good Tree? Anthropology and Paraenesis in Romans," *Concordia Journal* 22, no. 2 (April 1996): 154–63.

7. P. Raabe and J. Voelz, 160–61.

receiving the Gospel by revealing what we cannot be and do. In our tem-poral affairs, He does the reverse. He uses the Law to promote and even coerce fair-play and just relations in this fallen world with rewards and punishments. He molds us for good earthly citizenship, and this is something that we sinners can be and do. In both instances, because we are sinful beings, the imperative *thou shalts* of the law hound us spiritually and temporally. Only in the Better Day coming, shall we who are in Christ be free of its slavish character. In addition to these divine uses, the Law unfortunately has some bad side effects. It mag-nifies sin and incites rebellion (Rom. 5:13, 20). As it is lodged in the heart (the Devil's playground), the Unholy Spirit uses the Law to con-vince us that we either do not need the Gospel or have forfeited our right to claim it. Here the Law is used as a weapon against the Gospel.

Second, we need to remember and appreciate that the Law when rightly applied, as noted above, is always eminently practical, even for Christians. It is surely practical in the management of our temporal affairs and dealings with others. The Law teaches us the stuff of temporal uprightness and that life will usually go better for us if we follow the rules than if we break them. Here, the law nurtures wisdom and civil righteousness—matters that Luther rightly distin-guished as matters *below us*—where we indeed exercise free will. All this, of course, applies also to the non-Christian. In this sphere, we must agree that the Law not only threatens, but it also encourages and may even entice in very practical ways. On this level we can frame out persuasive arguments. We can even cajole: *C'mon do what the law says. You will be glad that you did! Life will go better for you if you follow the rules.*

From this point on, however, we must draw a big line—but not to rule out a practical use of the Law in the spiritual sphere of life. Yes, there are exhortations in Romans and elsewhere through-out the New Testament that deal with more than civil righteousness. However, we must draw a line that would exclude all pretensions of human free will. Luther reminded the Church first in his *"Heidelberg Theses"* and later in his monumental *Bondage of the Will*: in spiritual matters, there is no free will, not even for the Christian! Any concep-tion of human freedom in *spiritual things above us* is a figment of the imagination. The analogy of the will acting as a charioteer does not fit any human being before or after the Fall in the area of spiritual matters. The Christian simply does not occupy a neutral position to be able to choose between sin and the Spirit. The will is bound, not obliterated, but captive and ruled *from above*. As Luther graphically put it, one is *ridden in life as a mule* either by God or by the Devil. When the Law is applied to spiritual matters, *things above us*, the human will must always be considered bound.

The Apostle taught that as we Christians are a New Creation in Christ, we are captivated—slaves to God and righteousness (Rom. 6:18, 22). Yes, we are free from the bondage of sin, death, and the Devil, but now bound in slavery to God and the works of God (Luther's analogy of a mule ridden by God). Thus we do as we are in Christ. Nevertheless, the Law is indeed recognized as still needed and applied by God in the lives of Christians for the simple reason that apart from Christ, we remain sinners. Apart from Baptism into Christ, Paul considered himself fleshly self, and thus we like him, are *sold as a slave to sin* (Rom. 7:14, 18). Because of this latter slavery, the Christian's sanctification is incomplete, and he needs the Law continually, but not for encouragement or choices in spiritual things. There simply is no level or dimension of spiritual works where the Christian can be encouraged to make an autonomous *right decision*. There are no decisions for Christ—not with faith nor with works. We simply do, willfully, as we are ruled in the flesh and in the Spirit, by the Devil and our Lord, Jesus Christ. We must interpret Paul's use of Law exhortation in light of what he teaches about the dual slavery of the Christian—*bound in Christ and bound apart from Him to sin*. The simultaneous character of this duality means that our works always have a mixed, good tree / bad tree character about them in this life. What makes good works good is that they are covered with the forgiveness of sins. This is because they flow from the duality of what we are as a slave to righteousness and a slave to sin. Therefore, if the non-Christian isn't impressed with some of your works, you should not be surprised.

Because the Christian in this life is still Old Adam apart from Christ, he always needs to be exhorted by the Law. Lutherans in their confessions use strong verbs like *admonish, exhort, teach, reprove, warn,* and *threaten,* but *not* encourage.[8] Christians, on account of

---

8. See the Formula of Concord, Solid Declaration VI 9, 24.

the Old Adam, need to be *roused* and *egged on* by the Law. Law, however, is never credited with empowering or producing sanctification or its works of faith—not ever and not on any level! The Gospel produces works of faith exclusively. Rather, the Law should be recognized as necessary to crucify the sinful Flesh, expose false godliness, and reveal what we ought to be and do. Christians need this on account of the old Adam and the Devil's deceit. All the while, a wrathful God indicts us for missing the mark: we aren't, we don't, and we can't measure up to how He created and redeemed us to be and do. *The Law always accuses!* Thus Christians always need the Law. It is as eminently practical as it is assuredly spiritual. The accusation of the Law, as we have discussed earlier, leads to and prepares for the Gospel to be received. Here God's foolishness justifies, sanctifies, and empowers the fruit of faith . . . entirely! As God has His way with us, the spiritual heartbeat in the sanctified life of the Christian remains always the same—Law/Gospel, back and forth, again and again—but never Gospel/Law, and surely not Law/Gospel/Law.

Might it be misleading to call these imperatives *Gospel-based exhortations*? Perhaps such terminology should be reserved to describe the imperatives in the New Testament that invite the blessings of the Gospel. *Believe on the Lord Jesus Christ. . . . Be baptized for the forgiveness of sin and you will receive the Holy Spirit. . . . Take and eat, this is my body,* and so on. The imperative case in such instances should be understood passively as in merely heeding an invitation to receive what is to be freely given. Others have called these Gospel mandates, divine imperatives, or Gospel imperatives. They are not Law. To use the word *Gospel* to describe what is clearly Law material is rather contradictory and likely to create confusion.

Concerning Jesus' encounter with the woman caught in adultery in John 8, what should we make of His words, *Go and sin no more?* Perhaps the key to understanding them aright is tied to how His preceding words, *neither do I condemn you* should be viewed. Is this another instance of Jesus exercising the keys to the kingdom? Are His words parallel with His speaking, for instance, to the paralytic in Matthew 9: *Your sins are forgiven?* Many interpreters throughout the history of the Church have thought so. We are not so sure, however.

The situation with the woman caught in adultery was different. First, Jesus is confronted by would-be Jewish vigilantes who were inclined to carry out the old prescribed civil penalty for adultery, death by stoning. This was required in the Law of Moses under the Old Covenant. Civil condemnation of this adulteress according to Moses was their intent as they looked for rocks. Yes, they would be vigilantes (taking the law into their own hands) because the Jews were now under Roman rule where only Roman due process could legally condemn one to death. Second, Jesus ruffled many feathers with His insistence that Caesar should be rendered his due (Matt. 22:21). The Apostle Paul did the same in Romans 13 and 1 Timothy 2. From these observations, it would seem natural to interpret Jesus words— *neither do I condemn you*—in the same civil condemnatory sense as the contextual threat. The woman was threatened to be stoned to death. What we have here from beginning to end is a confrontation over civil judiciary issues of due process—not confession and holy absolution! Jesus shows compassion by putting down anarchy. His words *go and sin no more*, could therefore be seen as operating within the same temporal context of civil righteousness and wisdom. His words encourage the woman to act wisely, as if to say, *Look lady, I helped you out on this one. Now do yourself a favor and get your sex life in order!*

To interpret Jesus as bestowing grace on the woman on a spiritual level and then encouraging her with practical advice of law on a down-to-earth level in order to produce the fruit of faith in the sanctified life is quite a stretch. It requires us to make assumptions about this woman's spiritual life that simply are not in the text. Moreover, it completely divorces the sense of Jesus' words from the entire context in which they were spoken.

Some Words about the Third Use of the Law

Many have become confused by the term *the Third Use of the Law*— especially Lutherans. One might ask if this is a program for preaching and teaching good works after the promises and gifts of the Gospel have been given to Christians. Can we talk about some use of the Law in the Church that is programmatic and excludes its accusation of sin?

Some background about Reformation language concerning uses of the Law may be helpful in gaining greater clarity. Luther discussed the Law in his writings differentiating two uses of the Law: (1) a *civil use* and (2) a *theological* or *spiritual use*. His *theological use* describes how God uses the Law in the hearts of sinners as it is proclaimed and taught in the Church's ministry. Theologically or spiritually, the Law accuses of sin and reveals God's wrath and condemnation.[9]

In the *"Heidelberg Theses"* of 1518, Luther stressed the condemnatory aspect of the Law, especially in Thesis 23 where he stated, *The Law brings the wrath of God, kills, reviles, accuses, judges, and condemns everything that is not in Christ (Rom. 4:15).*[10] Nevertheless, Luther did believe that the Law also serves to inform Christians concerning the nature of good and God-pleasing works of faith. His 1521 *Treatise on Good Works* emphasizes this instructional use of the Law.[11] He expounded the nature of good works as works that are in accord with God's revealed Commandments in his Word, and not according to the traditions of men. If God has not commanded it in His Word, it cannot be considered a good work. Furthermore, if it has not been forbidden in His Word, it cannot be considered a sin. What God's Word does not forbid is permitted in Christian freedom. His treatise is simply an expanded commentary on the Ten Commandments and a forerunner to the first chief part of his catechisms that he would write a few years later.

The term *Third use of the Law* was introduced to Reformation terminology by Luther's colleague and close friend, Philip Melanchthon. As Melanchthon summarized Luther's evangelical doctrine in his *Loci Communes*, he changed Luther's twofold division concerning the Law into a threefold division.[12] The *civil use* remained the same, but Luther's *theological* or *spiritual use* became a *second use* accusing and condemning function, and then his *third use* enumerated Luther's insistence of the Law's instruction concerning good works. Melanchthon did not, however, advance any

9. *AE* 26, 308–17.

10. *AE* 31: 54

11. *AE* 44, 15–114.

12. See Melanchthon's discussion in his *Loci Communes* 1555 in *Melanchthon on Christian Doctrine*, trans. Clyde L. Manschreck (New York: Oxford University Press, 1965), 122–28.

instructional use separated from the accusatory function in the life of the Christian. Indeed, it was Melanchthon who coined the phrase (not the idea) *the Law always accuses.*[13] He simply itemized how God uses His Law in his systematic presentation of doctrine.

Some have argued that Luther did not teach that the Law instructs Christians about the nature of good works, as if Luther held that the Law *only* accuses when taught and proclaimed in the life of the Church. Such, however, is not the case. Luther did teach an instructional function of the Law. Note his words in his Conclusion of the Ten Commandments in the *Large Catechism*: "Here then, we have the Ten Commandments, a summary of divine teaching on what we are to do to make our whole life pleasing to God. They are the true fountain from which all good works must spring, the true channel through which all good works must flow. Apart from these Ten Commandments no deed, no conduct can be good or pleasing to God, no matter how great or precious it may be in the eyes of the world." Luther wrote his catechisms to instruct. The first chief part was written (like his earlier *Treatise on Good Works*) with the intent that believers would profit, in part, by understanding the true nature of good works, the fruit of faith in the justified life of the Christian. This is exactly what Melanchthon and the *Formula of Concord* in the Lutheran Confessions call, *the Third Use of the Law* (see Article VI of the *Formula of Concord*). Nevertheless, listing or understanding uses of the Law does not present programmatic methods or strategies for how it should be proclaimed. What needs to be clarified and emphasized, however, it that the Law always needs to be proclaimed at full strength regardless of its accusation or instruction about good works.

Why does the Christian need any instruction concerning good works, especially since the new creation just does them in accord with its nature? The problem, as our discussion has previously noted, is that the Christian is not simply a new creation in Christ. He is also, apart from Christ, a fleshly slave to sin (Rom. 7:14). Christians still require the teaching of the Law to prevent them from relying on their own sense of holiness and piety or creating works that lack His Word

---

13. The Apology to the Augsburg Confession IV: 128.

and command. The instruction of the Law helps the Christian guard against fleshly self-appointed works. At the same time the Law may curb, coerce, and co-opt the sinful self (motivated by self-interest) to go along with the outward character of works that have God's command. To be sure, the fleshly sinful self never contributes anything positive to the works of the Christian. All it can do is sin.

Uses of the Law and Going Soft on Good Works

The reformers clarified how *God uses His Law* in the life of the Church. They also explained how He works in the lives and hearts of sinners when the Law is rightly proclaimed at full strength and rightly divided from the ministry of the Gospel. It is God Who accuses, condemns, and instructs in good works when, where, and as He chooses through the proclamation and teaching of the Law. It may be that one hearer is accused, but not condemned (living under grace through faith), another is condemned (and finally brought to despair of his own righteousness) and another, at any given moment, learns something new about the fruit of faithfulness that was not understood before. These things that God would accomplish through His Law are not to be understood as programmatic elements for the preacher to organize his sermon. He is just to preach the Law at full strength and then the pure, sweet Gospel. Period! There is not to be a *third part* of the sermon after the Gospel for a programmatic and independent instruction in the Law to inform and press the Christian to do good works after he has heard his forgiveness in Christ.

The accusatory and instructional uses of the law are to be distinguished as we teach about how God uses His Law, but this distinction is not to be made into separate programmatic installments, as if the servant of the Word is supposed to orchestrate the accusation of the Law before the Gospel, but then instruct in good works afterward. Instructing and exhorting the believer about works after hearing the life-giving freedom of the Gospel can have the effect of erasing its impact. It is as we pointed out before; the Law *always* accuses. The Gospel predominates in the Church's ministry when it is heard as God's final Word and thus most appropriately followed by an *A-men* and then silence. Do we not all understand the final word has been heard, when silence follows?

In addition, Christians need to beware of exhortations and descriptions of the works of faith that are watered-down, or soft. Soft works are moralistic where any do-gooder can perform and parade them from pure self-interest. Servants of the Word are not to go soft on good works. Soft good works are the relaxed kind that Jesus railed against in the Sermon on the Mount (Matt. 5:19-22). They are the kind of works that sometimes shove godly virtue in your face because it is written on the face of the would-be do-gooder. Soft good works include calculated works where the right hand knows exactly what the left hand is doing (Matt. 6:1-4). The most distinguishing characteristic of soft good works is that they are doable—by anyone. Encouragement and soft good works just feed the sinful flesh and rob believers of the power and freedom of the Gospel.

Yes, good works are normed by the Law of God, but they need to be preached and taught at full-strength. This means that whatever outward actions they may demand, they will always include what is demanded in and from your heart. They need to be exhorted and admonished to flow from faith in Christ and love of God and neighbor. The fleshly self in all believers needs to be reminded that if nice outward righteous doing does not flow from faith and love of God (and your neighbor), they are just what Isaiah compared to filthy rags (Isa. 64:6). Yes, such preaching about good works is not particularly uplifting but it is not supposed to be. It is intended to be instructional, not inspirational.

Proper preaching of good works is never for our encouragement. Rather, it is intended do two things at the same time: inform us about the character of real God-pleasing works; and then, where they are lacking in our life. If it does not do the former, it cannot do the latter. The preaching of soft good works does neither. Proper preaching and teaching good works with appropriate admonitions are not designed to reveal your virtue or make you feel good about yourself. They are intended to expose your poverty—what you should do, but don't. This is a good thing for your spiritual health and, oddly enough, such preaching has an important role in doing good works.

Because good preaching of works commands the internal as well as the external aspects of the Law, it always exposes our weak faith and nails us for our impoverished often self-centered works. The fleshly self is always there in all our works. While this may make us squirm, it is a good thing. The Spirit of the Lord uses this to expose false works and indict our poverty to make us hungry for the Gospel—to make us hungry for the all-sufficient works and righteousness of Christ. So, is proper preaching and admonishing of good works a setup for the Gospel? Yes! When the Gospel gives you the all-sufficient perfect works of Christ and sets you free from their legal necessity, something magical happens. This is the hilarity of the Gospel. When you realize there is nothing you have to do, the impact of the Gospel produces both the desire and the freedom to do them flowing from a *want to* in the heart rather that a *have to*.

God is sneaky. Christ is the end of the law so that there may be righteousness for everyone who believes (Rom. 10:4). Works of faith without Legal compulsion from a free spirit was His plan for you all along (John 15:1–5; Gal. 2:10). Luther understood that this is what St. Augustine meant by *Love God and do as you please*.[14] Encouragement and exhortation about soft good works may motivate you to ratchet up more or better outward moral living—perhaps to satisfy a guilt trip—but it will not produce any hunger for the works and righteousness of Christ. It will not take you to the Gospel—the power of God unto salvation and the power of God that alone produces the fruit of faith.

It must also be clarified that right preaching of full-strength good works will not show us our own good works. God uses his Law to reveal our sin (Rom. 3:20) and what good works are, but it does not reveal ours. Our good works are God's secrets. He accomplishes this work in the hidden recesses of the believer's heart and mind, where fear, love and trust in God are nurtured. The bottom line is that our good works are to be believed simply because Christ promises they are there (John 5:1–5; Gal. 2:10). Christ will reveal them to you as a prelude to His Awards Banquet on Judgment Day (see Matt. 25:31–40). For now, however, size up properly how good

---

14. Actually what Augustine said was "Love God and do as thou wilt." The whole quote is this: "Once for all, then, a short precept is given thee: Love, and do what thou wilt: whether thou hold thy peace, through love hold thy peace; whether thou cry out, through love cry out; whether thou correct, through love correct; whether thou spare, through love do thou spare: let the root of love be within, of this root can nothing spring but what is good." Seventh Homily on 1 John 4:4–12.

works are being preached by Servants of the Word. And then either listen up . . . or walk.

So to summarize, Servants of the Word are simply to proclaim pure Law at full strength as preparation for the ministry of the Gospel. If on such an occasion God wants to condemn Mr. Schmidt sitting in the second pew right to the depths of Hell that is God's business. If He wants to expose the fleshly living of Mrs. Mueller in the back row and accuse her of using her family ties in an idolatrous manner, again that is God's business. If God uses our preaching to curb and discipline teenager Billy's gross rebellious behavior with the threats of Hell (notice, I have even brought in the civil use of the Law!), again that is God's business. *And* if God uses the pastor's fine proclamation to teach Mr. Hauptmann that the fruits of faith include even the ordinary duties around the house as a husband and father that is God's business. Even if Mrs. Smith sleeps through it all and Mr. Jones is simply provoked to greater levels of sinful rebellion—well again, that is God's business. He works His curbing, instruction/accusing unto repentance when, where, and as He chooses.

The servant of the Word is simply to rightly divide Law and Gospel in all its strength and purity and then leave the uses (in Luther's twofold sense or Melanchthon's threefold sense) up to God. The same point can be made about uses the Gospel. Again, the term, use, describes what God accomplishes through his Word according to His promise and good pleasure. From the Scriptures, we understand God uses His Gospel to create saving faith, bestow forgiveness of sins, mature the New Creation, and empower good works. Therefore, as clarified above concerning uses of the Law, these are not to be understood as separated elements that the Servant of the Word is to separate programmatically as if the Gospel should be proclaimed in one instance or method to bring about faith, but another to bestow forgiveness, yet another to mature life in Christ, and so on. These uses should certainly be taught about what God accomplishes through His saving Word. However, the Gospel is simply to be proclaimed at full-strength with the understanding that God will accomplish these saving works in the lives of sinners when, where, and as He chooses.

Some Concluding Observations

Let us close this discussion about the sanctified life of good works with a couple of important clarifications. First, instruction about good works provided by the Law presents only the framework or the parameters within which the good works of the Christian are to be found and beyond which his projects may not go. God's revealed Law sets up a bare-bones framework for the creative expressions of loving service as faith expresses itself out of *fear, love, and trust in God.* Within the framework of the Law of Love, the concrete duties and tasks of the Christian are shaped and particularized by the callings of his vocation. Moreover, the Scriptures simply assume that we know what love is when they exhort us to love our neighbor as ourselves. Christians need to resist a kind of *handbook Christianity.* Making the Bible into a rule book legalistically stifles the tremendous creativity and ingenuity that God wants his people to employ in their vocational settings as faith expresses itself in love, serving Christ in the needs of the neighbor.

Second, this brief discussion about good works constitutes only *talk about.* And *talk about* sanctified living and good works never produced a gnat's breath amount of either. Gerhard Forde wisely noted that talk about sanctification can be dangerous if it gives the false impression that sanctification and good works can be produced by simply concentrating a lot of correct teaching about them in discussions like this.[15] Such talk about the sanctified life and how Christ accomplishes it, even when joined with exhortations unto good works, is not the same thing as the impact of the proclaimed Gospel in Word and Supper. We can incant the words *power of the Gospel* and *love of Christ ad nauseam* and still have imparted neither. What sanctifies and empowers good works is the actual proclaimed Gospel—the very bestowal of the saving gifts of

---

15. "Even under the best of conditions, talk about sanctification in any way apart from justification in dangerous. It has a tendency to become a strict verbal exercise in which one says obligatory things to show one is 'serious about it'—but little comes from the discussion. Perhaps one feels sanctified just by talking impressively about it." G. Forde, "The Lutheran View," 16.

Christ. It is captured in such liberating words of Christ as *your sins are forgiven* and *given and shed for you*.

Nevertheless, straight talk about the sanctified life of good works is not trivial. It does have an important role. It can build a proper awareness of the faith/life into which we are baptized, a right focusing of the *eyes of faith*. Sanctification and good works are God's secrets. We cannot view them as we would the construction of a house. He accomplishes this work in the hidden recesses of the believer's heart and mind, where fear, love and trust in God are nurtured. We must simply believe that He has His way with us in the Gospel, building and maturing us into a full-stature image of Christ. We must also trust that works *are* empowered and produced by the same Gospel that pardons and gives eternal life. Such things, like all the blessings of the Gospel, are hidden, and thus only perceived by the eyes of faith. Yes, to truly center one's trust in the gifts and impact of the Gospel—to really believe the divine foolishness that, in Christ, we do as we are—there is the challenge!

CHAPTER 10

Vocation

Ordinary Life for Ordinary Saints

Luther's depiction of faith faithfully going to work in the world presented the Christian with a regimen for life that looks rather indistinguishable from would-be citizens of the Kingdom of the Devil. For Luther, saving faith is called to exercise a life of faithfulness that, compared to much of Western Christian thinking before the Reformation, is decidedly worldly and mundane in its appearance. He urged the Christian to leave behind the exercises of monastic life, pilgrimages, Eucharistic parades, and various acts of pious self-denial in a struggle for personal holiness. The righteousness of Christ shall be your holiness already accomplished and bestowed. You cannot get any more righteous or holy than you already are in your Baptism. Therefore, the Christian is directed to channel his efforts toward meeting the ordinary temporal needs of his neighbors as they are encountered where they commonly live, work, and play. Such a life of faith renders the believer rather unidentifiable in general society. Indeed, for Luther, the good pious Christian called to live in the cross of Christ is, and remains in this life a bit of a phantom, a sociological uncertainty; indistinguishable from the average citizen of this world. The character of godliness and piety that Luther advocated involved the call to a life of faith and faithfulness with a decidedly worldly accent.

The Call to Faith and Faithfulness

Christian life for the individual believer expresses who and what we are as addressed by the God's judgment of Law and Gospel. As such, the Christian is as we have earlier described in Luther's thinking: *righteous and beloved of God, yet he is a sinner at the same time.*[1] Let's examine this more closely. As the Christian lives in the flesh, he stands under the judgment of Law as a sinner. The Law presents all sinners in this life a security and peril. Outwardly, the Law presents this fallen world with the security of social orders; the creational structures of community by which our temporal life is ordered. Moreover, a reasonable civil application of the Law provides a modicum of security for peaceable relations in the social orders of the world. The civil use of Law boils down to a reasonable application of the golden rule: life will go well for me if I treat others as I would have them treat me.[2] Such behavior, however, does not make the believer extraordinary or unusual. Civil righteousness neither makes the believer pious nor does it focus on the essential nature of Christian piety. Common to believer and nonbeliever alike, it is rooted in self-interest. Civil righteousness is not intrinsically the stuff of godliness. It is the stuff of practical wisdom.

Spiritually speaking however, the Law presents a peril. It pronounces the Christian a sinner and threatens all sinners with the sentence of death. Through the Law, God produces self-honesty and repentance in the heart. The Law, however, is only God's preliminary word. It is His provisional judgment, not His final judgment. God's judgment of grace is His final verdict that pronounces the permanent truth of the Christian's identity that sets us all free. *The Law was given through Moses, grace and truth through Jesus Christ* (John 1:17). This is the word of truth about our identity that proclaims us saints—holy, righteous, pious ones—this is the truth that embodies all our godliness and sets us free.

It is the righteousness of Christ bestowed by God's gracious word that makes the Christian good and holy. In Christian Baptism,

---

1. *AE* 26, 235.

2. Werner Elert, *The Christian Ethos*, trans. Carl J. Schindler (Philadelphia: Fortress, 1957), 73.

God has declared the Christian pious. True piety or holiness is essentially a hidden possession of the Christian not a demonstrable attribute, nor a bundle of some uniquely pious activities. On the demonstrable side of things, the Christian is and remains an impious sinner in character, and in word and deed. And about this seeming nonsense, Luther rhetorically asked, "Who will reconcile these utterly conflicting statements, that the sin in us is not sin, that he who is damnable will not be damned, that he who is rejected will not be rejected, that he who is worthy of wrath and eternal death will not receive these punishments? Only the mediator between God and man, Jesus Christ."[3] The Law judges *what* we are in this fallen creation. We are sinful ungodly human beings and everyone in world can see this. The Gospel declares *who* we are in Christ. We are holy and righteous for the sake of Christ. This is a reality in this life that is only perceived by faith. For this reason, the essential expression of the Christian's piety is subjective in character. It is faith in the heart and hence, it is hidden from the view of others. The essence of true piety and godliness in cross theology is the obedience of faith and outward expressions of faithfulness. The outer limits of Christian piety—what the Christian is and does—are tied to the call of God. This call renders the individual Christian a provisional life in this old fallen creation that can be described extraordinarily ordinary. To understand this, and survey briefly the alternatives to this stance, we must explore how cross theology renders the Christian's vocation.

Luther often used a special term to designate the Christian life of faithfulness—*vocation*. The word *vocation* comes from the Latin term, *vocatio*. A *vocatio* is a call or calling to a given way of life. It grants an individual a particular standing and position in relation to others within a community. Moreover, it defines how one meaningfully participates in and contributes to the life of the community. In other words, our vocation tells us who we are within our social structures of life and what kind of duties we are to be about for the welfare of the community. These features of life make demands on us to live lives of faith and faithfulness. We must trust our standing to live securely as a member and our faith is expressed, in part, by

---

3. *AE* 26, 235–36.

faithfully being about the tasks that are assigned to our particular station within a community. In summary vocation addresses the following questions about our life in Christ: (1) What is our status or standing in community? (2) What or whom must we trust to make our place secure? (3) Whom are we to serve? (4) What are our tasks and responsibilities?

To illustrate, consider a young son living with his family. His vocation is first of all a call to *be* a son. Second, he is called to trust in his sonship, to trust that he truly and securely is a child of his parents, a legitimate member of the family. He must trust that his parents have a claim on him to be their own, a claim of love that has made him a son and a member of the family. Flowing from this standing in the family, he lives daily under a call to be a faithful son—that is, to live out his sonship using his time and abilities to contribute to the welfare of the family in countless ways as directed by mom and dad.

Notice that the son's call to serving the household is a secondary aspect of his vocation. It flows from his primary call to be a member of the family. At every point, what he does is dependent upon who he is. Second, who he is in the family is totally dependent upon his parents' initiative, not his own. His faithfulness neither made him a son nor does it ensure his sonship in the future. These are established and preserved by his parents love and commitment. And of great importance, we see the necessity of faith. The child must trust his parents and their love for him to live secure in his sonship. From such faith, faithfulness may flow. His life of faithful service to the family takes shape and develops as he matures. His tasks give him opportunity to express his love for others in the family and live out his faith in his sonship, his trust in who and what he is.

How we are called to live a life of service is dependent upon who we are. Our identity and status in community are received as gifts. They are not of our making. How we are called to live a life of service is dependent upon our station—where we are placed in community. Our tasks and our faithfulness to them are expressions of our trust in who and what we are as members of the community.

The Dual Citizenship of the Christian

Christian life is lived as a calling, a vocation that flows from God's call and love for us in Christ. Through the Gospel, He has called us to be sons and daughters in His family. This call is first and foremost a summons to a life of faith—a call to trust in the saving work of Christ and who and what we are by his grace—forgiven and adopted children of His love. Christians have received their vocational call from God in Baptism. Baptism bestows on each of us God's gracious claim to be His child. His call brings full and secure membership in his Kingdom. The tasks that God has given to us act out our faith in His calling. They are the means of expressing our faithfulness to Him and His family. True piety expresses or acts out our trust in who we are in God's call. *Vocation shapes the expressions of true Christian piety.*

Major questions about Christian vocation must be addressed. How and where in the world should we live and serve our God as His children? What are our tasks? What should be our relationship with the citizens and social structures of the world? What do our attachments and commitments to our family, our work, and our civic involvement have to do with living in the call of God? The Church through the ages has grappled with these questions and provided quite a spectrum of responses.

St. Augustine, the great thinker of the ancient Church, set forth his vision of God's call in his monumental work, *The City of God.* Augustine conceived of the Church as a pilgrim people, citizens of another age who are journeying through life in this world to their real home, *the City of God.* The call to faith is a call to faithful living as we travel on our way to the eternal Kingdom that God will usher in at the close of the age. Augustine saw citizenship as an exclusive status. Therefore, since believers are citizens of God's eternal Kingdom, they just inhabit the social structures of this world as foreigners, sojourners on their way to their real home. During the journey, God schools and outfits his people for the coming age. This was Augustine's vision of what Jesus meant in his call for his disciples to be in the world, but not of the world. We live in the world, but as foreigners—citizens of the Kingdom that is not continuous with any temporal community.

Our days on earth are focused on God's gracious power, transforming us in holiness—making us fit for life in the Kingdom.

This vision of Christian vocation created for Augustine a kind of ambivalence toward the social communities of this world. Christians are to live peaceably within them, but because they are fallen and will pass away with the dawning of the Kingdom, we must see the call of God and the higher tasks of faithfulness as transcending our involvement in them. True godliness involves for the faithful Christian a higher life that we pursue over and above the obligations and commitments that arise from our sojourning in the world's communities. The responsibilities of old world living are not of the same stuff as the works within a calling to divine citizenship. The Christian pilgrim may have to be involved with the former, but true godliness flowing from faith issue a higher order of duties that flow from divine citizenship. For Augustine, one is either a citizen of this world or the City of God—but not both. His portrait of the pious expressions of faith involved an extraordinary set of tasks, largely entailing self-discipline and spiritual devotion. They stood over and beyond the everyday duties that spring from our sojourning in the social orders of this world. Here within the ordinary of life is the extraordinary duties of a higher calling and these are the stuff of true Christian piety.

If this is really what true Christian piety is all about, why not simply separate from the entanglements of this world and pursue godliness full time? In the second and third centuries, some radical Christian thinkers had just such a plan in mind. They placed an extreme emphasis on the negative side of the call of God, *to be not of the world.* Influenced by Greek stoic philosophy, they conceived of the call of Christ as a call to live in seclusion, divorced from all human community. Guided by this vision, they equated the call of God with a life of isolation and self-denial. Many believers went out into the desert and lived solitary lives in caves. For them true Christian piety was tied up with an ascetic life of self-denial. They maintained a meager physical existence with just enough food and water to keep themselves alive. They were *Hermits for Christ* who devoted themselves to reading the Scriptures, prayer, and meditation while waiting for God to usher in the fullness of the Kingdom. For them, the Christian life was certainly extraordinary and remarkable.

During the Middle Ages, a variation of the hermit movement became the standard form for what was termed *the higher calling* of God. Rather than caves with one hermit per cave, Christians pursued the higher calling of God by cloistering themselves as groups inside monasteries. As holy fraternities, monks and nuns dedicated themselves to a pious life of devotion to God, separated from all commitments and attachments to the social orders of this world. Again, the highest order of true godliness was depicted as a life of self-denial and seclusion. Poverty, celibacy, and strict obedience to monastic order were seen as virtuous sacrifice, the epitome of faithfulness. Unencumbered by secular concerns, the believer could become absorbed in a higher regimen of worship, prayer, and meditation. Monasticism flourished in Western Christianity for over a thousand years as the exemplary form of Christian vocation and piety. It was a synthesis of Augustine's vision of Christian citizenship and the Hermit Movement. Christian's had a choice. They could be ordinary or extraordinary. They could live a life of mediocre piety sojourning in the old-world communities; trying to do pious things on top of the time-consuming tasks of earthly maintenance. Or they could pursue the more godly life (the higher calling) and do the pious things of divine citizenship *full-time* within monasticism.

While a young monk himself, Luther's searched the Scriptures and rediscovered the centrality of the Incarnation and cross in the call of God. As he developed his theology of the cross, he recognized that God's saving work and call involves a kind of *salvific worldliness* in His method. He chooses to enlist worldly elements and structures of His fallen creation as instruments or means to accomplish His saving purposes. Think for a moment of the whole cycle of events in the extended Joseph narrative from Genesis. The words "and the Lord was with Joseph" (Gen. 39:2 NASB 1977) signal for the reader that in, with, and under all the worldly and tragic events that happened to Joseph and his brothers, God was at work graciously blessing the family of Israel. Joseph knew with all his senses that his brothers and others were at work for evil purposes, but by faith he recognized God saving activity at work for their good (Gen. 45:5–8; 50:20).

Think also more centrally about God's method of salvation in the incarnation of His Son and the cross. God takes up and hides Himself in ordinary human flesh. He then enlists earthly family life, the carpentry trade, and the political and religious movements of the day into the service of His saving work. He works out but hides His righteousness and pardon for us in the grisly act of capital punishment by crucifixion (a tragic political event). By ordinary perception, we see His chosen worldly instruments and events. However, it is only by faith that we see the glory of God in the Suffering Servant and our righteousness acquired. To understand God at work in the world is to hold on both to what we see and to what is given to faith. Neither dimension is to be denied or omitted from the Church's faith and confession. In the Incarnation and the cross God reveals the ultimate of expression of salvific worldliness where the extraordinary work of God is tied to and hidden in ordinary events of this fallen world. As Luther observed, *Man hides his own things in order to conceal them; God hides his own things to reveal them.*[4]

Salvific worldliness is also how we should understand the Christian's vocation and true Christian piety from within a theology of the cross. We have become a new creation in Christ and a temple of the Holy Spirit, but God has called us to a life of faith and faithfulness in the flesh and blood of the old creation. This means that Christian vocation calls us to be simultaneously members of the communities of this fallen world *and* citizens of the Kingdom of God. Jesus carried out His call from the Father within the old creation communities of earthly family, work, and the social structures of general society. So also must we who now live in Christ. Christian life and vocation involve a duality. Christian citizenship involves an extraordinary one within the ordinary one. They present an extraordinary membership in the Kingdom of God, lived out within an ordinary membership in the old creation communities and structures of everyday life.

On one level, faithfulness in Christian vocation involves being about the ordinary living out of our commitments and projects that arise from our membership and specific station in our families, workplace, and general society. God's call to a life of faith and faithfulness always touches us within our space, where we live already. It does not demand that we go off and live in caves or separated communities. On this level, the outward character of Christian life is not radically

---

4. A sermon of Luther's delivered on February 24, 1517, WA 1.138.13–15, as cited in A. McGrath, *Luther's Theology of the Cross*, 167.

different from the average citizen of this world. In this sense, it is decidedly ordinary. However, in, with, and under this secular life, God is calling the believer to a life of faith and faithfulness as citizens of His Kingdom.

The higher calling of the Christian is not a summons to some state parallel or separated from our participation in our existing communities, but rather it is embedded within it. True Christian piety is the extraordinary life of faith and faithfulness in Christ. But it is the obedience of extraordinary faith expressed in the duties and responsibilities of ordinary life. True Christian godliness is tied to the common and often mundane tasks that make up life in our old-world citizenship. This is what the apostle Paul meant in 1 Corinthians 7:17, where he instructed Christians to retain the places in life that the Lord has assigned and to which God has called each one of us. Our roles and commitments within these structures of life are the schooling by which our Lord teaches us how to live out our faith. Here He would teach us how faith is to be expressed in life as loving service.

Christ indeed intends for our works ultimately to be of service to Him. There are some important qualifications, however, that are not very flattering. First, we do not have anything He needs. Second, all that we are and all that we have that is good, He made and gave to us. Anything of real worth, we call a blessing, and we praise God from whom *all* blessings flow. It is our neighbor who needs our gifts, skills, time, and blessings that the Lord has entrusted to us. Our spouse, our children, those who live next door, fellow employees, the customer, the client, those whom we encounter where we live, work, and play—these are the ones who need our goods and works of service. Jesus instructs us that as He served the neighbor (and the servant is not above his Master; John 13:16), so also must we. And then the Lord makes this kind of arrangement. When we serve these, He will credit it as service rendered to Him (Matt. 25:35–40). Here then is the economy for faith and works: place your faith in God and give your works to your neighbor.

Perhaps the most dramatic and yet humbling object lesson that Jesus provided about the works of our vocation was at a high-class inn when he celebrated the Passover and institutes his Supper privately with his disciples (John 13). Absent was the usually stationed servant who washed the feet and ankles of the guests who entered, providing a nice touch of class. The large bowl, towels, and pitcher of water were there in waiting. We know the story. After all were seated, Jesus got up, wrapped one of the towels around his waist, poured water into the basin, and proceeded to wash the feet of his disciples seated at the table. When Jesus was about to wash his feet, Peter freaks out. He demands that Jesus stop right there telling him that he would never allow such a thing (vss. 4–8). He could not stomach the idea that the One he had recognized as the Christ, the Son of the living God (Matt. 16:16), would stoop to take on some lowly dirty business that he himself would not do.

Washing the disciples' feet was the prop Jesus used to illustrate some important things about the works of vocation—theirs and ours. It was an object lesson for all who would call him Lord and are therefore his servants. As he washed the disciples' feet, all servants ought to wash one another's feet as service rendered to our Lord.[5] Serving our Lord will be service rendered indirectly through our neighbors (John 13:13–15). So as an example of work that serves Christ, he puts on a display of taking care of our neighbors' soiled conditions—like washing their dirty feet. Can you imagine that? When Jesus wants to exemplify quintessential good works in the Kingdom of God, he grabs a towel and engages in ordinary dirty business. This is what grossed Peter out. How would you have reacted if you were in his sandals?

While we may occasionally be called to do something amazing, even to engage in courageous deeds, it is the ordinary, dirty business of life that Jesus here reveals as the kind of labor that ultimately serves him as Lord. How could we translate foot washing into today's mundane dirty labors? How about the lowly domestic task of weekly laundry around the house? Imagine what doing the laundry might mean according to our Lord's example. When you throw in the soiled clothes and dirty socks; when the bleach and fabric softeners go in;

---

5. Only Christ in his vocation forgives penitent sinners. Jesus here is giving the disciples an example about elements of their vocation (vss. 14–15)—washing one another's feet. This is not an extension of Christ's vocation in the apostolic vocation involving confession and absolution authorized in John 20:23. This is horizontal reciprocal human service, not some metaphorical reference to the Office of the Keys.

the angels in Heaven are going crazy as they witness the performance of quintessential works in the Kingdom of God. So because we serve our Lord by serving our neighbor, it is ultimately our Lord Jesus who gets a clean set of clothes for the coming week.

When faith serves out of fear, love, and trust in God even the least among us in the most mundane of ways, we serve Christ and glorify our heavenly Father. Luther understood that every Commandment of God starts with fear and love of God. The First Commandment is embedded in all the others. This heart-centered dimension is hidden from the world, but perceived by the eyes of faith. When the Christian shopkeeper sweeps the sidewalk outside the store, the householder does the laundry, the parent helps the child with homework, or the Christian salesman offers quality service out of trust in Christ and love for those served—faithfulness to the call of God is rendered. Here is the essence of pious Christian living that glorifies God and for which the heavenly hosts are praising God. Faithfulness flows from the heart of faith and love as we are about the full range of duties and tasks that arise from our ordinary commitments. The outward works of worldly service are seen and perceived by all. But faith in Christ, and fear, love, and trust in God are all hidden. Christian living in God's *vocatio* from faith to faithfulness in the world, as with Christ and his saving work, are extraordinary as hidden, and ordinary as revealed.

On another level, Christian vocation calls us into an eternal fellowship with Christ and all the saints that belong in His Church. This church is the family of God that transcends our space and time reaching also into the heavenly mansions. On earth, this community of faith is scattered, but hidden, throughout the world. But through faith, we confess the presence and fellowship of this eternal Kingdom when we gather together around the proclaimed Gospel and the administered sacraments. The Kingdom of God and its fellowship in the world are also hidden and revealed.

We are indeed, as Augustine recognized, a pilgrim people on our way to our ultimate home in the coming age. We await the coming of our King and the fullness of our calling as citizens of a new age, to dawn when He returns. Life here within our old creation communities is temporary and provisional. Our vision of our final calling is shadowy and vague. It is not yet clear what we shall become. For now, our Lord directs our attention and energies to the tasks He has called us to be about here, as we hope in the life to come. On the whole they are not very spectacular or compelling in the eyes of the world. Perhaps we could describe them as by-and-large remarkably unremarkable. Let's explore them more closely.

The Tasks of Faithfulness

As Luther worked out from the Scriptures his theology of the cross and its application to Christian vocation, he realized that the call of Christ in the cross was a call to freedom. The Gospel abolishes slavish obedience to the Law and excludes the commandments of church authorities that have no clear basis in God's Word. Two major essays written in 1520 expressed the essence of Luther's thinking about the character of Christian vocation under the cross: *The Freedom of the Christian* and the *Treatise on Good Works.*

In *The Freedom of the Christian*, Luther captured St. Paul's central point in his letter to the Galatians that the Gospel of Christ is the end of the Law. Living in Christ's righteousness imparts a polarity of freedoms; there is a *freedom from* and a *freedom to* for the children of God in the Gospel. We have *freedom from* any and all slavish forms of obedience and from the curse of the Law. And we have *freedom to* live a life of faith and walk in the power of the Spirit. This, for Luther meant that obedience to the Law was replaced for the Christian with the obedience of faith. He wrote, "Is not such a soul most obedient to God in all things by this faith? What commandment is there that such obedience has not completely fulfilled? What more complete fulfillment is there than obedience in all things? This obedience, however is not rendered by works, but by faith alone."[6] Faith grants to the Christian *freedom from* a slavish self-love, and *freedom to* love others secure in God's love. The bondage of ordering all our projects to achieve a self-justification has come to an end. The call of the Gospel is not a summons to deny or denigrate self-love, nor does it forbid us our own commitments and projects in life. Rather, the righteousness of Christ is the fulfillment of self-love

---

6. *AE* 31, 350.

in God's love. Self-love may take a back seat and rest in the freedom and security of being OK. Sin distorted our loves by placing the self at the center and forefront of life's priorities. But now secure in the verdict of the cross, the claim of Christ calls forth a reordering of our loves that sin has perverted, back to an expression of God's original intention. The faith through which we are justified is expressed—it is acted out in life—through our loves as God originally ordered them. Faithfulness in Christian vocation is faith's activity in love. As a new creation in Christ, the freedom of the Christian is hearing God now address us with the following question: *What would you like to do, now that you don't have to do anything?*[7]

Luther's second writing, his treatise on *Good Works* is largely an extended exposition of each of the Ten Commandments. It was a forerunner to the First Chief Part of his catechisms, which he wrote eight years later. Luther recognized that the Commandments of God are a comprehensive summary of the Law—the Law that always unmasks our sinfulness and reveals God's judgment. Yet Luther also recognized that these Commandments also express all that the Christian needs to know from God about good and God-pleasing works.

He realized that the Commandments sketch out both the context of where Christian vocation is to be lived and the order of our loves as God would have faith in Christ express them. Good works are not some extraordinary deeds that we take time out from ordinary life to perform. Nor are they expressions about some intrinsic value about a life of self-denial. Rather, the Commandments describe the natural outworking of faith in the everyday affairs of daily living in our families, work, and community. Indeed, the Commandments presuppose living life in these social orders of the old creation.

The First Table of the Commandments presupposes that all human living flows from a personal involvement of a holy God in our lives. He created us, He graciously preserves us, and daily He provides for all our needs. The Fourth Commandment takes for granted that we live in the context of family and a general society of others ordered by the structures of government. The Fifth Commandment

---

7.   G. Forde, *Justification by Faith*, 57–58.

presumes interaction with others that can affect bodily welfare. The Sixth Commandment takes for granted sexual contact and the community of marriage. The Seventh, Ninth, and Tenth Commandments presume private possessions, and some kind of appropriate exchange of goods and services. The Eighth Commandment reflects the reality that we touch and interact with one another through communication. The Commandments have just reflected the interpersonal character of how we live, work, and carry on our ordinary projects of life.

The greatest insight of Luther in his *Treatise*, however, was his recognition of the primacy and all-embracing thrust of the First Commandment. First, this means that we must approach all our tasks and commitments in life from the perspective of *fear, love, and trust in God*. Indeed, we are to orient our whole being within such a relation to God. Second, Luther recognized that the First Commandment is embedded in all the others. All doing that involves the concerns in the remainder of the Commandments Luther understood as a *doing with faith*. He called this *a theological sense* of doing rather than a moral sense of doing. To this point he wrote, "In theology, therefore, 'doing' necessarily requires faith itself as a precondition. . . . Therefore 'doing' is always understood in theology as doing with faith, so that doing with faith is another sphere and a new realm, so to speak, one that is different from moral doing. When we theologians speak about 'doing' therefore, it is necessary that we speak about doing with faith, because in theology we have no right reason and good will except faith."[8] Faith in Christ is first expressed in fear and love of God. Then our love of God becomes channeled into loving service toward others. Our justification through faith in Christ is thus expressed in life through loving service to our neighbor.

Our neighbor is determined by where we are placed in life. We are limited and dependent creatures who have been called by the Gospel to live within the communities that make up our vocational call. This context we could call "our *circle of nearness*," which particularizes our neighbors and limits our works that serve them. Here we encounter real flesh-and-blood people with names and faces. We have not been called to love some abstract humanity. This does not

---

8.   *AE* 26, 262–63.

mean that love is limited to simply *my station and its duties*. Our circle of nearness may also include the stranger whom we encounter in our path as we tend to our station and its duties. This is what the *certain Samaritan* in the parable understood that apparently the priest and the Levite did not. Jesus implied the same thing when He told us that in as much as we serve the least of His brothers, we serve Him (Matt. 25:40).

Each of the interpersonal spheres reflected in the second table of the Commandments becomes a context where God calls us to act out our trust in Christ and love of God. Our tasks of loving service will vary according to our relationships and commitments within the communities we inhabit. The character of loving service will be different toward our spouse than toward the student in the classroom or the checkout person at the local supermarket. The Commandments do not define love nor do they present an exhaustive list its duties. Rather they set parameters within which our duties can be found and beyond which our projects and our loves may not go. Given the boundaries of the *shall* and the *shall nots*, vocational duties may be recognized as they arise out of the authority and responsibilities that fall to the individual according to the offices one occupies in our human communities. These are the tasks that we may be confident have God's command. Luther closed his extended commentary on the Ten Commandments with the sarcastic advice that we should not ask God for more things to do for Him until we have first mastered the duties of love that these ten imperatives outline. They shall keep us occupied for a lifetime.

The Vocatio of the Church

Our discussion of Christian vocation up to this point has focused on God's call of faith as it is lived and expressed within the social communities where we live. We have explored the life of faith as a life of service and reordered love. Now we want to turn our attention to the corporate dimension of God's call that relates to our vocation to be a *fellowship of faith*—to be a called-out community of God's people—what we more commonly refer to as Christ's Church. We may think of our individual vocations within the old creation structures of life as callings to be the *Church-scattered*. Here Christian vocation flows from the obedience of subjective faith in the projects of loving service. Individual Christian piety is usually extraordinarily ordinary. We now want to briefly consider the piety of the Church corporate and for that we must investigate the contours of vocation for the Church-gathered. This is what Werner Elert called *we piety*.[9]

The Church gathered is called to be the family of God that lives by faith under the grace and headship of Christ. This is what the Church is called *to be*, and it is its primary vocation. And flowing from its primary call is a call to its duties. Unlike individual Christian piety, however, the Church's piety is expressed in objective tasks that need not flow from the subjective faith of the individual Christian to be valid. While the piety of the individual Christian is largely subjective in nature and thus hidden in the ordinary tasks and duties that arise from membership in the old-world communities, Christian piety considered corporately in the Church is objective and made up of specific commands of Christ that are open to the observation and measure of all. This is *we piety*—where Christian vocation is *ordinarily extraordinary*. Here is where Christians show off, exhibit, and display their righteousness and holiness—here it is made manifest to all. In manifesting its righteousness and holiness, the Church shows of its Head and distributes His gift of holiness. This is *Divine Service*: the holy Bride of Christ expressing her faith objectively in proclamation of the Gospel, as Christ taught it to His apostles, and in administration His sacraments as He instructed. In addition, the Church is called to admonish and discipline its impenitent members and restore them through His grace when they repent. Through the performance of these tasks as means, Jesus and His righteousness are made manifest in the world and bestowed on sinners. Moreover, by these means as marks, the Church is located and its piety unmistakably observed.[10] The Church-gathered has no phantom existence in the world. Indeed, unlike the individual Christian, The Church is

---

9. W. Elert, *Christian Ethos*, 336–45.

10. The true proclamation of the Gospel and the right administration of the sacraments are noted in the Lutheran Confessions as marks of the presence of the Church of Christ. Sometimes confession and absolution has been listed as a third mark rather than subsuming it under the category of the proclamation of the Gospel. This distinction is a matter of semantics not substance.

identified through the vocation of its Head, the righteousness and holiness of Christ as manifested in the Gospel and Sacraments.

Through the Church's vocation, its head continues His ministry of building up and extending the Kingdom of God. To carry out this vocation of the Church, Christ calls pastors today, as He called the apostles before, to carry out the Church's corporate call to the ministry of Word and Sacrament. To consider the Church scattered, is to see individual Christians who receive their vocational call from God in their baptism. It is a call to live in the grace of Christ by faith as a member of God's family primarily and then express that faith in a life of service in the duties and commitments of the communities of this world. The Church-gathered received its call from Christ before He ascended into heaven and it is called to express its faith in the public proclamation of the Gospel and the administration of the sacraments.

Individual members of God's family relate to the call of the Church-gathered in two ways. First, we are called in the Third Commandment not to despise the fellowship in the Word nor absent ourselves from it. But rather, we are called to regularly partake of God's Word as it is proclaimed and as it is applied in the sacraments. This is of crucial importance, for through the means of grace, Christ nurtures our faith and equips and empowers it for our daily duties of service. Second, the Church-scattered is to witness to Christ and mutually admonish and console one another within our circle of nearness as part of our duties of service. When Jesus was with His disciples in the upper room, He schooled the Church-scattered about the life of loving service. It even includes the ordinary dirty business of life, like washing feet (John 13:14–15). But when He came to "This is my body. . . . Do this in remembrance of me," He called the Church-gathered to a part of its vocation (Luke 22:19 ESV).

The primary piety of the Church-scattered is sacrificial in nature, and the primary piety of the Church-gathered is sacramental. The sacrificial life of the Church scattered through loving service in the world flows from the grace-bestowing sacramental life of the Church-gathered. Church-gathered piety is always logically prior to individual piety. As need and opportunity arise, however, we witness to Christ in our individual callings. And as need and opportunity arise, the Church-gathered offer sacrificial service. At

Paul's request, the churches in Greece took up a collection to aid the famine-stricken church in Jerusalem. The Church-gathered has similar projects today. The Church is hidden within the old-world structures of society and even in the structures of church government; but it is revealed to faith in terms of its presence by its Word and Sacrament service. Individual Christian piety is extraordinarily ordinary for its godliness is largely hidden. Corporate Church piety, however, is ordinarily extraordinary—and its godliness that is the righteousness of Christ is made manifest in Word and Sacrament. If you want to see Christian piety on bold display, followers of Luther's theology of the cross say, *here it is*!

On this count Church historian, Mark Noll, had some remarkably favorable things to say about the contributions that American Lutheranism can make to the American Christian scene well. He wrote:

> The Protestant tendency in America has been to preserve the importance of preaching, Bible-reading, the sacraments (or ordinances), and Christian fellowship, but to interpret these as occasions for human acts of appropriation. That *God* saves in baptism, that *God* gives himself in the Supper, that *God* announces his Word through the sermon, that *God* is the best interpreter of his written Word—these Lutheran convictions are all but lost in the face of American confidence in human capacity.
>
> Finally what Lutherans can offer Americans is the voice of Luther, a voice of unusual importance in Christian history . . . because in it we hear uncommon resonances with the voice of God. . . . For whatever reason, in the affable wisdom of God, the speech of Martin Luther rang clear where others merely mumbled.[11]

† † †

Some Important Words of Clarification

When considering matters that involve vocation, Christians have not been called to do everything, for everyone, all the time. Just because you recognize that someone is in need, does not mean that you have

---

11.   Mark Noll, "The Lutheran Difference," *First Things*, February 1992, 39.

either the authority or responsibility to meet the need. Except for life-threatening situations where even strangers may cross our path, our duties and neighbors are usually limited by our vocational offices and those within the communities these offices serve. Moreover, Christians have not been called to redeem time. Yes, idleness is condemned on several occasions in Scripture (e.g., 2 Thess. 3:11; 1 Tim. 5:13), but at the end of the day, you can be done. The labors (and troubles) of the day are sufficient thereof and when you are done you may take up your own elected projects and you may rest.

If we go beyond these outer limits of a piety that lives in a theology of the cross as Luther enunciated it with such clarity and power, we will inevitably lapse into a false piety born from the many theologies of glory that Church history has strewn about. Here piety usually lapses into pietism, legalism, and Phariseeism. Pietism creeps into the Church's thinking when it begins to develop a negative attitude about participation in the worldly interests and concerns of this life, when the works of God are tied to a *higher calling* in this life that ought to separate us from the affairs of secular life in family, neighborhood, and state. When the piety of the Christian is measured by a certain outward code of demonstrably holy acts, even if they are drawn from the Bible, we have launched into a theology of glory. Historically, pietism was Christian orthodoxy stood on its head. Orthodoxy embraces the objective presentation of Christ and his gifts as they are mediated by Spirit-connected external Word and Sacraments. Flowing from these gifts of righteousness and holiness, a subjective personal piety is expressed in faith that is active in works of loving service. Pietism argued for a subjective mediation of Christ and the Spirit within the heart of the Christian, while the expressions of Christian piety are objectively delineated and divorced from the tasks of worldly concern.

Luther depicted a piety of outward works that are devised by the religious opinions of men as *Churchyard piety*. Monasticism was the contemporary expression of Churchyard piety that Luther condemned as a false and empty piety that burdened consciences and took Christians away from the real tasks in the world that God would have them be about. This was cloistered monasticism. Today we must beware of church body or congregational Churchyard piety, modern ecclesiastical monasticism that seeks to inundate the Church membership with a veritable plethora of programs, activities, and organizational events that lack the context of true Christian vocation of sacrificial service in the communities of this world. Piety as program involvement and participation can involve everything from *quilting for Christ* to *living prayer chains for endangered animals*. In some churches, if you are not scheduling life and the use of your gifts according to all of the week's calendar of events, something is seen as terribly wrong. You have not been assimilated into the regimen of *real* Christian living. Some congregations are even calling a special pastor in charge of assimilating you into all these superspiritual events—The Pastor or Director of Assimilation. The thinly veiled message seems to be; *blessed are the involved and assimilated, for they shall inherit the Kingdom of God*. Activism in works that do not flow from one's vocational call is present is every age as a temptation to leave ordinary duties of Christian piety for the extraordinary. This is Churchyard piety.

Luther had a warning about one more variety of false piety; what he called *Nave piety*. This is where the obedience of faith that lives in the righteousness of Christ is replaced with obedience of the Law. Today some are seeking to replace the obedience of faith with a faith that must then become obedient. This we are told is the real goal of the Gospel. The Gospel has the central objective to turn us all into obedient people under God's legal system. Life with God is said to terminate not evangelically on the Gospel—it is not the Good News of death to life—rather the Gospel just provides the ticket of admission to a legal life of obedience to the precepts of Law. Gospel is to Law as means are to end. The Lordship of Christ is not the dominion of grace, but the rule of Christ the lawgiver. This is the notion of the Gospel in the service of the Law—the idea that God has saved us for obedience.

Away with these things. We must follow Luther from the Churchyard, from the Nave into the Sanctuary where Life with God, the truly godly and pious life, begins and ends with the righteousness of Christ, which is the obedience of faith. When it goes to work in the world is may seem rather ordinary, yes even dead, when not looked upon through the eyes of faith. But here in the old-world tasks of everyday life are the outer limits for the expression of the righteousness of faith. The inner limits however are found in the sanctuary. When we gather together in the sanctuary, when we parade our *we piety* through the manifestation of Christ in Word and Sacrament, there is the extraordinary righteousness of us all—our true piety that has set us free. And that, Mark Noll and all Christians can recognize and confess, is and will always remain, *remarkable!*

CHAPTER 11

The Freedom of Grace and the Bondage of the Neighbor

The Paradox of Christian Nurture

Although not a Lutheran, David Hicks eloquently described a fundamental paradox inherent in classical Christian education, particularly when viewed from a Lutheran perspective. Hicks described a pedagogical tension in an education that would seek simultaneously to equip young minds for *the world's fight and the soul's salvation.*[1] By world's fight, Hick was referring to all the challenges of the Christian living the life of faith in a fallen world. Taken together, these two aspects closely parallel the paradoxical character of the Christian's life in one of Luther's early, but most profound essays, his *Treatise on Christian Liberty*, better known as *The Freedom of the Christian* (1520). In this essay, Luther stated it this way: "a Christian is a perfectly free lord of all, subject to none. A Christian is a perfectly dutiful servant of all, subject to all."[2]

The intent of this chapter is to explore the centrality of these paradoxes. More than ever, parents and Servants of the Word need to understand them for the nurture of our children with an education that is distinctly shaped by a Theology of the Cross. And this is the education that they vitally need. In this interest, I would add another

---

1. David V. Hicks, *Norms and Nobility: A Treatise on Education* (New York: University Press of America, 1999), 2.

2. *AE* 31, 344.

way of describing Luther's paradox that shapes the Christian's walk of faith. The Christian life is characterized by living in *the freedom of grace and the bondage of the neighbor.*

On the one hand, a distinctively Christian education shaped by Luther's theology of the cross needs to nurture understanding and attitudes that are shaped by the faith into which we are baptized. That faith centrally proclaims a life of secured freedom—a freedom just to be the children of God enjoying life with our Creator for the sake of the grace of Christ. When it comes to securing and maintaining God's favor, when it comes to grappling with the gap between the people we are and the people we ought to be; when it comes to securing our own welfare, there is nothing for us to do, nothing to accomplish, nothing to perfect. We must teach that getting saved is a matter of our doing nothing.

The real offense of the Gospel as it addresses the soul's salvation is that it calls us to a ridiculously passive life, not unlike that of a beggar. Beggars lack the basic things that are needed to live. Moreover, should they be given what they need for life, they have nothing to offer in return. They just stand there—hat-in-hand—ready to receive again and again whatever they can get. It is recounted that Luther's last spoken words on his deathbed were these: *We are all beggars, and that's the truth.* And so here is our task: to raise up young beggars who make it a habit, simply to go—spiritual hat-in-hand—to the throne of grace and receive all the donated dignity and sustenance for life they can get from the bleeding charity of a crucified Christ. They are to learn how to have and maintain a spiritual appetite simply to receive from the bloody hands of Jesus, all that they are and all that they need for life today and every day. And as beggars, they are to do this with the clear conviction that they do not, nor will they ever, have anything to offer their Lord in return. And this is just how it ought to be. When God has His way with us—we passively grow in an awareness and appreciation of our poverty and His graciousness. We may experience our spiritual poverty by the inner workings of Law and the external events that bring *tentatio*—trial and temptation—but we grasp the graciousness of God by faith alone. We are to teach our children to enjoy a freedom from being obligated ever to do anything for God. As we have noted how Luther eloquently put it in his Heidelberg Theses, *The Law says, "do this," and it is never done. Grace says, "believe in this," and everything is already done.*[3] What Luther learned from the Apostle Paul is that we can live life under the Law, or we can live it under the Gospel. Under the Law, when all is said and done, there is always more to do. But under the Gospel, when all is believed about the promises of Christ, all is already done, and there is nothing left to do. And with nothing, you get everything. You are free. This is the grace by which we are saved, and it brings outrageous freedom, an outrageous freedom that has God whispering to us what Gerhard Forde has called the hilarity of the Gospel: pondering what you will do when there is nothing you have to do.[4]

By the standards of the world and good old-fashioned religion—even that which often seeks to pass itself off as Christian—this is an understanding of grace that is both outrageous and hilarious. We get everything we need in our baptismal inheritance, even adoption into the royal family of His Son, yet we remain beggars. We become kings in the Kingdom with the Lord Christ, who also made His appearance to the shout of *hosannas* as a royal beggar.[5] That makes us royal beggars! Our God is a God who demands perfect righteousness, yet it is this God who gives us just what He demands in the righteousness of Christ, given in the Sacred Things to us, again and again. And remember the paradox about that righteousness: We are now perfectly sufficient in the righteousness of Christ, yet we always are in need of more. Royal beggars for life.

The freedom of the Gospel is God's wisdom, but it is usually seen as foolishness—religious foolishness from the human perspective. With man's sense of justice, everybody gets what they deserve.

---

3. *Heidelberg Disputation*, 1518, Thesis 26, *AE* 31:41.

4. G. Forde, *Justification by Faith*, 33.

5. Our royal beggarly identity flows, in part, from our union and inheritance with Christ, whose royal reign was hidden under a beggarly appearance. Luther refers to Jesus as the royal beggar as he expounds on Matthew's connection with the prophecy of Zech. 9:9 concerning His triumphal, yet humble, entry into Jerusalem. *He rides there so beggarly, but hearkens to what is said and preached about this poor king. His wretchedness and poverty are manifest, for He comes riding on an ass like a beggar having neither saddle nor spurs. But that He will take from us sin, strangle death, endow us with eternal holiness, eternal bliss, and eternal life, this cannot be seen. Wherefore thou must hear and believe.* WA 37:201–2, as cited in David Steinmetz, *Luther in Context* (Grand Rapids: Baker Book House, 1995), 28.

Yet as we have observed, with God's justice, everybody gets what they do not deserve. The righteous Christ receives the wrath of God and punishment for sin, and we wretched sinners received mercy. For us, it is all about getting saved, doing nothing. From the human standpoint, it sounds like a con job to keep us uncaring and lazy. Worldly wisdom operates with the assumption that the more important the issues connected with human existence, the more we need to get busy. The more God commands us, and He certainly commands us in his Law (they are not the Ten Suggestions!), the busier we think we need to be. Man's religion always advances the notion that there is Divine help for those who help themselves; thus, the apex of spiritual commitment is manifested in what we do. But against such a sensible perspective, we must teach our children to understand and appreciate the divine foolishness of the Gospel, which operates with different logic. The Gospel teaches, ironically, what is contrary to what well-meaning Christian parents often teach, especially around Christmastime: *Tis better to give than to receive.* The logic of the Gospel, ironically, is just the reverse: *Tis better to receive than to give.* When it comes to the soul's salvation; we must teach that all commitments to giving produce just what Aristotle promised: a growth in worldly virtues, but when it comes to the soul's salvation, when such things are trusted in, they also produce a ticket to Hell. Conversely, the passive reception of the saving gifts of Christ produces just what the Apostle Paul promised: perfect righteousness and a ticket to Heaven.

Our challenge, today more than ever before, is to provide the experiences, vantage points, and the theological logic by which our children can see (first of all) and then appreciate (second of all) the freedom that the grace of Christ imparts. In this regard, Christian pedagogy for our children has often made a critical mistake—one that, unfortunately, has been passed on for generations. We think that life in Christ can best be nurtured and appreciated by our small children by engaging their hands in meaningless handicrafts and their minds in unnecessarily watered-down Bible stories. We then mix this formula with bland thoughts about a milk-toast love of Jesus for bunnies and butterflies. We have witnessed how this regimen of soft religious pabulum produces mischievous boredom in our strong-willed boys by age eight and utter rebellion by many of both sexes by age thirteen. In the eyes of these children, the youth culture of today may not be seen as very wholesome, but it certainly is not so boring! We need to recover a distinctively Lutheran understanding of how hearts and minds are prepared for the Gospel. We must renew our faith in what Professor Ronald Feuerhahn has called *the power of negative thinking*.[6] The power of negative thinking is harnessed by frequent sojourns in the way of full-strength Law. Spiritual Beggars are made—and renewed in their passion to beg—by a continual experience of their own spiritual poverty. Only those who die to sin may live in Christ. This is as true for the young baptized children as it is for their parents.

The theological logic that anchors the freedom of the Gospel entails three very important adversaries that must be overcome—sin, death, and the Devil. Without a real awareness and appreciation of these three enemies, the foolishness of the Gospel will be simply foolishness and progressively uninteresting foolishness at that. We must continually expose our children to these evils in their own life and world in order to nurture and maintain a beggar's mind-set for life. Sin has rendered our little children dead in their trespasses, prone to make idols out of almost anything or anyone, and curved in upon themselves with inordinate self-love. As with all of us—to use the botanical metaphor—they have become bad vines, in a bad vineyard, producing nothing but sour grapes.[7] We are and remain in this life—apart from Christ—wretched sinners.

One of the biggest challenges for the Christian nurture of our young people is to make these realities clear, important, concrete, and related to the fabric of how life must be lived in a fallen world. The freedom to live as beggars of God's favor in Christ Jesus and the peace and security that it brings makes little sense apart from an awareness and appreciation of the magnitude of the problem of evil. For this, the Law needs to have more than its instruction; it needs to have its impact. The power of negative thinking needs to have an impact on the lives of our children early and often, not just for discipline, but also for appropriate character formation. The problem

---

6. The late Rev. Dr. Ronald Feuerhahn has been a faithful and stimulating professor of Systematic Theology at Concordia Seminary, St. Louis, MO for many years.

7. An allusion to the metaphor in Isa. 5:1–4.

of sin needs not simply to be discussed in instruction; it needs to be experienced. The power of negative thinking is the conviction in the hearts of our children by the work of the Spirit that they can either die to sin—or they can just die. This conviction is what creates a passionate life of begging for God's outrageous grace without any concern over what they might give in return. And not just for the children, their parents must have this conviction about the problem of sin as well. For them, as for each of us—they can live by grace, or they won't live at all.

But thanks be to God, they will live by grace. The awareness of the riches of God's grace may be no greater than the awareness of the magnitude of one's sin. Our children can only grasp the wonder of the way of the Gospel, as it is balanced by the impact of the Law. They will make progress maturing in the image of Christ bit-by-bit, as Luther put it, by always starting over again—dying to sin in the way of the Law and rising up unto new life in the freedom of the Gospel.[8] This is as true for our little ones, as it is for our teenagers, as it is for each of us.

The Bondage of the Neighbor

Now at this point, you may have been thinking, *But . . . but . . . but you are leaving things out, important things!* Yes, that is true. There is another side of the life of the Christian. The freedom of grace we have covered. But now we must turn our attention to the other side of the paradox: the bondage of the neighbor. We must prepare our children for what Hicks calls *the world's fight.* Christians are simultaneously free and bound. Strangely, the notions of freedom and slavery are not always opposites from a biblical perspective. In the civil sphere, our forefathers closely linked the idea of freedom with the idea of liberty that is self-government or autonomous self-rule. Our Declaration of Independence declared that we would be a free people, determined to govern ourselves, independent of the British Crown. However, when the Scriptures address what Luther called *things above us*—spiritual matters—they know nothing of human

---

8.   *AE* 25, 478.

autonomy. We are either ruled at all points by the powers and princi-palities of evil, or we are ruled by God.[9] The Scriptures do not tie the notion of freedom to autonomy; rather, they tie the idea of freedom to purpose—God's purposes. The Christian's life is free, and yet it is a life of slavery. Yes, Jesus taught that *if the Son has set you free, you will be free indeed.*[10] But He also instructed His disciples that as they rightly acknowledged Him as Lord, this meant that they are slaves, and a slave is not above his master.[11] In the same vein, the Apostle Paul explained that in our Baptism, we have been set free from the slavery of sin and are alive to God in Christ Jesus. But we have also thereby become slaves to God and righteousness.[12] As slaves are bound to their master, so we are bound to Christ. We are a new cre-ation fashioned after His human nature and created for works that God has planned from eternity that we should be about.[13]

The sense of bondage here involves a necessary connection between our being and our doing. When it comes to spiritual things, we do as we are. Good fruit comes from a good tree as bad fruit from a bad tree. Grapes come from grapevines because that is how God has made them. Jesus taught that He is the vine and we the branches and that abiding in Him, we can produce some pretty good vintage. What we do flows from what we are. It is God Who has so connected our being and doing. There is freedom here, for this is how God has designed us to be, but it is not autonomy. This, again, is Aristotle on his head. Aristotle taught that we are perfected in our being by

---

9. This means that in Christ we are bound to His righteousness, which produces the fruit of faith; and apart from Christ, we are bound to sin. Luther used the unflattering illus-tration of a mule who is ridden by its master in this regard. In spiritual matters we are as a mule, either ridden by the Devil or ridden by Christ. Oberman's discussion of *man as a mule* is a delightful explanation of Luther's analogy here. He writes, For Luther, *man is not the mule that, stupefied by ignorance, cannot decide between two haystacks—education could help that mule. No the condition of man does not depend on the breadth of his education but on his existential condition as a 'mule' ridden either by God or the Devil, but with no choice in the matter, no freedom of decision, no opportunity for self-determination.* H. Oberman, *Luther*, 219.

10. John 8:36.

11. John 13:13–16.

12. Rom. 6:7, 17–19, 22.

13. See Rom. 5:17; Eph. 2:10; 4:13–15.

a progressive perfecting of what we do. *Doing* is an investment in *becoming*—for good or ill. For this reason, Luther saw Aristotle's *Nicomachean Ethics* as of the Devil, for it runs counter to the whole sense of the creating and saving work of God.

Recall Luther's observation in his Heidelberg Theses: *The love of God does not find, but creates that which is pleasing to it.*[14] God never comes to us as a beggar with His hat in hand—hoping to get from us what he desires. (For example, God really would like you to become a Christian. How about it? What do you say?) Whatever God wants, He just makes all by Himself. He needs no help from us. As we have maintained, the general interpretive rubric for the Bible is this: whatever God commands, God creates. And whatever God demands, God gives. He commanded the creation of human beings in Genesis 1, and through the power of His Word, it was so. He demands of us a perfect righteousness in his Law, and He gives us just that in the righteousness of Christ through the Gospel. In the Gospel, he exhorts faith, and that is what He creates by the power of the Spirit through the Word of Christ.[15] His redemptive will is that we become a New Creation in Christ, and that is just what he fashions by the power of the saving Word in the waters of Baptism. We are as He has made and remade us, and we do as we are in accord with His will and work.

Any Christian might naturally conclude that if God has regenerated us to be slaves of the Lord Jesus, then we must above all serve and be obedient to Him. Indeed, this is how much of the theology in the Church through the ages has seen it. The Christian has been called to a life, bound by a higher calling, to perform special spiritual works for our Lord Jesus out of obedience to Him. The more pious you are, the more time you devote in your life to doing them. Such an idea flourished in medieval monasticism. You go to the monastery to perform super spiritual works for your merit and for Christ's benefit. Today we see the remnants of such thinking even in our congregations. We dream up special works to serve Jesus in our congregations and then we implore our members to come and do them regularly.

---

14. *Heidelberg Disputation*, 1518, Thesis 28, *AE* 31:41.

15. Rom. 1:16; 10:17; 1 Cor. 12:3.

Congregations that can fill up a monthly calendar with such activities are called *alive*. Those who busy themselves doing them are called *active members*. We could call this congregational monasticism, and it is a misunderstanding about Christian piety and works.[16]

To engage the world's fight is to leave the confines of monastery and church building and enlist your talents and energies in the temporal orders of life—to be of some earthly good. In the thinking of Luther, it is to make things in this life a little bit better. The Christian life proclaims a bondage to our neighbor and his welfare. This point was made in the previous chapter on Christian vocation, but it bears repeating here. We cannot serve our Lord Jesus directly for two rather unflattering reasons. The first is that we do not have anything that He needs. The second—equally unflattering—is that whatever we have that is worth anything, He gave us. Faith generates love. God would have us channel our fear, love, and trust in Him (things that are just part and parcel with being a new creation in Christ) distributing as stewards the blessings that God has entrusted to us. He binds our deeds to our neighbor and thereby gives us some significant things to do in this life. At the same time, He schools us in the gentle art of loving—something that we shall be doing for an eternity. And then He makes this arrangement: serving the neighbor in faith is reckoned as service rendered to Him, even when that service is rendered to those one might consider the least of His brothers.[17]

The bondage of the neighbor is to be understood in a twofold sense: in the way of the Gospel, and in the way of the Law. As a new creation in Christ, this bondage is composed of the compelling demands of gratitude and love. In the way of the Gospel, we serve the neighbor out of delightful gratitude for all that our Lord has done and given to us.[18] This is a bound freedom from all concerns about our own welfare as these are put to rest in the secured

---

16. For a more complete discussion of the false piety exhibited in monasticism and contemporary congregational forms of the same thing, see my essay, "The Outer Limits of a Lutheran Piety," *Logia—a Journal of Lutheran Theology* 3, no. 1 (January 1994): 4–10.

17. See Jesus' teaching about the works of the sheep on Judgment Day in Matt. 25:31–40.

18. We serve out of a sense of loyalty to Christ who is Lord and has made us servant/ slaves—not out of a sense of legal compulsion but by grace. The life of service flows from an ethos under grace, not law.

gifts and promises of Christ. Moreover, we serve our neighbor out of love because that is just what the New Creation has been created to do. We are God's piece of work, and we do as we are. These realities undergird the usually taught *because-you-want-to* side of things. This is the delightful bondage of love. The neighbor becomes a beloved, and it is love's compulsion to serve and bestow gifts for her welfare. Little Suzie falls down and skins her knees. Her loving mother picks her up, comforts her, and tends to her wounds. Now should we be so silly as to ask the mother why she did this or if she thought she *had to*, she would surely think we were crazy. Works of love have a bondage about them—even a compulsion—as one is captivated by the needs of a beloved, but legal considerations of duty and calculation have no place.

Such is the bondage of the neighbor as the Christian, as seen in light of the realities of the new creation in Christ brought forth from the waters of Baptism. There is another side to the bondage of the neighbor because there is another side to the Christian. Apart from Christ, the Christian remains a fleshly sinner, sold as a slave to sin in which nothing good dwells, and nothing good comes forth.[19] The bondage of the neighbor offers occasions for the Christian to carry on the subduing and disciplining of the flesh. Moreover, it is a significant hill on the battlefield where spiritual warfare is to be engaged against the world, the flesh, and the Devil. To our children, we are to say, *You don't want to? Well, you have to.* This is the bondage of the neighbor in the way of the Law.

We need to be very clear about this. There is no liberty in the bondage of the neighbor. There is no liberty in our doing or in the nurture of our children's doing. We can be constrained by the love of Christ and captivated by the needs of the neighbor, or we can be strained by the Law and serve our neighbor for our own good, or as is often the case, we can be constrained by both.[20] It is a win-win

---

19.   See the Apostle Paul's description in Rom. 7:14–20. Luther expressed this *you do as you are* understanding between faith and unbelief in the following way: "So it is with the works of man. As the man is, whether believer or unbeliever, so also is his work—good, if it was done in faith, wicked if it was done in unbelief. But the converse is not true, that the work makes the man either a believer or an unbeliever." *AE* 31:361.

20.   Forde expressed this duality of motivation as rather typical of ordinary saints, and even more so. To be realistic, this side of the eschaton we shall no doubt have to say that

situation in either case. In the paradoxical nurture of our children that addresses the bondage of the neighbor, we are to use discipline with all its rewards and penalties to teach what *the fat relentless ego*[21] in all our children needs to understand: life will go better for them if they follow the rules than if they break them. We call such service that flows from discipline, *civil righteousness*. It is not intrinsically the stuff of godliness; it is the stuff of practical wisdom. So we teach our children this: *Do yourself a favor, follow the rules!*

A good tree bears what the Lord considers good fruit, and a bad tree bears what is considered bad fruit. But the Lord can use either or both to feed your neighbor quite sufficiently. Warming the heart of our children by the Gospel produces the bondage of love, and warming the butt of our children—or other such applications that get the message across—produces the disciple of the Law. Both Law and Gospel are needed to nurture the bondage of the neighbor.

A Bitter Parable: Where Did We Go Wrong?

There is a tragic parable that repeats itself all too frequently in many of our best parishes and Christian homes. While it has many variations, there are common threads that run through all its versions. The concluding punchline is usually a question raised very quietly: *Where did we go wrong?* The story is seldom told publicly, and when shared, it is delivered in hushed tones, usually by mothers with shed tears.

The story is about how many of our baptized sons and daughters—twentysomethings or even older—have made their exit from the Kingdom of God. They do not attend Christian worship services, they no longer confess Christ, and they often have animus toward those who do. In the Christian's spiritual warfare against the world, the flesh, and the Devil, it seems they have lost. Take Jennifer.

---

in our actual deeds there is something of a mixture of the have to and the want to, maybe even a good deal more of the former than the latter. But we must not lose sight of the hope, the vision, inspired by the absolutely unconditional promise. For in the end, that alone will survive—true sanctification. G. Forde, *Justification*, 57.

21. A delightful term for the central enemy of moral life coined by Iris Murdoch. See her *The Sovereignty of Good* (London: Rutledge & Kegan Paul, 1970), 52, 66.

Jennifer, baptized as an infant, grew up in a church-going family. Her congregation championed the historic Christian faith as Luther recovered it, and so did its long-term pastor. The family attended worship services regularly, and Jennifer went to Sunday School and VBS as a young girl. Her father shied away from participation in the educational hour on Sundays, preferring instead, to talk congregational business out in the parking lot. Managing the physical and financial assets of the congregation was where he felt most comfortable. Jennifer's mother often attended adult Bible class. She also was an occasional teacher in the Sunday School and VBS when her daughter was young. Aside from memorizing some verses and studying for confirmation between Jennifer and her mother, any articulation of faith life at home was largely restricted to saying grace at dinner time.

Jennifer attended the public schools in the local school district because they had solid reputations for being excellent. Her high school was recognized for consistently high academic achievement, and most of its students went on to college. Academically, she thrived at high school, making the honor roll more often than not. While occasionally attending the congregation's high school youth group, her most significant peer group friends were from the public high school. Beyond her studies, Jennifer's high school life was filled with sports, drama club, listening to hip-hop music, going to movies, and hanging out with her school friends.

Upon graduation, Jennifer went off to State University as a resident student. During her first year away from home, her phone conversations with her parents sometimes included this question from her mother: *Are you going to church or involved in a campus ministry?* Jennifer often replied in a somewhat pained tone of voice; *Oh, Mother! Sometimes, when I can. I have to spend a lot of time on my studies, you know.* The fact is, as only learned later, Jennifer went a couple of times when she first arrived on campus, but since then, quit going entirely. She did attend worship with her parents, however, when she came home during Thanksgiving, Christmas, and other school breaks.

After the first year, visits home became less frequent. During her second year, Jennifer found a part-time job off campus working as a waitress. She now stayed at school to work during most school breaks. She also explained to her mother that she usually had to work the Sunday morning shift and could not attend campus worship. Phone calls to her folks back home became less frequent as well. Usually, it was Jennifer's mother who made the calls, which often became strained. On one occasion, Jennifer indicated to her mother that she believed that there were many valid expressions of human spirituality other than the traditions of Christianity. Each person needs to find what best suits them. On another occasion, she argued with her mother, indicating that she thought the Church had been guilty of hate and intolerance toward the LGBTQ community. The Church should not be so judgmental. It turns people off, she said. Jennifer accused her mother of being narrow-minded and indicated that she felt that sexual preferences are personal matters that everyone should respect.

When questioned by her mother concerning her living arrangements, Jennifer responded nonchalantly, "It's no big deal, mom, most of my friends here at school, are living together. I know you don't approve, but I have to live my own life." To Mom's question, "Do you think God approves of what you are doing?" Jennifer shouted back, "Don't give me any of your God-crap, Mother, I'm doing just fine without it!" She hung up.

Sometime, somewhere, after she left home, Jennifer graduated from the Church's confession before graduating from State University. Her father has had very little to say about any of this. Occasionally, he tries to console his more concerned wife, "We raised our daughter as best we could. She's a big girl now and has to live her own life. We have to accept her the way she is and be here when she needs us." She is not consoled. Jennifer's mother is hurt, angry, and confused. While she is embarrassed to talk to her pastor or any of her church friends about Jennifer, she has many questions and is filled with self-doubt. She ponders over and over again, Where did we go wrong?

What is it that the Christian community needs to understand and implement here in North America in the twenty-first century to meet the challenge of faithfully nurturing our young baptized in the Lord? More pointedly, what do we need to know and do as parents, pastors, and parishes to prepare our children for the spiritual assault that they face today in our current anti-Christian culture? What do we need to provide that so often is not being provided, so that future

Jennifer parents will not be pondering the question, Where did we go wrong?

The last things needed to conclude reflection on this parable are some sentimental spiritual platitudes or words that gloss over the severity of the spiritual warfare our children face to retain and grow in their faith. Yes, we will pray for our now not-so-young children who no longer confess Christ. Yes, with God all things are possible, and He has not given up these children. Jesus is the Good Shepherd who leaves the ninety-nine in search of the one who has strayed and is lost (Luke 15:3–7). Let us take comfort in these realities about our gracious Lord and God. Nevertheless, it may be helpful to take into account what was presented about our baptized children in chapter 7:

> Often not taught or explained to parents, especially to fathers, is that their child's Baptism has landed her in a spiritual war zone where the Devil relentlessly prowls to get her back. The often-unspoken truth is that the Baptism of our kids has landed them in a life-long spiritual war with the Devil. Jesus taught; he who endures to the end will be saved (Matthew 24:13). With his close allies—the fallen world (say, youth culture) and the Sinful Self—Satan is working to see that your child is not one of them. They are out to make her collateral damage in the Kingdom of God. (137–38)

The Christian faith is all about understanding and appreciating that the problem of sin will always be our children's greatest problem. Sin has resulted in a death problem, and as with all of us, they have it 24/7 (Rom. 5:12, 21). Unsolved, it cancels the possibility of having a Happy Forever. About our death problem, Christianity presents only two options: you can die to sin in Christ, or you can just die. Dying and rising in the cross of Christ and being covered with His righteousness is the only solution to the death problem (Rom. 5:3–11, 20–21). All other avenues just present escape and coping mechanisms. These biblical truths must command our greatest attention in the care and spiritual nurture of our children regardless of their age. Life with God in Christ means enjoying His undeserved forgiveness and favor, but it also means sharing in His undeserved suffering and the world's disfavor. If these realities about human existence and life in Christ are not understood and appreciated, being or remaining a

Christian can make little sense. Then other options, most any other options, can easily be seen as more attractive and fulfilling. We pray that God may enlighten and use parents, Servants of the Word, and Christian friends as His instruments to help our children deepen their understanding and appreciation of these realities or, as with Jennifer, recover them for a Happy Forever.

Nurturing children in the midst of their spiritual warfare to live in the freedom of grace and the bondage of the neighbor corresponds to a dual citizenship that God has called all His Children to occupy as the Church Militant. Under the lordship of Christ, we are simultaneously citizens of the Kingdom of God and worldly, earthly communities. We live a secure life as beggars of the grace that makes us free, and we live significant lives with works that bind us to our neighbors. These are great and wondrous truths about the fundamental identity of all of us, including our children—yes, even the smallest of these. Yet we must always remember our children's very real spiritual warfare that will continually attack her in both communities. Attacks that will assault the life-giving freedom of grace, the bondage of the neighbor, or both. These children are simply on loan to us from their Heavenly Father and, through adoption, our brothers and sisters in the Gospel. Let us put away (or demand to be put away) the glitter, the finger painting, and the silly things that we do in the name of Christian education and teach this paradoxical identity of life in the Cross of Christ. Let us rightly divide the Word of Truth, teaching and applying God's Law and His Gospel that our children might adopt a lifelong habit of dying to live—dying to sin, and rising unto newness of life, serving Christ in the neighbors need—lords of all, beholding to none, and servants of all and subject to all. Let us nurture our children with the goal and confident hope that in that day, when you gather your earthly family together in the fullness of salvation, by the grace of God, they will be there.

CHAPTER 12

Some Reflections on Heaven and Hell

Where Are Heaven and Hell?

As we may seek to get some kind of mental grasp on the eternal realms of Heaven and Hell, how should we conceive them? What is their relationship to where we live our life of faith right now in the cross of Christ here in space and time? One of the great divisions coming out of the Reformation era was over the question, When Jesus ascended into Heaven, did He go away to some specific place? Should we understand Heaven (or Hell) as a distant place such that the ascended body of Jesus must be understood as now gone? If it is gone, it would logically follow that the body of Jesus cannot be present in the Supper. This is the perspective taken by Protestant reformers against Luther and the Wittenberg theologians. Reformers such a Zwingli and Calvin argued that while the divine nature of the ascended Jesus can be considered anywhere and everywhere, His human nature, especially His body, must be understood as now absent. Jesus bodily ascended into Heaven, and since Heaven is a *place*, and human bodies only occupy one place at a time, we must insist on the *real absence* of the body of Christ in the Lord's Supper. The Lutherans protested that such a position does violence to the simple words of Jesus: *This is my body.* They also argued on the basis of the permanent personal union of the two natures of Christ. Where the divine nature of Jesus is, there also is the whole Person of Jesus with all His divine powers, including His human nature. The body of Jesus can be wherever He desires it to be.

There are additional considerations here that are important, not only for understanding the real presence of the body of Jesus in the Sacrament, but also for how we ought to understand Heaven and Hell; indeed, the entire realm of eternity in relation to space and time. It is faulty thinking to conceive of Heaven and Hell as places despite the limitation of our language, which is forced to speak of them as such. Let's examine some of the words of our Lord shortly before He ascended into Heaven. He indicated to His disciples in the upper room that He was going to the Father and in a little while they would see him no more (John 16:16). But should we understand His words to mean that He was no longer going to be with them? He said, "Lo, I am with you always, *even* to the end of the age" (Matt. 28:20 NKJV) and "For where two or three are gathered in my name, there am I among them" (Matt. 18:20 ESV). Notice His use of the personal pronoun. He says, *I am with you; I am among you.* He does not say, "My divine nature is with you." The *I* refers to the whole person, Jesus. The human and divine Jesus will be with us *to the end of the age.* The heavenly, exalted Christ is still with us. It includes also His body in the Holy Supper. In the Sacrament He is both host and menu as He speaks to us; Take, eat; this is my body.

The simple meaning of these passages is that Jesus is both in Heaven and also with us. In other words, we should adjust our thinking about Heaven. It is not some other or distant place as opposed to where we are. Rather, we need to think about Heaven and Hell, all the heavenly hosts, and all the demonic powers of Hell as closer to us than the shirt on our back, or the nose on our face. Listen to Luther's description about the presence of the Devil: *A Christian should know that he is sitting among devils and that the devil is closer to him than his coat or shirt, nay, closer than his own skin.*[1] While certainly recognizing a mystery here, it might be helpful to conceive eternity and the realms of Heaven and Hell as similar to another dimension that interfaces at every point in space and time with our three-dimensional universe. They are not places within created space and time although we must use spatial/temporal language to talk about them because these are the limits of our thinking and our language. We may describe them as infinite and eternal; that is speaking negatively as realities that are not limited or bound by space

---

1. WA 32, 112, as cited in Ewald Plass, ed., *What Luther Says* (St. Louis: Concordia, 1991), 399.

or time. We must speak by negation, because we really do not know what they are in positive terms for they are beyond our conceptual reference. Nevertheless, we should not view Heaven and Hell as if we are talking about some places beyond the farthest reaches of the universe. Rather, they are closer to us, as Luther alludes concerning the Devil, than the nose on our face.

Some Whimsical Reflections on Eternity

In the interests of stretching our understanding, let's consider a couple of imaginative illustrations. The first is somewhat philosophical; the second is rather corny, but perhaps helpful nonetheless. Think for the moment about the conceptual problem for two-dimensional life-forms pondering the reality of the third dimension, *depth*. Imagine a philosophy class of amoebas on a slide smear trying to grasp the concept of *depth* in a germ-based philosophy class. The professor amoeba indicates that depth should not be conceived as some distant place at the far reaches of length or width. He insists that it should not be seen as *out there* in any sense. Rather, he says, depth should be understood as *here*. He then offers this negative definition of depth: *not limited by length or width*. There is a smart-alecky amoeba sitting in the back row who wants to stump the professor. Raising his hand, he asks this question: *Tell us professor, How should we understand the relationship of depth to length and width? How does depth interface with length and width?* The professor answers, *Depth interfaces directly and completely at every point along length and width. There is no point along length and width that is closer or farther from depth. It is just here, there, and everywhere.* What do you think of his answer? We who inhabit a three-dimensional world know he did pretty well. Perhaps by analogy, this illustration might help us conceive how eternity interfaces with our three-dimensional universe. Heaven and Hell, indeed all eternity, interface equally at every point in space and time. No point in space or time is closer or farther from Heaven or Hell. We may think of them of as here and there—wherever, and whenever.

Let's consider another illustration that is rather mundane. We might compare this conception of eternity with space/time somewhat crudely by considering the relationship between a bathtub and the bathroom. The bathtub represents our world of space and time. Eternity, the realm of Heaven and Hell, is represented by the bathroom. We live here in the bathtub. Being in the bathtub, where must we say the bathroom is? It is simply understood as *here*, isn't it? And it does not become closer or farther from us if we stand at one end of the tub or the other. Moreover, the bathroom does not become any closer or farther from us in the tub today than yesterday or tomorrow. Accordingly, we ought to understand Heaven and Hell. They are simply here and there, and now and then. The mystery is that we cannot perceive them with our natural senses. But then, there is the shower curtain, which provides an interface between the bathtub and the bathroom. When you are in the tub, the bathroom is here, but you cannot see it.

Perhaps we may understand a similar mysterious interface between this created order and eternity. Prior to the fall into sin and the curse of the ground, there was an interface between space and time and eternity that seemed to have been transparent. We have a picture in Genesis chapter 2 where God and Adam almost walked hand-in-hand in the cool of the day. The Lord God in Heaven was just as present to Adam and Eve's senses as they and all in the garden were to each other. But when our first parents fell into sin and their natures became corrupted and their bodies subject to the curse of the ground, the splendor and glory of the Lord God, and all of what is Heaven became more than corrupted human nature could bear. It was sensory overload. Perhaps, God turned the shower curtain (the interface) translucent, hiding the bathroom of eternity and the heavenly hosts from our natural perceptive abilities. If we can no longer bear to see the heavenly glory and splendor that we were intended to see by the fullness of our senses—God out of His grace and mercy provided a veil to block that which we cannot handle while fallen and frail here on earth. So now to fellowship with us, God gets into the bathtub and chooses masks—ordinary things of this world—to both hide and reveal Himself to us here in our worldly space and time. Think of Moses and the burning bush, the human nature of Jesus, water, bread, wine, and ordinary human language.

Beyond these considerations, we might ponder questions about what Heaven and Hell are like. What can we know about them now given our conceptual limitations? What are things that we must wait to understand when the glory of eternity crashes in on us at the Second Epiphany of Christ? The problem of how we might understand Heaven in the here and now might be compared to a blind man from birth trying to understand a world filled with color. We can only use shapes, texture, and sounds to convey colors that they are not, but must serve to represent them. If you tell the man that he shall one day *see* heaven, what is he to make of that promise? How is he to understand, in a positive way, what he can only know by experiences still yet to come? So we tell him a lot of negatives: *No more painful bumps and bruises.*

Heaven and Hell as Fulfillment of the Heart's Desire

Perhaps the most common picture of Heaven and Hell goes something like this. Heaven is a place where everything you want and like will be there for you in overflowing abundance; and Hell is just the opposite. It is a place where everything that you hate and least desire will be yours forever. I have had a running argument with my thirty-eight-year-old special needs son about these things. He has stubbornly insisted that Heaven will be a place where everything that he wants to be there will be, and simply because of his strong desire. And most of what he desires is simply a more sophisticated version of *The Big Rock Candy Mountain.* For him and many who are not in the special needs category, Heaven is understood to be the place where God is going to give us all the things we want that He chooses not to give us now or at least in the abundance that we desire. I have tried to convince my son that Heaven will be what God has planned for him and he will be fully and completely happy and contented with it. I have not been able to budge him. He grants me a right to my opinion, but that is all. I seem to have little authority on such spiritual matters and that is very humbling for his father. However, there is a grain of truth in my son's understanding. There is a connection in eternity with our deepest yearnings and desires. How Heaven and Hell relate to the desires of the heart comes down to the spiritual condition of the heart, and the nature of its desires. In the final analysis—Heaven or Hell—all will end up getting just what is supremely desired.

While we have noted how some Christian authors today try to sell Bible-based principles of spiritual doing with promises mirroring the beer slogan: *It just doesn't get any better than this*, in Heaven, it really does get better! The days of true glory are on the way. Since sin is not a something, but rather it is a corruption or lack of what God created as good, Heaven delivers us from the curse of a spoiled creation and existence. While we are here, we do not grieve for a departed loved-one who dies in the faith; we grieve for ourselves in our loss of that beloved person. Uncle Judd, who has departed this life in the faith, is doing just fine, thank you very much. He has finally arrived at the green pastures beside the still waters. But we have been left behind and must continue to struggle here in the valley of the shadow of death for a while longer. As described in chapter 7 about *Tentatio*, "We experience life as bitter/sweet: our cup is somewhere between half empty and half full. We long for much more than daily living provides. For that reason, the voice within can hammer us with a painful conclusion: the life we are living falls woefully short of our longings for what it ought to be for would-be citizens of the Kingdom of God." The book of Revelation is especially rich with pictures of Heaven accentuating important things about death's shadow valley that are not there. In Heaven, it's what you no longer get that counts a great deal. Listen to the interlude between the sixth and seventh seal in the second vision of John in Revelation 7:13–17 ESV:

> Then one of the elders addressed me, saying, "Who are these, clothed in white robes, and from where have they come?" I said to him, "Sir, you know." And he said to me, "These are the ones coming out of the great tribulation. They have washed their robes and made them white in the blood of the Lamb.
>
> "Therefore they are before the throne of God, and serve him day and night in his temple; and he who sits on the throne will shelter them with his presence. They shall hunger no more, neither thirst anymore; the sun shall not strike them, nor any scorching heat. For the Lamb in the midst of the throne will be their shepherd, and he will guide them to springs of living water, and God will wipe away every tear from their eyes."

In Heaven, the corrupted things we suffer from being fallen in a world that is cursed will be no more. What you get is the Lamb who was slain and in whose blood you have been washed clean. In Heaven you get to finally be with your Heavenly Lover. As the beloved bride of the Heavenly Bridegroom, you are able to throw away the love letters that have been the stuff of your love relationship with Him and you finally are brought home and into His everlasting arms forever. What you get in Heaven, in a positive sense, is your new creation heart's desire. What you get in Heaven quite simply is God . . . your Creator and the Redeemer—and more richly than you have ever known Him or had Him in this life. Again it was C. S. Lewis that well expressed this:

> Most certainly, beyond all worlds, unconditioned and unimaginable, transcending discursive thought, there yawns forever the ultimate, Fact, the fountain of all other facthood, the burning and undimensioned depth of the Divine Life. Most certainly also, to be united with that Life in the eternal Sonship of Christ is, strictly speaking, the only thing worth a moment's consideration. And in so far as *that* is what you mean by *Heaven*, Christ's divine Nature never left it, and therefore never returned to it: and His human nature ascended thither not at the moment of Ascension but at every moment. . . . I allow and insist that the Eternal Word, the Second Person of the Trinity, can never be, nor have been, confined to any place at all: it is rather in Him that all places exist.[2]

Now you have Him in the cross under the masks of the appointed sacred things given to His Church. He comes to us veiled in the mundane things of this world such as water, bread, wine and even crazy servants of the Word who dress up in Jesus suits for Divine Service. But being finally glorified in Heaven, you get your honest-to-God God in all His splendor and glory. Heaven is not a place; it is a full-to-the-brim presence of the glorious Lord of all. He, in all His glory and splendor is what Heaven is—not a place but a rich fellowship that you take in with all that you are and all that you have with your physical senses and your spiritual faculties all united together. The body is no longer in competition with the spirit. No more masks or veils. Remarked C. S. Lewis, *It is safe to tell the pure in heart that they*

---

2. C. S. Lewis, *Miracles* (New York: Macmillan, 1960), 155.

shall see God, because only the pure in heart want to.[3] Those who do not want *Him* and who do not want *that* really do not want Heaven. All else is beside the point. Only the Godlike would like Heaven, for there you get to be purely and completely . . . like-God. *If you do not have at least some of these qualities already, it is very hard to imagine this as being "Heaven" to someone.*[4]

In Hell, it stays the same. In the Fall, our parents wanted to be lord of their own lives and this bent has been passed on to all the sons and daughters of Adam. It is a struggle that cannot be attained in this life; it is only fully accomplished in Hell. It takes rebirth from the Second Adam to yearn to be merely *like* God, letting everyone, like the true God, be simply who they are. In Heaven only God attempts to wear the big *G* on His sweat shirt and both He and we would have it no other way.

Heaven and Hell and the Justice of God

It has been a common notion that the difference between Heaven and Hell and the work of God is that in Heaven God rules with mercy, but Hell is the abode where His justice holds sway. You either eventually receive God's mercy and are saved or receive His justice and are damned. Actually the true picture of Heaven and Hell are in many ways almost the opposite. Heaven is really the only place where the justice of God reigns supreme, while at the same time, ironically, it is the only eternal condition that is patently unfair. Yes! Unfairness is the name of the ethos of Heaven. It absolutely reeks of unfairness. Yet at the same time, Heaven is also where God justice reigns supreme. With the justice of God, you get mercy. But with God's justice as opposed to ours—everybody gets what they do not deserve. God's execution of justice for the sins of the whole world is found in the universal vicarious atonement of the cross of Christ. The innocent Jesus receives the punishment for all our sins and we guilty ones get off, scot-free. Through the vicarious sacrifice of the Lamb of God,

---

3.   C. S. Lewis, *The Problem of Pain* (New York: Macmillan, 1962), 145.

4.   C. S. Lewis, *Mere Christianity* (New York: Macmillan, 1960), 78.

all bound for Heaven live by undeserved grace—but grace that is through the execution of God's justice, not in spite of it.

It is the will of God that reigns here. Heaven is where God's will is not simply to be done; it *is* done. It is all that there is. However, if you will have nothing to do with the bleeding charity of His justice where His will has been done, but rather you insist on your will over against His, then Hell is God's consequential provision for you. Hell is where nothing but your will is done, because that is all there is—just your curved-in-upon-yourself passionate desires, unending, forever. Matthew characterizes Hell as the darkness where *there is weeping and gnashing of teeth.* The darkness is simply the absence of God's fellowship and all that He has made. There are just your passions unending that long for what you deserve but do not have, because you deserve it. Hell is populated with all who insist on their rights and what they deserve . . . and they are willing to die for it.

The common view of Hell is that it is a place of God's punishment for being incorrigibly naughty. It is God's eternal penalty for wrongdoing and as such it brings those who land there an existence foreign to all their desires and sentiments. They don't want to go there; they don't want to be there; and if they had a second chance for Heaven, they would take it immediately and consider it sweet deliverance. But it is a fiction that Hell is a place where God's justice is meted out against unrepentant sinners. He already executed His justice against all evil and evil doers with His Son on Calvary's cross. Jesus died for all, not simply the repentant. Here Lutherans part serious company with the Reformed who champion a Limited Atonement on the cross. All in Hell are both forgiven and justified. They just insist on living separated from these realities and the Author of them. Rather than say to the Lord God, *Thy will be done.* The Lord God reluctantly has said to them, *Thy will be done.*

The other fiction is that upon physical death, those who are consumed by self-love and cannot stand the scent of the true God will somehow have a complete change of heart. Enemies of God in this life remain the same after they pass into the next. Think of it for a moment from the rebellious unbeliever's perspective: If you were told that you would have to spend eternity separated from someone you spent your whole life hating, would you have any objections? Remember what St. Paul tells us: *While we were enemies, Christ died for us.* Or take the fanciful question entertained in Lewis's *The Great Divorce:* if rebellious sinners in Hell were given a chance to transfer to Heaven and live in and for the full presence and glory of God, would any want to do so? No. Think gals of that geek that made your skin crawl who was after your heart. You would die first than have him, right? That is the way the unbeliever is wired to feel about the true God, the supreme Geek of Heaven. They would rather die that live with Him, and God reluctantly allows just that. Hell is God's provision for those who would rather die that live with Him. In this sense, Lewis concluded, *The doors of Hell are locked from the inside.*[5]

In Hell, the fat relentless ego in all of us fallen creatures becomes ensconced as the jailor of our own eternal prison. For Lewis, the question about whether we should believe in an *actual* Hell was answered with the thought that *one's own mind was actual enough.*[6] You start down the road to Hell when you are bitter and resentful for getting in life what you do not deserve and you are quite certain that God is responsible. And of course, you are right. The road you are on includes your intention of seeing that things are turned around so that you can get your just desserts. Stick with it and you will be successful. We call the whole thing, Hell. Hell is not simply a destination; it is also the kind of journey you take to get there. You have already been there, before you arrive. The Highway to Hell is paved with pure ego-entitlement and you will end up at a destination where everything and only what you think you have coming to you will be yours for eternity. Is there such a thing as Hell on earth? Yes there is. Hell is where you are on earth when you get on the what-I-deserve highway. It is the very nature of the journey and it is the destination. When you and what you desire—for simply the love of yourself—is finally all that consumes you, you are in Hell, whether in this life or in the next. Is this frightful to you? Listen to Lewis then. *In all our discussions of Hell we should keep steadily before our eyes the possible damnation, not of our enemies nor our friends . . . but of ourselves.*[7]

---

5. C. S. Lewis, *Problem of Pain*, 127.

6. C. S. Lewis, *The Letters of C. S. Lewis to Arthur Greeves* (New York: Macmillan, 1986), 508.

7. C. S. Lewis, *Problem of Pain*, 128.

And of course, we understand that death is the gate into either state, Heaven or Hell. The difference for all sinners living under the curse of the ground is this: you can either in this life die to sin or just die. If in this life you are totally committed to yourself as your ultimate concern—then you live in Hell already, dead because of sin. Your after-physical-death will be a continuation of the same with no chance of change. But joining Christ the crucified in your baptism, when you die to sin, you get life. With Hell, you get the complete fullness of yourself: your rights, what you deserve, the passions of self-love above all; the final outcome of the self-curved-in-upon-the-self; the self finally and forever collapsed upon the self. Hell is a state of mind. Conversely, Heaven is reality, total reality. It is all that is real in the fullness of time—God and all things that He has made, free from the corruptions and spoilage of sin, gloriously forever.

CPSIA information can be obtained
at www.ICGtesting.com
Printed in the USA
LVHW112115030821
694437LV00009B/122/J

9 781948 969680